SPORTS AND AT. PERFORMANCE, AND PSYCHOLOGY

PACING IN SPORT
AND EXERCISE

A PSYCHOPHYSIOLOGICAL
PERSPECTIVE

CP046175

SPORTS AND ATHLETICS PREPARATION, PERFORMANCE, AND PSYCHOLOGY

Additional books in this series can be found on Nova's website under the Series tab.

Additional e-books in this series can be found on Nova's website under the e-book tab.

SPORTS AND ATHLETICS PREPARATION,
PERFORMANCE, AND PSYCHOLOGY

PACING IN SPORT AND EXERCISE

A PSYCHOPHYSIOLOGICAL PERSPECTIVE

ANDREW EDWARDS
AND
REMCO POLMAN

New York

For permission to use material from this book please contact us:
Telephone 631-231-7269; Fax 631-231-8175
Web Site: http://www.novapublishers.com

NOTICE TO THE READER

The Publisher has taken reasonable care in the preparation of this book, but makes no expressed or implied warranty of any kind and assumes no responsibility for any errors or omissions. No liability is assumed for incidental or consequential damages in connection with or arising out of information contained in this book. The Publisher shall not be liable for any special, consequential, or exemplary damages resulting, in whole or in part, from the readers' use of, or reliance upon, this material. Any parts of this book based on government reports are so indicated and copyright is claimed for those parts to the extent applicable to compilations of such works.

Independent verification should be sought for any data, advice or recommendations contained in this book. In addition, no responsibility is assumed by the publisher for any injury and/or damage to persons or property arising from any methods, products, instructions, ideas or otherwise contained in this publication.

This publication is designed to provide accurate and authoritative information with regard to the subject matter covered herein. It is sold with the clear understanding that the Publisher is not engaged in rendering legal or any other professional services. If legal or any other expert assistance is required, the services of a competent person should be sought. FROM A DECLARATION OF PARTICIPANTS JOINTLY ADOPTED BY A COMMITTEE OF THE AMERICAN BAR ASSOCIATION AND A COMMITTEE OF PUBLISHERS.

Additional color graphics may be available in the e-book version of this book.

LIBRARY OF CONGRESS CATALOGING-IN-PUBLICATION DATA

Pacing in sport and exercise : a psychophysiological perspective / Andrew Edwards and Remco Polman , editors.
    p. cm.
  Includes index.
  ISBN 978-1-63321-245-9 (softcover)
  1. Sports--Psychological aspects. 2. Sports--Physiological aspects. 3. Cardiac pacing.
4. Endurance sports. I. Edwards, Andrew. II. Polman, Remco.
  GV706.4.P335 2011
  796.01--dc23
                              2011047268

Published by Nova Science Publishers, Inc. † New York

For all my friends and family who have supported me over the years.
In particular this is for my wife Tracy, son Alex and father Harry Edwards.

Andrew

To my mother for all her love and support throughout my life.

Remco

CONTENTS

LIST OF FIGURES

LIST OF TABLES

FOREWORD

Pacing is one of the most important concepts in sport and exercise. The regulation of effort is a choice that every athlete and exerciser must make continuously (if not always with awareness) throughout every workout and competition, and this choice has a profound effect on outcomes. The difference between successful and unsuccessful pacing is often the difference between achieving and falling short of goals; between benefiting and failing to benefit from the work that is done.

Athletes, coaches, exercisers, and trainers have long recognized the importance of pacing and employed experience-based strategies and methods to teach and practice successful pacing. But until recently pacing received relatively little attention from exercise scientists. There was a tendency to view pacing as a psychological phenomenon and therefore outside the purview of mainstream exercise science, whose focus has always been physiological. Inasmuch as pacing *was* studied, it was studied from a physiological perspective that tended to "explain away" the obvious psychological dimension of the phenomenon.

Recent advances in our knowledge of the brain have lately brought long overdue attention to pacing in the exercise science community. There is a growing recognition that pacing is a phenomenon with both psychological and physiological dimensions that are deeply mutually interpenetrating. Improvements in our understanding of how the exercise pacing mechanism really works are opening up exciting new possibilities for the practice of effective pacing in sport and exercise. A need has therefore emerged for a comprehensive and authoritative resource that summarizes what we now know about exercise pacing and more fully realizes the potential for practical application of this new knowledge for a broad audience of scientists, coaches, trainers, athletes, and exercisers.

Andrew Edwards and Remco Polman have met that need masterfully with this book. *Pacing in Sport & Exercise* presents a cogent and compelling explanation of pacing that, while certainly not representing the last word on the subject, is as close as anyone has yet come. On the solid foundation of their persuasive model the authors have constructed a perception-based system of monitoring and controlling pace, as well as of quantifying and controlling training loads that is easy to comprehend and apply, whether you're a football coach or a beginning jogger seeking weight-loss.

The bias toward physiology and technology that has dominated sport training and exercise prescription for many decades has discouraged people from developing the refined sense of effort perception, the trust in such perception, and particular psychological tools without which optimal pacing is not possible. *Pacing in Sport & Exercise* holds the promise to correct this imbalance with a single stroke, and I expect it to have a revolutionary effect in a wide range of sports and exercise modalities.

For me personally, Edwards and Polman's book fills a big hole that was left open in my own efforts to help endurance athletes conceptually tie mind and body together and become better pacers, hence better racers—most notably in my books *Brain Training for Runners* and *RUN: The Mind-Body Method of Running by Feel*. I intend to rely heavily on Edwards and Polman's invaluable new contribution to the field in my future work as a writer and coach, and I know I will not be alone.

Matt Fitzgerald
Author of Brain Training for Runners
San Diego, California, US

PREFACE

The study of pacing is a relatively new and exciting area of investigation, owing much to original studies by leading academics such as Professors Carl Foster, Veronique Billat and Tim Noakes. These researchers, among others, have demonstrated that pacing is not simply a muscle-driven outcome of performance; it is an important regulatory process that determines performance. Yet, the concept of pacing is not merely confined to elite performance; it underlies all human movements in which voluntary effort is required. As such, the mechanisms by which we regulate pace are complex, requiring mind-body interaction. Therefore, we have considered this topic from a psychophysiological perspective.

Pacing in Sport and Exercise: A Psychophysiological Perspective is, to our knowledge, the first book which comprehensively examines the way humans pace exercise and sporting activities. Research on pacing has been dominated by physiological investigations despite the acknowledgement by many authors on the interdisciplinary nature of pacing. Therefore, we consider both physiological and psychological influences on pacing, before developing an interdisciplinary perspective. This approach explains metabolic regulation during exercise and also facilitates the development of a practical (self-regulatory) means with which to optimise training.

Chapter one of this book provides an overview of the factors associated with the evolutionary development of human athletic performance. It presents a historical view on human training and conditioning perspectives and also on methods including the use of linear and non-linear periodization systems. Chapter two introduces the concept of pacing in sport and exercise. We define pacing as *'the goal directed distribution and management of effort across the duration of an exercise bout'*. Evidence from both animal and human studies is presented to illustrate the way species adapt behaviour to contextual and personal constraints and pace activities accordingly.

A guiding principle is to see pacing as a neural buffering process preventing premature physical exhaustion. In chapter three, both physical and psychological limitations to human performance are discussed. Limitations of traditional physiological models and also the contemporary central governor model of metabolic control are outlined. We propose a new *'conscious brain regulation'* model as a variation to the central governor model, which provides a simpler but more comprehensive explanation of the many phenomena associated with pacing and fatigue in sport and exercise from a psychophysiological perspective. In chapter four, self-regulatory systems for developing skills and also for monitoring training outcomes are identified and discussed. In particular, the rate of perceived exertion (RPE) for monitoring training is suggested as a practical way of both setting and monitoring training across all modes of exercise. The facilitating and debilitating role of psychological factors like mental toughness, coping strategies and self-confidence are also discussed. Pacing in relation to endurance activities is explored in chapter five. The physiological and psychological demands of activities like marathon running, cycling, rowing and triathlon are outlined. Although the ability to sustain high rate of work output continuously over time is important, from a strategic perspective, front loaded, fast start pacing appears to be optimal for most endurance events. Also, associative coping strategies appear to be related to better performance outcomes in high performance athletes. This chapter provides the reader with a practical example of setting and monitoring endurance training using an example of a RPE-based training programme allowing adoption of an individualised training load.

Although the role of pacing may not be intuitively apparent for power, strength and speed events, in chapter six we provide the reader with information on the relevance of appropriate pacing strategies across anaerobic events. High intensity activities might also benefit from preparatory strategies to control arousal levels or expectancies. This chapter also contains a self-paced system and practical example for training in power, strength and speed activities. In chapter seven, pacing for team (invasion-type) sports is discussed. Most team sports are intermittent in nature requiring utilization of both aerobic and anaerobic energy systems. Pacing strategies are apparent in team games, yet are more complex as energetic demands vary by position and the game situation. A multi-level pacing model is discussed based on observations in soccer, yet which is applicable to all invasion games. A practical example of self-regulatory training for team sports is provided. Finally, in chapter eight we outline a number of situations in which self-regulation of exercise might need to be accompanied by other extrinsic (support) techniques. For example, accuracy of self-perception is less developed in children because of their inexperience and can also be distorted among all individuals when homeostasis is compromised by illness or medication. The regulation of exercise behaviour in children, in individuals with Multiple Sclerosis and the obese are examined.

ACKNOWLEDGMENTS

The authors would like to thank friends, colleagues and family for all their help, advice and assistance with preparing and proof reading this book. Tracy Edwards (MSc, Oxford) patiently led the proof reading process and for this we are very grateful. Erika Borkoles (PhD, Hull) provided much appreciated assistance and additional perspective.

As inspiration, we would like to acknowledge Professor Tim Noakes who, in our opinion, remains the undisputed champion of exercise physiology. For Matt Fitzgerald, we greatly appreciate his foreword to this book and his meaningful contributions to the literature which promote self-regulatory exercise via a collection of books.

AUTHOR BIOGRAPHIES

Andrew M. Edwards BEd (Hons 1), MPhil, PhD

Andrew Edwards gained a PhD in Exercise Physiology from Sheffield Hallam University in December 2003 and has since worked as an academic in the UK, New Zealand and Australia. He is a British Association of Sport & Exercise Sciences (BASES) accredited scientist and is the Director of the Institute of Sport & Exercise Science (ISES) at James Cook University, Cairns, Australia. Andrew's main research interest is the inter-relations between fatigue, pacing and high performance sport. He has written many original research articles and worked as a consultant to several professional UK soccer clubs.

In addition to his academic achievements, Andrew is a former UK nationally ranked 400m hurdler and elite level rower/sculler. He competed at many national events in both sports, such as the AAA athletics championships and Henley Royal Regatta. In recent years he won the 400m and 400m hurdles at the New Zealand and Pan Pacific Masters games respectively. He is committed to examining theory-practice interaction in sport and exercise science.

Contact details: andrew.edwards@jcu.edu.au

Professor Remco Polman DPhil, CPsychol, AFBPsS, Csci

Remco Polman's initial training was in the Faculty of Human Movement Sciences at the 'Vrije Universiteit', Amsterdam, The Netherlands where he gained a 'Doctorandus' qualification (1992). Following this, he completed a PhD degree at the University of York, England.

Prior to commencing his current post as Professor and Research Leader in Active Living at Victoria University (Melbourne, Australia), Remco was Professor of Sport and Exercise Sciences and Director of the Centre of Applied Sport and Exercise Science at the University of Central Lancashire, Preston UK. He is a chartered psychologist by the British Psychological Society (BPS) and an accredited sport and exercise psychologist by the Health Professions Council in the UK. He is also accredited for psychological research by BASES and for practice, research and teaching by the Dutch Association of Sport Psychology (VSPN). Remco has fulfilled a number of roles with the Division of Sport and Exercise Psychology (DSEP) of the BPS, including chair, chair elect and honorary secretary. His research interests are diverse and include stress, coping and emotions in sport and exercise, the psychology of (sport) injury rehabilitation; personality and sport and exercise (Mental toughness, Type D personality), exercise psychology (special populations, exercise prescription) and ageing (interaction between psychological and biomechanical factors).

Contact details: Remco.Polman@vu.edu.au

Chapter 1

EVOLUTION OF TRAINING AND PERFORMANCE

1.1. ABSTRACT

The aim of this chapter is to identify and discuss influential factors pertinent to the evolutionary development of human athletic performance. Elite and world record performances are tracked from the beginnings of accurate recordings to the current time. This analysis demonstrates the commonalities of performance change over time and the relative performance plateau now commonly observed in elite athletic events. The methodological evolution of training practices is also examined, thus comparing and contrasting systems with which to organise, distribute and monitor training. The chapter concludes with an examination of issues surrounding the potential for sustainable performance gains.

1.2. INTRODUCTION

The study of pacing in sport and exercise in a relatively new phenomena [1], yet the practice of distributing effort to finish (and perhaps win) a race is not new. To win a race requires the willingness to outperform others and such a desire produces behaviours to achieve that goal. As one race is won, other competitors seek to gain the upper hand and will also adopt new behaviours. This means future strategies for both training and performance must be developed to attain, or re-establish the competitive edge. Such competition inevitably drives up the general standard of performance and the emphasis placed on innovative and effective training practices. The distribution of effort (pacing) therefore applies acutely to an exercise bout and also to the effort applied to systematically improve performance through dedicated training.

Striving for excellence in athletic performance has historical basis [2] and the desire to win may be considered cornerstone of contemporary society. However, there are many factors that contribute to athletic success. By understanding the evolutionary development of elite performance, changes to training practices and the challenges faced in sustaining performance gains we may better understand the place of pacing in sport and exercise.

1.3. EVOLUTION OF HUMAN ATHLETIC PERFORMANCE

It is easily observable that in the immediate years following the introduction of the modern Olympics, frequent improvements were rapidly made to world record performances (Figure 1.1a and 1.1b). However, such gains have now slowed to such an extent that it is possible the human species may be approaching its physical limits [3]. Based on evidence of exponential data trends, it has been estimated performances have reached approximately 99% of human capability and unless there is an unexpected change to human evolution, it is further predicted that most world records will not be improved by more than 0.05% over the next 15-20 years [3].

Numerous investigators have applied exponential mathematical models (e.g. [4]) to predict future athletic performances and estimate the probable limits of human capability. One event anticipated to demonstrate minimal improvement is the 100 metres sprint. The 100m is the shortest Olympic track running distance and therefore represents an interesting test case for examining speed generation in humans. The first men's 100m world record to be ratified by the International Amateur Athletics Federation (IAAF) was set in 1912 by Donald Lippincott of the USA who recorded a time of 10.6s [5]. This performance has now been improved to the current world record of 9.58s set in 2009 by Usain Bolt of Jamaica; however, this only represents a performance gain of 9.6% across 99 years to the present time (Table 1.1).

For women, the first ratified 100m world record was set in 1922 Marie Mejzlikova II of Czechoslovakia who recorded a time of 13.6s [5]. This performance was approximately 23.5% slower than the comparative male world record of that time (Charlie Paddock: 10.4s) but that world record has now improved to the current time set by Florence Griffith-Joyner in 1988 (10.49s).

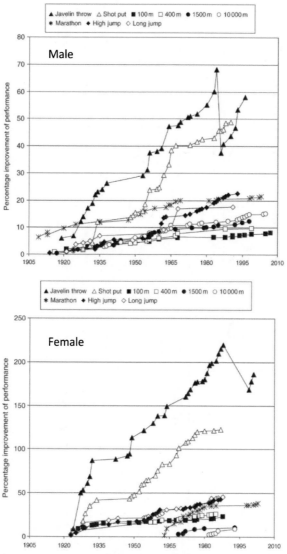

Figure 1.1a (male) and 1.1b (female). Progression of male and female world record performances across selected track and field events (taken with permission) [6]. Note the rate of change in the javelin declined in the 1980s due to altered equipment specifications as competitors began to reach a level of performance that would mean throwing the javelin beyond the length of an athletics stadium.

Table 1.1. Progression of selected world track and field records from 1900 to 2011

	Men			Women		
	First record	Current record	Improvement (%)	First record	Current record	Improvement (%)
100m, time (date)	00:10:60 (1912)	00:09:58 (2009)	9.6	00:13:06 (1922)	00:10:49 (1988)	19.7
400m, time (date)	00:47:08 (1900)	00:43:18 (1999)	8.3	01:04:04 (1922)	00:47:60 (1985)	25.7
1500m, time (date)	03:55:08 (1912)	03:26:00 (1998)	12.4	04:17:03 (1967)	03:50:46 (1993)	10.3
10,000m, time (date)	30:58:08 (1911)	26:17:53 (2005)	15.1	32:17:20 (1981)	29:31:78 (1993)	8.5
Marathon, time (date)	02:55:19 (1908)	02:03:59 (2008)	29.3	03:40:22 (1926)	02:15:25 (2003)	41.2
Long jump, distance (date)	7.61 m (1901)	8.95 m (1991)	17.6	5.16 m (1922)	7.52 m (1988)	45.7
Shot put, distance, (date)	15.54 m (1909)	23.12 m (1990)	48.8	10.15 m (1924)	22.63 m (1987)	123.0

Time is represented as h:min:s.

Griffith-Joyner's 100m record considerably closed the gender difference to its current level of 8.7% and the progression of the women's record represents a 19.7% improvement from the first ratified world record to the present day. As Griffith Joyner's record is often debated for legitimacy (e.g. it was windy that day) even substituting in the winning performance from the last World Athletics Championships (Shelly-Ann Fraser of Jamaica: 10.73s), it still represents an improvement of 21.1% across almost 90 years. This is over double the performance change in men and explains the closed gap (23.5% to 8.7%) between genders [6]. There remains considerable debate as to whether world record performances between genders are narrowing to the extent that males and females may one day compete equally, or whether this gender difference will ever close. However, the gap between elite sprinting performances of males and females has ceased to narrow substantially during the last 50 years and has even widened in some athletic events since the mid-1990s [7]. It is possible that current gender performance differences may reasonably reflect true physiological differences between males and females [7]. Nevertheless, it remains a viable possibility of natural selection that gender-specific differences in performance could continue to reduce.

An explanation of the limited change in the men's 100m sprint performance over the last 100 years is obviously related to the short performance time/duration, but may also be specific to that event in so far as sprint ability has generic usefulness to a wide range of sports activities. In 1912, the ability to sprint would have been a useful attribute for athletic males wishing to perform in Soccer, Baseball, American Football or other well known sports. Therefore, elite male sprinters in 1912 were probably already well trained and likely more so than comparative women for whom competition was less significant and opportunities for participation in organised sports less readily available.

If sprinting to some extent represents an innate ability to maximally exert physical power on an athletics track, long distance running exemplifies different attributes such as the willingness to resist the developing sensations of fatigue and boredom over prolonged activity. This is not to diminish the amazing achievements and hard work of elite sprinters or the value of dedicated sprint training; however, it is possible long distance events may, to a greater extent, demonstrate the impacts of more recently evolving training developments such as periodization and biotechnological training techniques. Long distance events such as the marathon demonstrate greater change in elite performance over similar time frames to sprint events, having progressed from the first male record of 2:55:18.4 set by Johnny Hayes of the USA in 1908 to

2:03:59 by Haile Gebrselassie of Ethiopia in 2008 [5]. This is a performance improvement for males of 29.3%, while for females, the world record marathon performance has improved from 3:40:22 in 1926 (Violet Piercy of the UK) to 2:15:25 set by Paula Radcliffe of the UK in 2008 (41.2% improvement).

Anti-doping control procedures, extrinsic rewards, political boycotts of major events, two world wars and rule modifications, have all impacted on sports participation and the development of world records over the last 100 years. Considerable expansion of participating countries and athletes in Olympic events has also occurred, increasing from only 14 nations competing in the first modern Olympics of 1896 in Athens (240 competitors), to 204 nations for the 2008 Beijing Olympics (11,028 competitors) [8]. Nevertheless, despite greater numbers of elite competitors, greater accessibility to modern training facilities and a growing world population, elite performance have not continued to improve linearly. This undoubtedly represents a slowing of gains in elite level performances and it is possible this may eventually impact on consumer interest in sports where spectators enjoy witnessing world records broken and new role models established based on their athletic achievements.

1.4. EVOLUTION OF TRAINING METHODS

It is tempting to assume that modern training techniques such as periodization and state-of-art technologies are modern phenomena exclusively derived from contemporary training practices outside of the scope and comprehension of athletes in antiquity. However, this perspective would be naive and do a disserve to our athletic predecessors who were well known to complete physical training, prepare themselves for athletic events and also demonstrated understanding of the association between physical activity and health [9].

The earliest known records of physical activity are documented in ancient tomb drawings of ritualised dance and hunting such as those depicted in the Lascaux Caves approximately 13,000 BC [10]. However, the earliest known records of planned, purposeful physical activity (exercise) for acquiring fitness or other health benefits appear from approximately 2500 BC in China. Surgeons at that time encouraged patients to participate in exercise for health benefits, modelled on the movement of animals, chiefly the tiger. In modern terms, this would barely constitute planned exercise as we might consider it, and so the earliest evidence of a like-for-like structured approach to physical training with which to compare our current practices is that of the ancient Olympians.

The ancient Olympics were first documented to be held in Olympia, Greece in the year 776 BC and continued to be celebrated for over one thousand years, broadly on a 4-year cycle [2]. This 4-year cycle has been replicated in the modern Olympics, although we are some way short of achieving the longevity of the ancient Olympics (approx. 112 years vs. 1000 years). There were three main criteria for entry to the Games: the participants had to be male, of Greek origin and had to be free men [11]. Women, slaves and non-Greeks were therefore excluded. The programme of events lasted for five days and only individual sports were contested. These included equestrian events such as horse-drawn chariot racing, pugilism (boxing), wrestling, athletic events such as the pentathlon (discus, long jump, javelin, running and wrestling), and selected running events. For the running events, straight line races were held as the stadium was rectangular and an oval track had not yet been introduced. Consequently, races were classified in terms of their relative length to the length of the stadium. There were four races [2]:

1. The *stade* (a sprint one length of the stadium: approx. 192m)
2. The diaulos (an extended sprint two lengths of the stadium: approx. 384m)
3. The dolichos (an endurance event, 7 to 24 lengths: approx. 1300 – 4600m)
4. The race-in-arms in which competitors raced in armour with helmet and carrying a shield.

Potential participants for the Olympics had to give an undertaking to individually train for 10 months prior to the Olympics before travelling to a dedicated training camp four weeks before the Games to join other participants for an intensive preparatory period. The specifics of either individual training practices or the intensive training camp are scant, but it is clear a final selection of suitable athletes was made once all training had been completed. This process would be analogous to satisfying a selection committee that the appropriate level of qualifying performance had been obtained.

Although it is common to view ancient training methods at that time as unstructured and inferior to modern practices, this viewpoint may be misguided. For example, Philostratus (ca. 172-250AD) described the traditional Greek athletic training system which was a four day cycle of activities, known as the *tetrad*:

"By the *tetrad* system we mean a cycle of four days, each one of which is devoted to a different activity. The first day prepares the athlete; the second is an all-out trial the third is relaxation; and the fourth is a medium-hard work out. ..[Regarding] exercise of the first day,[it] is made up of short, intense movements which stir up the athlete and prepare him for the hard workout to follow on the next day. [This] strenuous day is an all-out test if his potential. The third [day] employs his energy in a moderate way, while on the day of the medium workout [or last day], the athlete [himself] practices breaking holds and preventing his opponent from breaking away." [12]

The *tetrad* system is similar to the modern concept of periodization and yet is given little credit as the basis for cyclic exercise in which work and rest are considered within the training plan (Figure 1.2). Each cycle of the *tetrad* was designed to avoid overloading the athlete with consecutive high intensity training days and thus follows a fairly conventional programme of 1) preparatory exercises (day one), 2) very heavy training (day two), 3) rest (day three) and 4) moderate intensity exercise (day four). The completion of one such cycle would be followed by the first day of the cycle, meaning that moderate exercise was followed by preparatory (or perhaps technical) training, and thus leaving a reasonable period for recovery between high intensity sessions. This organisation of the training cycle would minimise the risk of overtraining and facilitate reasonable recovery from training with which to manage overload and physiological adaptation to training stimuli. Such concepts are obvious to athletes and coaches undertaking training in modern times and yet it is apparent this was in the case in ancient times too.

Interestingly, the limitations of following a regimented, generic and inflexible training programme not accounting for diet and a holistic approach were also noted. The *tetrad* was therefore not without its critics:

"While the gymnasts [coaches or athletic trainers] are following this fixed routine of the *tetrad*, they pay no attention to the condition of the athlete they are training, even though he is being harmed by his food, his wine, the secret snacks he eats, mental strain and fatigue...How can we [prepare athletes] by a schedule of *tetrads*?" [13, 14]

Lucian (AD 120-ca 180) identified the need to vary the training stimulus, manipulate the training environment such as ground surface, and demonstrates an understanding for the need to train for distance as well as speed work for the preparation of Olympic runners:

"We train [young men] to run, getting them to endure long distances as well as speeding them up for swiftness in the sprints. This running is not done on a firm springy surface but in deep sand, where it is not easy to place one's foot forcefully and not push off from it since the foot slips against the yielding sand." [14]

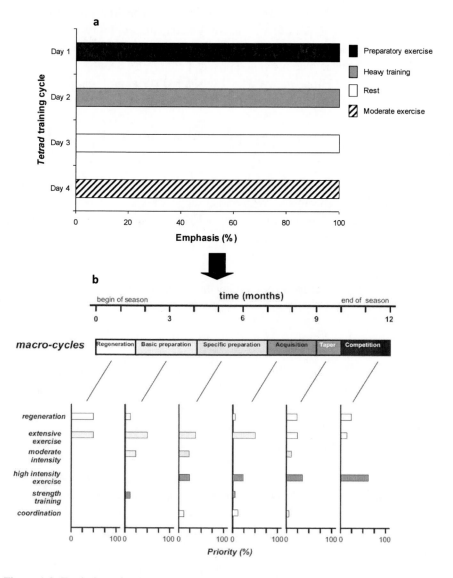

Figure 1.2. Evolution of training periodization from the Greek *tetrad* (a) to modern periodization (b). Periodization (b) diagram taken with permission [19].

Professional coaches had therefore learned a practical appreciation of basic exercise physiology and the principles of athletic training; however, medical philosophers at the time did not always agree that high volumes of training were positive. Galen (c. 200-129BC) for example, wrote an extensive essay on gymnastic exercises in a major work on health. He perceived that too much exercise was not necessarily positive for health, an observation consistent with modern observations of greater susceptibility to illness in response to high training volumes. Full-time athletes therefore did not always find favour with those who promoted physical culture for health.

Galen quotes Hippocrates who considered that professional athletes trained to excess:

"..the perfect condition which these fellows strive for is dangerous."
[2].

As a consequence, the science of training theory was referred to as 'Health Science' and was considered within the scope of the trainer, while a new subject 'hygiene' was taught by the physician and could perhaps be described in modern terms as 'Sports Medicine'.

"..athletes live a life quite contrary to the precepts of hygiene, and I regard their mode of living as a regime far more favourable to illness than to health." [14]

It is interesting to also note at this time that Nike was involved in the Olympics even in antiquity. The Greeks considered it was the gods who decided to grant victory to an athlete. Victory was often represented in the form of a winged female character known as Nike, meaning 'victory' in Greek. However, as competitors performed nude in the ancient Olympics one could also assume performance was free of commercial endorsement.

During the Roman Empire (up until c. 500 AD) physical fitness was an essential military skill but was also seen in a more general context. There was a difference between the Roman attitude to athletic events and the Greeks. Romans, although willing to develop fitness through sport, did not enjoy public participation in the same way as the Greeks. Public spectacles of athletic pursuits were through combat-based activities such as gladiatorial events. Gladiator training was highly specialised, event specific work that was overseen by teams of coaches/trainers, many of whom were former gladiators. Equipment was state-of-art for that period of history and training was highly intense. Nevertheless, multi sport festivals modelled on the early Olympic

Games were never popular among the Romans. After the downfall of the Roman Empire and the beginning of the Dark Ages, the Church became a dominant influence in many countries.

The role of sport in society such as in England at this time was largely dictated by religion and affairs of state. Sport was not consistent with Puritanism and only became a more acceptable feature of society (particularly in Britain) with the decline of Puritanism. The later emergence of the public school system in England re-established the benefits of sport, such as where sport was seen as exerting a positive, character forming, and stabilizing influence on the youth. With these changing attitudes, sport was not only encouraged for its physical benefits but also spiritually. In contrast to the Dark Ages, exercise was now considered a practical component of religion, hence the 'muscular Christian' ethos, but as sport evolved further, it became not so much a means to an end, but an end itself [15].

Galen's early view that vigorous exercise could be harmful persisted into the nineteenth century. It may have been this perception that prompted JE Morgan (1873) [16] to study the health of those who had participated in the Oxford vs Cambridge University Boat Race. Morgan studied longevity and subsequent effect on health of university oarsmen who had participated in the first 40 years of the boat race from the years 1829-1869. He found that the average length of life for each oarsman after the boat race, assuming an age of 20, was 42.2 years. The normal expectation of life at that time based on contemporary English life tables was 40 years. This supported a positive role of exercise on long term health outcomes.

Although the *tetrad* of ancient Greece identified athletes working in four-day training cycles, the modern schema of dividing a training programme into stages or cycles (periodization) originated in Europe in the early twentieth century (~1910) [17]. Coaches began to structure training programmes to incorporate different stages for emphasis to training, such as general, preparatory and specific (pre-event) considerations [17].

In the 1920s and 1930s, more clearly defined cycles of training began to emerge. Experts began to recognize the need to clearly alternate periods of work and rest, to gradually progress from high-volume/low-intensity to low-volume/high-intensity training close to a race and to have each phase of training build on the training completed in the previous phase.

During the 1950s and 1960s, prominent New Zealand running coach Arthur Lydiard refined the periodization concept to include base training, hill training and sharpening work [18]. Lydiard was one of the first to divide a training cycle into distinct phases and establish a defined order for the different types of training within them; however, it was not until the latter half of the 20th century that the idea of periodizing an athlete's training became common practice.

The modern periodization training method divides a year of training into major periods called macrocycles, each about three to four months in duration [19]. These macrocycles are further subdivided into smaller mesocycles, which typically last three to four weeks (but can last up to 6 weeks) and even smaller microcycles, which are typically one week long [20]. Thus, three to four microcycles comprise one mesocycle; and three to four mesocycles constitute one macrocycle (Figure 1.2). The final week of a mesocycle is usually designed as a restorative microcycle before undertaking the work of the next mesocycle. This restoration period can involve both reduced training loads and periods of rest.

The basic goal of periodization training is to introduce a series of training loads and recovery times that provide a stimulus for adaptation and super-compensation [21]. This causes overload (Figure 1.3), whereby the body (e.g. muscles and physiological systems) is periodically stressed in response to higher than normal work. The body adapts and thereafter is able to work more efficiently at a higher work. If the training stimulus is too small in either intensity or duration, little or no adaptive overload will take place (Figure 1.3). Conversely, if the stress is too severe, the adaptation could be delayed or may even be compromised. Therefore, determining an appropriate training load for each individual is a key consideration to optimising athletic potential. A one-size fits all approach to training is rarely the answer.

The Lydiard-style periodization of training is known as linear periodization because the various major training stimuli (e.g. aerobic, anaerobic, strength or speed) are largely segregated from each other in the training process and are arranged in a line such that each makes way for the next. This approach is distinct from nonlinear periodization, in which the various training stimuli are mixed together throughout the training programme and only the emphasis or importance of each component changes from cycle to cycle.

There are several major criticisms of Lydiard-style linear periodization systems. For example, many experienced coaches and athletes believe that the sudden introduction of high-intensity training after a lengthy period of low-intensity training carries a high risk of muscular injury. A second criticism is that the various important aspects of running fitness are not developed in unison [22]. This is particularly the case when strength and speed characteristics are developed in different phases of training, only for the athlete to experience some extent of detraining in one while the other is practiced. Finally, linear periodization systems are also criticized for requiring months of dedicated (linear) preparation towards a specific goal rather than facilitating numerous goals across a competitive period or season.

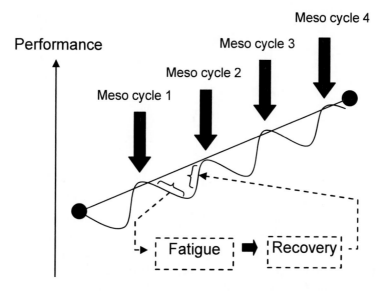

Figure 1.3. Principles of overload whereby performance in response to each cyclic period of training (mesocycle) results in fatigue and subsequent adaptation and progressive performance gain. The solid diagonal line represents performance gain in response to four consecutive mesocycles.

Nonlinear periodization attempts to address all of these limitations by mixing together the various major training stimuli throughout the training cycle. The presence of simultaneous strength and speed training across the training period may minimize injury risk and retain performance to a greater extent [20, 22]. It also gives athletes more flexibility to compete when required. As athletes are therefore continually in a reasonable broad-base state of conditioning, they can achieve a peak for a particular event fairly quickly by appropriately increasing the emphasis and prevalence of race-like training characteristics. There is therefore no requirement to wait for each fitness component to be added to the programme linearly one by one. In linear periodization, outcomes can be difficult to quantify though as training intensities and loads can be much more difficult to discern amid a series of training targets within the overall training plan (Figure 1.4).

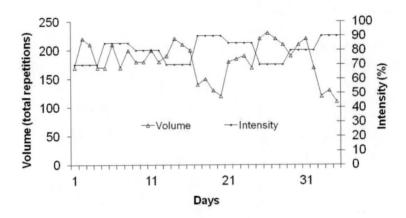

Figure 1.4. An example of outcomes for training volume and intensity in response to nonlinear periodization resistance training.

Most of the more recent periodization systems are based on nonlinear principles [22]. One example is the multi-pace training method developed by David Martin and Peter Coe [23], which changes the emphasis within cyclic training periods without dedicating the whole training schedule to one modality, or specific focus. This enables several strands of training to be progressed simultaneously while the specific emphasis can still be maintained. This has been suggested to minimise risk of injury as it removes the necessity for broad base change of training when changing the phase of training [20].

Training methods have certainly evolved to the extent where phases of training, emphasis of components of fitness, specific goals, and methods of determining intensity of effort are all paramount to achieving optimal balance. However, rather than being a completely new concept it appears such training is an evolution rather than a modern invention. In many ways, training methodologies may have reached the stage at which they have become too complicated and a simpler intuitive approach such as self-paced and self-regulated exercise may prove optimal. Fleck summarised [20]:

> "We have, in the USA, overdone overanalyzed and overplayed periodization. We have created too many rules, to the stage where it is too daunting to wade through the plethora of literature to gain or imply any practical use."

1.5. THE CHALLENGE OF SUSTAINING PROGRESS

In antiquity, body masses were approximately 70% of current values [24]. In modern times, (1900-2002), the mean height of humans has increased by approximately 5cm, while over the same period, the mean height of elite swimmers and runners increased by 11cm and 16cm, respectively [25]. For many sports there appear to be specific physical or anthropometric characteristics that indicate suitability, or potential, to compete at the highest level. In basketball, the heights and masses of all retired NBA players are significantly positively associated (p < 0.01) with the length of career and regression analysis suggests player body mass equates to, on average, an extra year in career length [26]. For example, it has been estimated that for every extra 1.0cm in height or 1.3kg in mass, this corresponds to approximately $US43,000 in additional player payments over a career [26].

In soccer, differences in age, stature, body mass and BMI have been observed and these differences vary across different European soccer leagues. For example, goalkeepers and defenders tend to be older than other outfield players suggesting that they have longer careers with increased earning potential. In addition, on average, players in the Spanish, Italian, English and German soccer leagues are taller and leaner than the secular population of their respective countries [27]. Spanish soccer players were, for example, 7cm taller than the general Spanish population [27]. Of course sport is evolving on a continuing base and so are the athletes competing in these sports. Olds [28] provided some evidence from Rugby union to suggest that changes in the physical characteristics of players is above and beyond that of the secular population. For example, rugby players showed significantly greater increases in body mass and BMI in comparison to the normal population. The demands of the different sports and the possible rewards mean that for many to reach and/or survive in professional sport they may be tempted to adopt illegal and dangerous behaviours with which to modify body size and shape.

Different sports and playing positions within team games appear to require specific morphologies for success and thus role-specific physical characteristic requirements are now common. Since 1980, the rate of increase in body mass and height has been observed through evaluation of BMI among sports people. This has shown an approximate increase in body size of 0.159 BMI units per year. In addition, studies involving the anabolic steroid androgen showed that, even in doses much lower than those used by athletes, muscular strength could be improved by 5–20% [29].

Although improved nutrition, biotechnologies and up to date training practices may contribute to the observed change in elite performer morphology; it is also likely that both legal and illegal ergogenic aids are influential. For example, Ben Johnson is suggested to have stood to gain an estimated $US30 million in endorsements for his 1988 Olympics sprint victory [30]. It is difficult to deny the attraction of such an incentive.

In response to announced drug testing, less than 1% of Olympic athletes during the 1980s (1984 to 1989) were found to test positive [26] which suggests drug taking in sport is a relatively minor issue. However, this low percentage is misleading as it is widely accepted that the use of illegal performance enhancing drugs is one of the greatest problems facing sport. To put this issue in perspective, [31] it has been reported that when the US Olympic Committee conducted unannounced drug tests involving no punitive actions, approximately 50% of athletes tested positive to anabolic steroids. There is also considerable colloquial evidence that in sports such as NFL American Football, steroid use in some positions may be as high as 90% [32]. The International Amateur Athletic Federation estimates that only 10–15% of participating athletes are tested in each major competition [33] and so most athletes are relatively unlikely to ever undergo testing. As a consequence, the risk of expulsion is relatively low in relation to the possible gains. This is unsurprising given the financial and publicity incentives for reaching the upper echelons in professional sport. Elite athletes can earn many millions of dollars every year in prize money, sponsorships and endorsements. The extrinsic rewards of success are therefore great, but the penalties relatively minor.

The issue of drugs in sport has been hotly debated for many years with researchers such as Haugen [34] predicting that where the risk of being caught is zero, all athletes will choose to cheat. The enormous rewards for the winner, combined with the effectiveness of the drugs, and the low rate of testing all interact to create an environment of loosely accepted cheating [35]. However, due to the apparent necessity of ideal physical condition, body size and shape for high performance sport, we may be placing modern athletes in an untenable position. It is conceivable that cheating could eventually be the only option for success as even athletes with ideal physical attributes may not consider elite level performance obtainable without pharmaceutical support. One could question whether is it morally right to place such expectations on athletes while denying them effective pharmaceutical aids.

Savulescu and colleagues [33] suggested that perhaps the answer to the dilemma of drugs in sport might be to simply allow all performance enhancing drugs. In support of this argument it has been pointed out that many classical musicians use ? blockers to control performance anxiety as these drugs lower heart rate and blood pressure, thereby reducing the effects of stress. It has previously been shown that the quality of a musical performance generally improves if the musician takes these drugs [36] and yet there is no stigma attached to the use of these drugs in the performance of music. The audience assesses the performance and the use of pharmaceutical aids is largely irrelevant to that context.

There are many examples of tenuous legality and selective morality in the limitations of acceptable cheating in sport. For example, there is little difference of intent between elevating blood count by altitude training, by using a hypoxic air chamber, or by injecting erythropoietin (EPO). The aim is largely the same for each, although results are only consistently effective with the latter [37]. It is the EPO form of blood doping which is the only activity not permitted. Assuming altitude and hypoxic training proved consistently effective, it is likely they too would be banned. Yet some competitors have naturally higher packed red blood cells, or have better suited muscular characteristics to a given activity, each of which is an advantage by genetic good fortune [35]. Some individuals can afford hypoxic chambers for training; some live at altitude, or can afford regular training trips to suitable environments. Some gymnasts are more flexible, and some basketball players are seven feet tall. It is apparent that nature has not dealt us all an equal hand.

It has additionally been proposed that any legalization of performance-enhancing drugs in sport, if it were to occur, would need to be subject to limitations [37]. However, this is a self-defeating argument as the presence of any imposed limit on permissible drugs encourages athletes to seek out and exceed such limitations in the quest of the competitive edge. An illegally obtained competitive edge is not so simply circumvented as to allow a free(er) environment for doping. If there were a legalization of performance enhancing drugs in sports, the athletes may be inclined to adopt greater risk taking behaviour which could mean world records are extended beyond the extent of that achievable in drug free performances. In the short term, this might satisfy the viewing public, media and sponsors but does not address the issue of whether this is a moral or fair situation for athletes who are seeking to reach the top in their event. If an athlete strives to reach the top, he or she can only realistically try to beat the competition at the time of racing. Whether or not this requires a world record performance is largely irrelevant compared to the specific goal of simply outperforming the opposition. Placing the athlete in an untenable position requiring personal health risks to achieve this goal is not consistent with a morally responsible modern society and surely cannot be permissible. It could be considered exploitative of impressionable, vulnerable individuals who are physically able and willing to dope for the avarice of spectators and media. This is not a situation we should condone.

Performance enhancing drugs primarily facilitate the desire of the athlete (or coach) to improve performance in excess of that otherwise perceived to be achievable. This is presumably in response to an identified need or deficiency recognised in the athlete, although this assessment may often be made under false assumptions. The desire to improve, to seek out ways to improve and adopt practices to outperform others is perfectly natural and entirely consistent with the evolution of sport. Improvements can also be accomplished legitimately, especially if appropriate drug testing is adopted systematically across all sports. There then remains the question of how performances can be optimised in the absence of illegal drugs? This question can be addressed by understanding the mechanisms of how physical performance is managed. The simple explanation is that humans distribute effort across the duration of an exercise bout (or race) in relation to: 1) the known demands of the task, 2) an innate sense of their physical capabilities and 3) their motivation to succeed. Nevertheless, this explanation requires considerable elucidation such as the ways in which effort is applied, whether or not it is possible to increase effort, where this effort is best applied, and what are the physiological and psychological mechanisms that potential restrict all voluntary efforts? Although the mechanisms underlying the application of effort are highly pertinent to performance of all physical tasks, it is an area often neglected. This is, in many ways, surprising as Triplett identified the concept of pacing as long ago as in 1897 [38], and yet his observation were largely ignored. As a consequence, the study of pacing remains an emerging area of research in contemporary sport and exercise science [39]. It is therefore the purpose of this book to thoroughly describe the role of pacing across contemporary sport and exercise situations.

CONCLUSION

- It is now predicted that without an unexpected change to human evolution most world records will not be improved by more than 0.05% over the next 15-20 years.
- Analysis of elite sprinting performance between males and females demonstrates that current gender performance differences may now

reasonably reflect true physiological differences between males and females.

- The ancient Greek tetrad system of training is similar to the modern concept of periodization and yet is given little credit as the basis for cyclic exercise in which work and rest are considered within the training plan.

- Each cycle of the tetrad was designed to avoid overloading the athlete with consecutive high intensity training days and thus follows a fairly conventional programme of 1) preparatory exercises (day one), 2) very heavy training (day two), 3) rest (day three) and 4) moderate intensity exercise (day four).

- The modern system of linear periodization training divides a year of training into major periods called macrocycles, each about three to four months in duration. These macrocycles are further subdivided into mesocycles, which typically last three to four weeks (but can last up to 6 weeks) and microcycles, which are typically one week long.

- Criticisms of linear periodization systems include: 1) many coaches and athletes believe the sudden introduction of high-intensity exercise after low-intensity training carries a risk of injury; 2) various important aspects of training are not developed in unison through this training system and 3) it requires months of dedicated preparation towards a specific goal rather than simultaneously facilitating several goals.

- Nonlinear periodization attempts to address all of these limitations by mixing together the various major training stimuli with differential emphasis throughout the training cycle.

- Different sports and playing positions appear to require specific morphologies.

- It has been suggested that to remove unfair advantage in sport, it may be simplest to allow all performance enhancing drugs. This could be considered exploitative of impressionable, vulnerable individuals who are physically able and willing to dope for the avarice of spectators and media.

REFERENCES

[1]   Foster, C., et al., Effect of pacing strategy on cycle time trial performance. *Medicine & Science in Sports & Exercise,* 1993. 25: p. 383-388.

[2]   Robinson, R., Sources for the history of Greek athletics 1980: *Ares Publishers.*

[3]   Berthelot, G., et al., Exponential growth combined with exponential decline explains lifetime performance evolution in individual and human species. *Age,* 2011. Online ahead of print (ONLINE).

[4]   Berthelot, G., et al., Athlete atypicity on the edge of human achievement: performances stagnate after the last peak, in 1988. *PLoS ONE,* 2010. 5: p. 1-8.

[5]   IAAF, IAAF world championships in athletics: IAAF statistics handbook. Daegu. *IAAF Media & Public Relations Department,* 2011.

[6]   Lippi, G., et al., Updates on improvement of human athletic performance: focus on world records in athletics. *British Medical Bulletin,* 2008. 87: p. 7-15.

[7]   Seiler, S., J.D. Koning, and C. Foster, The fall and rise of the gender difference in elite anaerobic performance 1952–2006. *Medicine & Science in Sports & Exercise,* 2006. 39: p. 534-540.

[8]   IOC, Factsheet. *International Olympic Committee,* 2011.

[9]   Galenus, C., De parvae pilae exercitio, in Medicorum Graecorum opera quae exstant, C. Kuhn, Editor. 1964, G. *Olms:* Leipzig.

[10]   Williams, J., Medical aspects of sport and physical fitness. 1965, London: *Pergamon Press.*

[11]   Crowther, N., Athlete and state: qualifying for the Olympic Games in ancient Greece. *Journal of Sport History,* 1996. 23: p. 34-43.

[12]   Philostratus, F., Concerning gymnastics (Translated), in *The Research Quarterly,* T. Woody, Editor. 1936, Ann Arbor: MI.

[13]   Bowie, E. and J. Elsner, Philostratus. *Greek culture in the Roman world.* 2009, New York: Cambridge University Press.

[14]   Grivetti, L. and E. Applegate, From Olympia to Atlanta: a cultural-historical perspective on diet and athletic training. *Journal of Nutrition,* 1997. 127: p. 860S-868S.

[15]   Holt, R., Sport and History: the state of the subject in Britain. *Twentieth Century British History,* 1996. 7: p. 231-252.

[16]   Morgan, J., University oars being a critical enquiry into the after health of men who rowed in the Oxford and Cambridge Boat Race from the year 1829–1869, based on the personal experience of the rowers themselves. 1873, London: *McMillan.*

[17]   Pedemonte, J., Foundations of training periodization. Part I: Historical outline. *National Strength and Conditioning Journal,* 1986. 8: p. 62-65.

[18]   Lydiard, A. and G. Gilmour, Run to the top. 1962: *AH Reed, NZ.*

[19] Flueck, M. and W. Eilers, Training modalities: impact on endurance capacity. *Endocrinology and Metabolism Clinics of North America* 2010. 39: p. 183-200.

[20] Fleck, S. and W. Kraemer, The ultimate training system: periodization breakthrough. 1996, New York: *Advanced Research Press.*

[21] Bompa, T. and G. Haff, Periodization: Theory and methodology of training. 5th ed. 2009, *Champaign IL: Human Kinetics.*

[22] Fleck, S., Periodized strength training: A critical review. *Journal of Strength and Conditioning Research,* 1999. 13: p. 82-89.

[23] Martin, D. and P. Coe, Better training for distance runners 2nd ed. 1997, *Champaign IL: Human Kinetics.*

[24] NHANES, National health and nutrition examination survey: average weight for an adult man, 1999-2002. 1999.

[25] Charles, J. and A. Bejan, The evolution of speed, size and shape in modern athletics. *The Journal of Experimental Biology,* 2009. 212: p. 2419-2425.

[26] Norton, K. and T. Olds, Morphological evolution of athletes over the 20th Century: causes and consequences. *Sports Medicine,* 2001. 31: p. 763-783.

[27] Bloomfield, J., et al., Analysis of age, stature, body mass, BMI and quality of elite soccer players from 4 european leagues. *Journal of Sports Medicine and Physical Fitness,* 2005. 45: p. 58-67.

[28] Olds, T., The evolution of physique in male rugby union players in the twentieth century. *Journal of Sports Sciences,* 2001. 19: p. 253-262.

[29] Hartgens, F. and H. Kuipers, Effects of androgenic-anabolic steroids in athletes. *Sports Medicine,* 2004. 34: p. 513-554.

[30] Lucas, J., Future of the Olympic Games. 1992, *Champaign (IL): Human Kinetics.*

[31] Voy, R., Drugs, sport and politics. 1991, Champaign (IL): Leisure Press.

[32] Yesalis, C., Anabolic steroids in sport and exercise. 1993: *Champaign (IL): Human Kinetics.*

[33] Savulescu, J., B. Foddy, and M. Clayton, Why we should allow performance enhancing drugs in sport. *British Journal of Sports Medicine,* 2004. 38: p. 666-670.

[34] Haugen, K., The performance-enhancing drug game. *Journal of Sports Economics* 2004. 5: p. 67-87.

[35] Noakes, T., Should we allow performance-enhancing drugs in sport? A rebuttal to the article by Savulescu and colleagues. *International Journal of Sports Science & Coaching,* 2006. 1: p. 289-316.

[36] Brantigan, C., T. Brantigan, and N. Joseph, Effect of beta blockade and beta stimulation on stage fright. *American Journal of Medicine,* 1982. 72: p. 88-94.

[37] Wiesing, U., Should performance-enhancing drugs in sport be legalized under medical supervision? *Sports Medicine,* 2011. 41: p. 167-176.

[38] Triplett, N., The dynamogenic factors in pacemaking and competition. *The American Journal of Psychology,* 1897. 9: p. 507-533.

[39] Foster, C., et al., Pacing strategy and athletic performance. *Sports Medicine,* 1994. 17: p. 77-85.

Chapter 2

AN INTRODUCTION TO PACING IN SPORT AND EXERCISE

2.1. ABSTRACT

The aim of this chapter is to identify, define and discuss the conceptual basis of pacing in sport and exercise. Evidence of behaviour consistent with pacing exists in animals and humans, yet levels of organism complexity differ between species. Decision-making and responsiveness to afferent sensory information are consistent features in many species, with each demonstrating a coping behaviour with which to avoid catastrophic physical exhaustion. This suggests that pacing is a mechanism with which to manage the completion of a specific task in relation to the known demands and the perceived physical capabilities of the individual. For humans, commonalities of pacing strategy also exist and it seems likely these are driven by personal and situational demands. Typical pacing strategies are categorised and their particular applications to performance are discussed in this chapter.

2.2. INTRODUCTION

Pacing is a relatively new area of research within sport and exercise science. To our knowledge, there is not yet a working definition of what is meant by pacing and it is likely that a definition to satisfy all the diverse attributes of pacing will still remain elusive. Nevertheless, for the purpose of understanding the authors' interpretation of pacing in response to sport and exercise, we propose the following definition:

Pacing:

'The goal directed distribution and management of effort across the duration of an exercise bout.'

This is a definition of the topic which best fits our view of pacing in this book. Pacing is a strategy with which to manage effort across an exercise bout in relation to a specific goal and in the knowledge of the likely demands of the task. It is widely recognised that individuals distribute effort throughout an exercise bout and it is this distribution of applied work that has already been loosely termed pacing [1]. Yet, pacing does not purely apply to elite athletic performances. It is also in evidence during all non-reflex exercise situations where individuals are able to receive and act on neural feedback from peripheral physiologic systems [2, 3]. Yet little is known of the specific physiological, cognitive and/or environmental factors that affect or control the distribution of work during exercise [4, 5].

2.3. THE CONCEPT OF PACING

The 1980 Olympics games held in Moscow was remarkable for several sporting and non sporting reasons. It was the first time a major sporting event had been subject to substantial political boycott, the last time a Caucasian male won the 100 metre sprint [6] and also because it was the arena for intense competitive rivalry between two British middle distance runners (Figure 2.1a and 2.1b).

Figure 2.1a and 2.1b. The agony (800m) and ecstasy (1500m) of Sebastian (Lord) Coe vs. Steve Ovett at the 1980 Olympic games (with permission from Topham Picturepoint).

Both runners were supreme athletes and each was in peak physical condition. Sebastian Coe was the current world record holder for the 800 metres (1:42.33 min:s at that time) and Steve Ovett had recently set a new world record for the 1500 metres (3:32.09 min:s), marginally bettering the previous record set by his rival, Coe [7]. Each was scheduled to compete in both 800m and 1500m events with Coe the favourite for the 800m and Ovett the 1500m. The fact that Ovett then won the 800m race while several days later Coe won the 1500m is not so remarkable in itself as middle distance runners are often able to perform similarly well across these two distances. However, it was the manner of Coe's defeat in the 800 metres that was unexpected, particularly as he was placed last after the first 400m lap. Considering the race leader completed that lap in a relatively modest time of 54.55s, it should have been well within Coe's capabilities to be placed somewhere other than last. At that stage of his career, Coe had a personal best performance of 46.87s for 400m [7] and yet, in the most important race of his career so far, he spent the 2nd 400m lap running in an outside lane and attempting to accelerate past all the other competitors from last place. It is not surprising he didn't win the race from that situation and it was actually quite an achievement that he managed to overhaul everyone else except for Ovett and claim the silver medal. Yet, Ovett's winning time of 1:45.4 minutes was 3s slower than Coe's world record. This duration represents a lifetime in the competitive world of middle distance running and it is perhaps a race Sebastian Coe has run over in his mind more than once, subsequently selecting a different race (pacing) strategy. A slow start to the race was also not the strategy he chose for the 1500m a few days later.

The scientific study of pacing has previously been described as 'the unexplored territory in sport performance' [1] and, until recently, few studies had examined the influence of pacing on exercise performance [8]. This is surprising as the distribution of effort is an integral part of racing, but this also suggests that a voluntary behaviour (effort) may limit performance rather than the absolute capacity of a single physiological system [9]. For example, many experimental studies have assumed athletes run to the point of exhaustion and cease exercise directly as a consequence of depleted fuel sources, severe local muscle acidosis, a limiting core body temperature, dehydration or other examples of a system failure [10, 11]. However, none of these factors has consistently been shown to be causal to exercise-induced fatigue. Each variable may be strongly associated with the sensations of fatigue and declines in work outputs, but such associations do not infer causality.

Perhaps the most logical way of viewing pacing is to consider it as a neural buffering process to prevent premature physical exhaustion. This buffering process may avoid the necessity to conclude an exercise bout prior to its scheduled finish, or attain an unnecessarily high peak power output prior to the specific point where it is most required, or expend too much energy on one exercise bout when the task requires sustained performance quality across a series of activities.

Pacing is not a perfect process and some people are better at it than others. Nevertheless, it is apparent that the ability to accurately pace oneself can be improved with training or, if not by training, with experience [12]. Prior experiences of similar circumstances whether in sports, day-to-day life, or clinical exercise rehabilitation settings are important features in the ability to pace [4]. If pacing is a buffering mechanism to enable people to successfully complete tasks, then prior experience and accurate knowledge of the task demands are crucial to success [9]. It is the coupling of prior experiential knowledge and accurate awareness of the task demands that enables us to consider the requirements for likely success in relation to our individual capabilities [12]. The more accurate this knowledge, the more likely pacing will accurately reflect our intentions or maximal capability. These intentions might be to simply complete a race, perhaps to win it, to work at a fixed effort level during training, or to complete a series of tasks while distributing efforts across each.

In sport, it is known that individuals perform less well in unfamiliar circumstances [9], when the demands of the task are unclear [13] and that impaired performance occurs prior to the absolute failure of any single physiological system [14]. In all exercise situations, voluntary power output is immediately reduced when individuals are confronted with adverse conditions such as extreme heat in comparison to neutral conditions [15] and certainly well in advance of any physical necessity to do so. It has also been demonstrated that differences in power outputs for endurance events are evident in the first minutes of exercise between carbohydrate loaded and normal carbohydrate conditions, while metabolic fuel storage of glycogen is still high in both [16]. This suggests pacing is established in anticipation of, and not after, physiological system failure, especially as individuals appear to run down fuel stores to similar post-exercise concentrations (i.e. not fully depleted) of muscle glycogen regardless of initial starting levels [16, 17].

The concept of pacing is not exclusive to sports and race performances. It applies to almost all exercise situations [18-21] as will be demonstrated in this book. The concept of pacing dictates that effort is distributed to facilitate task accomplishment at the perceived intensity required by the individual. The requirements of the individual depend on many factors and are not restricted to the physiological limitations of the human body. As subsequent chapters will identify, no single physiological system demonstrates catastrophic system failure during exercise in healthy subjects. Also, no single physiological variable accurately predicts athletic performance [9] and it is the purpose of this book to identify the role of pacing in this conundrum and more importantly to discuss the factors that influence pacing. It should be apparent at this stage that the protective buffering role of pacing cannot be investigated purely from a physiological perspective. As pacing is an informed decision based on accurate knowledge of past and present factors [4], it must also be considered a psychological issue. The interaction of physiological and psychological factors is crucial to pacing and more generally to human performance. Therefore the philosophy of this text is to view the human body from a psychophysiological perspective whereby physiological and psychological components contribute to the complexities of behaviour.

2.4. THE ORIGINS OF PACED ACTIVITY

Although the study of pacing is a relatively new concept, the premise that both humans and animals exhibit behaviour consistent with pacing is not novel, new, or even speculative. The abilities of efficient and effective locomotion are important to the survival of all species [22, 23]. Hunting, foraging, or avoiding predators are all achievement based outcomes [24] and the more complex the organism, the greater the complexity of behaviour and task execution. The principles of natural selection [25] infer that the most successful at achieving their outcomes will provide the future genetic basis of their population. A slow moving animal, prone to premature fatigue, and unable to respond to environmental demands would seem an unlikely evolutionary forerunner. Organisms adjust behaviour to the stimulation they receive from the environment [26] and the origins of pacing are perhaps best described through investigation of behaviour-environment interactions.

It is well noted in laboratory studies that single cell amoeba display simple avoidance behaviour in response to stimulation with mechanical shock, weak electric currents, and light [26]. This is as a consequent to sensitization to a single stimulus. Amoebas do not possess a brain; however, as organism complexity increases, greater sophistication of behaviour is observed.

The concept of conditioned learning was neatly demonstrated by Ivan Pavlov [27]. Pavlov observed that dogs salivated when a bell was rung if the sound of the bell had previously occurred while the dog had the pleasurable sensation of meat in its mouth. Pavlov proposed the overlap in time of the meat in the mouth with the sound of the bell resulted in the creation of a neural association between the two stimuli, such that the sound was able to substitute for the meat and elicited salivation. Pavlov called the meat an unconditioned stimulus, the bell a conditioned stimulus and the salivation resultant to the conditioned stimulus a conditioned response. The salivation of the dog was therefore a learned (conditioned) behaviour in response to a stimulus.

The cognitive abilities of birds are also now appreciated as more complex than previously assumed [28]. Pigeons for example, have been shown to be able to memorize up to 725 different visual patterns, while parrots can learn human words and use them to communicate reciprocally with humans. In cold environments, birds adjust their posture to contribute to heat conservation [29] while in hot environments they voluntarily seek out shade and remain inactive [30]. This is inherently sensible behaviour.

Reptiles have brains similarly organized to birds due to their common ancestry. Reptiles are capable of both non-associative (response-stimulus reflex) and associative learning such as when a saltwater crocodile notices a routine pattern of behaviour in a potential prey and lies in waiting for an opportunity to strike. Reptiles are also the first vertebrate class in which a neocortex is present in the brain (site of conscious thinking), but this is minimally developed and so high order conceptual learning is generally considered beyond their scope [31].

As amoeba, mammals, birds, and reptiles all demonstrate the ability to interact with their environments it seems unlikely that environmental triggers would not form part of a sensory process informing exercise behaviour. If a bird is able to recognize the need for shade on a hot day [28, 30] so to avoid overheating, then a human is also perfectly capable of this behaviour.

Animals demonstrate a multitude of complex behaviours. Predators such as large cats (e.g. lions) are only ever intermittently active, while lizards also exhibit stop/go movement patterns, even when pursued. Migratory birds sustain constant motion during long flights and dogs such as the Cape Hunting dog or wolves are capable of tracking prey for extensive periods [32]. Despite this obvious diversity, the commonality of all animals is the outcome driven nature of their locomotion. Each animal has morphological and biochemical differences which make it suited to its unique lifestyle and aims. It is uncommon to observe an animal fall short in achieving its aim. It may fail to execute the task (e.g. a lion may miss capturing a gazelle) but we do not observe it continue the chase until it reaches absolute exhaustion. That is unless some unexpected environmental circumstances deny the animal its usual means of recovery. Therefore, a lion does not run itself to exhaustion, a Cape Hunting dog tracks an animal for 25-50 minutes before resting and reassessing new prey targets [33], migratory birds land early if adverse wind speeds preclude reaching the expected destination [28], and lizards do not exhaust themselves, even when pursued [23, 34]. None of these animals possess the cognitive abilities of human and yet all are able to respond effectively to their environments. All these organisms have a brain which receives sensory feedback and each adopts behaviour in response to this sensory information. The main difference between species rests on whether that behaviour is instinctive, or consequent to a conscious cognitively-derived decision.

Instinct is an innate, unlearned pattern of response [31]. Instinctual behaviour is therefore fixed by permanent neural patterns which are genetically determined and passed on to future generations. In contrast, learned (acquired) behaviour is generally considered to be a result of experience. Laboratory-bred rats, for example, will freeze if they encounter a cat, despite never having previously seen one [35]. Freezing is therefore a built-in (innate) response and simple behaviours do not require conscious decisions (i.e. they are automated, sub aware behaviours). Humans, like other animals, receive afferent feedback to inform us of such sensations of hunger, thirst, excessive heat storage or nausea in the presence of metabolic disturbance. These sensations gradually grow in severity if we try to ignore them and if we do not change our behaviour; they therefore stimulate us to adopt sensible behaviours to avoid physical damage. In some situations, the sophistication of the human is also its limitation; in other words, our superior cognitive abilities enable us to ignore, rather than immediately act on the feedback information our bodies are providing.

2.4.1. Case Study: Cheetah, *Acinonyx jubatus*

The cheetah is a rather special animal and worthy of closer inspection in the study of pacing and behaviour. In many ways, the behaviour of the cheetah is similar to our own, in so far as it recognises the demands of a given task, has a plan of how to execute the task, recognises when the desired outcome is likely or unlikely to be achieved and it also learns from experience.

The cheetah has a deep chest, small waist and proportionally longer limbs than the other big cats [36]. An average adult male cheetah weighs 43 kg [37], it has relatively small canines which allows for a larger nasal aperture, facilitating increased air intake during recovery from activity while it suffocates its prey by throttling it. However, what makes the cheetah a *cause celebre* of the animal kingdom is its ability to reach incredible speeds.

A captive cheetah has reportedly been observed to reach 112 kph over a short distance with 0-60 kph acceleration not uncommon within 3 seconds [38]. Antelopes, the main prey of cheetah reach top speeds of 80-97 kph [34] and so although the peak speed of the cheetah is exceptional; it is a necessary capability for its hunting practices. Nevertheless, cheetah hunts are relatively brief and seldom last longer than 200-300m (e.g. 10-15s).

Cheetahs have been observed to have a successful hunt to kill ratio of approximately 6:1, although this improves to 4:1 in open grasslands where it has the best opportunity to use its pace [38]. Studies in the Nairobi National Park found that cheetahs had significantly longer chase distances in successful (189m) than in unsuccessful hunts (96m). The success of longer chase distances indicates that cheetahs are able to gauge their chances of success and decide to give up early if failure is predicted. In this way, energy is conserved, exhaustion avoided and further hunts remain viable. Any longer distance (>300m) unsuccessful hunts are generally initiated by juvenile cheetah, suggesting that, as with humans, (prior) experience is a key factor in the hunting process. Learning and gaining experience from trial and error is of course a key feature in developing successful behaviour. Thus earlier recognition of likely success in animal hunting in relation to the specific task is consistent with human (anticipatory/predictive) paced behaviour (Figure 2.2).

Figure 2.2. Humans and Cheetahs: both exhibit pacing behaviours in response to the known demands of a task (www.scenicreflections.com).

2.5. PSYCHOLOGY OF PACING

Whilst physically active or exercising, humans have the ability to consciously process afferent sensory information arising from the internal and external environment and make decisions based on this information. In comparison, a system based entirely on hardwired reflexes to deal with all sensory signals would be infinitely large, slow to respond and cumbersome. The capacity to make conscious decisions in this respect has allowed humans to optimise their behaviour [39]. This provides a huge evolutionary advantage.

Information reaching the central nervous system has four characteristics: quality, intensity, duration, and hedonicity [39]. Quality, intensity and duration provide positive information and are multiplicative. Hedonicity (how useful or harmful an event is) provides positive, negative or neutral information and is additive in nature. Hedonicity refers to our capacity to associate different sensations with pleasant or unpleasant responses.

It is highly likely that the conscious sensation of effort consists of a combination of peripheral and central sensory information. Hence, the perceptions of effort or perceived exertion are not based on a single sensation but an amassing of multiple signals. The Borg scale of perceived exertion [40] in this respect assesses our global perceptions arising from the internal environment. This mental representation has been shown to be as good a measure of exercise intensity as physiological parameters such as heart rate [41].

According to Cabanac [39], behaviour is regulated by hedonicity, commonly known as the pursuit of optimizing pleasure. Pleasure in his view equals usefulness. Engagement in muscular exertion therefore is the result of direct or indirect motives. There is evidence that muscular exertion in itself is rewarding and improves mood [42, 43] and its instigation can thus be intrinsically motivated. Also, acutely sustained muscular activity itself can be unpleasant, however the resulting reward compensates for the feelings of unpleasantness.

In sport, individuals often engage in training regimes which are extremely strenuous and not pleasurable at all. So why would athletes be motivated to experience high levels of displeasure? Cabanac [39] has suggested that there is a trade off between our ability to tolerate displeasure and the anticipated future rewards. An athlete might train extremely hard because his desire to run faster, jump further or make the soccer squad outweigh that of feeling immediate pleasure. The athlete is able to delay gratification to a future point in time. As such, the selection of a behavioural response or the way we pace our self during exercise is based on physiological properties (e.g. anaerobic threshold) as well as the immediate or future needs of the individual (achieving future gains). The latter would explain why an exerciser or athlete engages in training practices whilst ignoring other hedonic messages (fatigue, pain). The athlete might not like the training session but continues because of the pleasure experienced in the foreseeable future.

To achieve ones goals, it is key that individuals are motivated. As outlined, this motivation might come from within the individual (intrinsic) because of the enjoyment or pleasure derived from the activity or alternatively from outside (extrinsic) sources such as rewards, threats or competition. Hence, competition indicates that the athlete participates in the event to beat opponents rather than for the inherent pleasure of the activity itself. Besides Cabanac's explanation why individuals might engage in exercise there are a large number of other motivational theories. A number of these motivational theories are concerned with the needs of individuals. One such theory is Self-Determination Theory (SDT) [44]. According to SDT individuals have three needs to be autonomous, competent and feel related and connected to others. SDT has been a successful theory in predicting engagement in sport and physical activity. A cognitive motivational theory relevant to pacing is goal theory or achievement motivation theory [45, 46].

According to this theory individuals can have two goal orientations. Task goal orientation refers to the individual being interested in the mastery of a particular skill, to get better at it. Ego goal orientation refers to individuals who are interested in demonstrating their superior ability in competition with others rather than self-improvement. Mastery and ego goal orientation are independent constructs and individuals could be high in both, low in both or high in one and low in the other [47].

More recently other goal orientations have been proposed. Social approval goal orientation refers to social acceptance through conformity to norms. In addition, Gernigon et al. [48] suggested that individuals might have an orientation to avoid embarrassment or defeat (in contrast to beating the opponent). Both goal orientations would have consequences for pacing. Social approval goal orientations are associated with displaying maximum effort whereas goal orientations to avoid failure would result in individuals putting in just enough effort not to fail.

Also important for pacing is the motivational climate created in which the sport or exercise takes place. The sporting environments can also be classified as either task or ego-oriented. A task oriented environment would emphasise and reward effort, cooperation and improvement, whereas an ego-oriented environment is characterised by encouraging competition and punishing mistakes or poor performance. There is evidence to suggest that the individual's goal-orientation and the motivational climate interact and might influence the way athletes behave in such an environment [49]. On the whole, both, individual goal orientation and motivational climate appear to be factors which are likely to influence the way athletes or exercisers regulate their behaviour and therefore pace their exercise bouts or competition performance.

Self-efficacy is defined as the 'beliefs in one's capabilities to organise and execute the course of action required to produce given attainments' [50]. Self-efficacy has been shown to be a consistent predictor of athletic performance and has been associated with more effort, persistence, and higher performance levels. For example, Moritz et al. [51] found, in their meta-analysis, a moderate positive relationship ($r = .38$) between sport specific skill-based self-efficacy and athletic performance. If an athlete believes to be in control and has the ability to produce certain outcomes than he/she will be motivated and happily engage in the activity. An athlete with high levels of efficacy is a motivated athlete who is likely to work hard to succeed. There is also evidence that group self-efficacy beliefs result in higher performance levels [52]. Although not specifically researched to date it is apparent that individual or group self-efficacy beliefs are likely to influence sporting or exercise behaviour and as such the pacing strategies adopted by athletes and exercisers during training and competition.

Two psychological concepts which have also been shown to influence athletic performance are anxiety and self-confidence. Since the work of Spielberger [53] it is now well established that there is a distinction between anxiety as a personality characteristic (trait-anxiety) and anxiety as a transient mood state (state-anxiety). State-anxiety is the 'right now' feeling of apprehension and tension in a specific situation [54] whereas trait-anxiety is a general disposition to feel anxious in certain environmental situations [55]. Research has shown that people with high levels of trait anxiety are more likely to interpret a situation as threatening than people low in trait anxiety [56].

To achieve sporting excellence it is generally believed that athletes need to possess a high degree of self-confidence [57]. This construct has been perceived by both athletes [58] and coaches [59] to be a salient characteristic in order to achieve success. Meta-analytic studies have provided evidence for this contention [60].

An additional psychological state associated with outcome in sport is pre-performance mood state. Mood has been defined as "a changing non-specific psychological disposition to evaluate, interpret, and act on past, current, or future concerns in certain patterned ways" [61]. Mood differs from emotions in terms of its cause, consequence, and intention. That is, emotions are specific to a particular event, focuses on specific objects, and influences behaviour. Mood, on the other hand is a consequence of minor events and internal metabolic or cognitive processes, is unspecific in its direction, and influences cognition [62]. A meta-analysis [63] found a small-to-moderate effect of mood on performance (mean Effect Size = 0.31). In particular, effects were moderate for vigour, confusion, and depression, small for anger and tension, and very small for the fatigue subscale of the Profile of Mood States questionnaire (POMS). Mood has been found to influence decision making [64] attentional-focus [65], and motivation [66]. Consequently, like state anxiety and self-confidence, mood is likely to influence the selection of the pacing strategy for the upcoming competition or training event.

It is apparent that a number of psychological constructs might have direct or indirect influence on the way an athlete select a pacing strategy. Although these relationships have not been explicitly tested some of the evidence suggests that these psychological constructs will determine the athletes intentions which in turn will influence the strategy adopted for the task at hand as well as the maintenance of this strategy during performance. It is also likely that these psychological constructs interact with physiological states and behaviour and that the interaction effects between these variables have additional influence.

2.6. PERFORMANCE AND PACING STRATEGY

The observation of Steve Ovett beating Sebastian Coe in the 1980 Olympics 800m final is hardly analogous to the tortoise beating the hare; however, it demonstrates that a runner with a slower personal best performance time is capable of winning if the margins between athletes are relatively minor and decision making is required as part of the activity. How an athlete distributes work and energy throughout an exercise bout can profoundly impact performance [5] and, in elite competition, a well executed pacing strategy may mean the difference between 1st and last place.

Strategy is a cognitive process of planning action(s) designed to achieve a particular goal [1]. In many exercise situations, strategy is pre-conceived prior to task execution, particularly in tasks of short duration such as vertical jumping. In these cases, all the necessary information is already held by the individual prior to the task. This situation is referred to as an *open-loop* control system as sensory information is either not required or the task is simply too brief to facilitate action modification as a consequence of the feedback. Where the individual has sufficient time to consider the implications of sensory neural feedback and consequently modifies action, it is referred to as a *closed-loop* control system [4]. Therefore, a single vertical jump may not require sensory feedback for the purpose of the performance (open loop control), but if the individual were requested to perform a series of repetitive vertical jumps (closed loop control) this would require the distribution of effort (pacing) in response to considerations such as the number of bouts and the physical condition of the individual [2]. Consequently, it could be expected that peak performances would be diminished in a series of bouts compared to a maximal single, one-off effort while energy is consciously managed across the entire series.

Closed loop control of exercise, forms the foundation of pacing. In response to exercise, *afferent* (towards the centre) information is sent by peripheral (e.g. muscle, skin, organs) receptors to the brain [2]. This sensory information is used to modify behaviour. It can also can be influenced by self-awareness (anxiety, self-confidence), previous experience of similar situations, environmental, and situational considerations such as the duration of the exercise bout [67]. These factors inform the strategy and its effective execution. Nevertheless, in many exercise situations there is often little time to deliberately plan a strategy, or even to adjust a pre-planned strategy. Therefore, greater familiarity with one's capabilities and the circumstances of the task can lead to reductions in the processing time of information and refine the execution of appropriate strategic action.

Pre-planning of pacing strategies for exercise situations not previously encountered can lead to misjudgments in pace [14, 68]. This is due to inaccurate estimations of individual capabilities and uncertainty of the specific demands of the task. In these circumstances it is relatively common to adopt a more circumspect approach to the starting pace of the exercise bout [1] while intra-bout sensory information is processed and the task demands are dynamically evaluated [4]. Inaccuracies of pacing can also lead to over estimations of individual capabilities (particularly among novice exercisers) and result in optimistically high initial power outputs or velocity. This potentially presents serious issues in situations where the individual has a pre existing health condition. In exercise cases among healthy individuals it is unlikely that an overly optimistic approach to pacing intensity will result in anything other than premature sensations of fatigue (e.g. overheating, muscle pain, nausea), which will require a behaviour modification to down-regulate effort at an earlier than optimal stage to avoid exhaustion.

Athletes generally learn pacing strategies in training as a consequence of physical practice [1]. This process is also informed by observations of other successful athletes, and advice from coaches. Therefore, optimal pacing may depend on numerous factors such as experience, prior knowledge and self-awareness in similar circumstances [12].

The type of exercise task being performed can influence the extent of strategic planning involved in the task execution. For example, in head to head competitions, athletes are required to directly compete against each other whereas in time-trial events, individuals compete against the clock [8]. For success in a head to head race the winner simply needs to be faster than that of the other competitors. The strategic plan in this circumstance, places greater emphasis on managing physical resources efficiently while retaining sufficient reserve of energy in case it is required for a final 'end spurt' to outsprint an opponent [69]. In contrast, time-trial performances tends to produce more even pacing as the aim is simply to finish the race in the shortest time with no requirement to retain energy for any other purpose than the avoidance of physical harm.

The evidence for pacing, rather than simply running to exhaustion in response to head to head racing has recently been demonstrated by Noakes and co-workers [70] in an examination of lap times for world mile record performances between 1886 and 1999. Over that period there were only 2 races (from 32) in which the final lap was the slowest of the four lap race. In 24 of the 32 races (76%), the final lap was either the fastest or slightly slower than the opening lap, while in 90% of the races, the middle two laps were slowest. The presence of this final end spurt of speed neatly supports the presence of a common pacing strategy in which a reserve of energy is retained in the final stages during head to head races (Figure 2.3).

Studies in short duration events (<80s) where athletes have been forced to start either faster or slower than the average speeds from their best performances have demonstrated better outcomes with a faster start so that energy is maximized early in the trial [8]. This is unsurprising as pacing is most likely pre-planned as an 'all-out' effort where sensory regulation and action modification is not required.

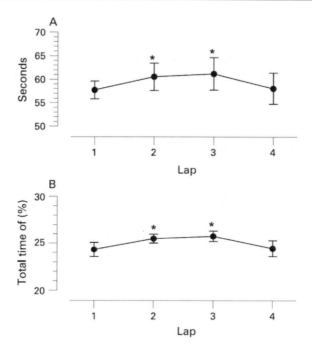

Figure 2.3. Average lap times (s) for 32 world record mile performances between 1880 and 1999. Note that the second and third laps are significantly slower than the first and final laps, between which there is no significant difference. (B) Average percentage of total time (%) spent in each lap in 32 world record mile performances between 1880 and 1999. *p,0.05 Values are expressed as mean (SD). (Taken with permission [70]).

A fast start approach to short duration events also appear to apply in elite 800m track running (e.g. 101-105s), where only 2 world records have been set in which the 2nd lap was faster than the first [71]. Nevertheless, Foster [8] showed that when power output decreased during cycling time trials ranging in length from 500 to 3000m, the subjects still maintained an ability to increase anaerobic energy production for a final acceleration. This suggests that performance even in short duration events is unlikely to be truly 'all-out'.

In both head to head and time trial events of longer duration events (>120s), laboratory studies have found that performances may benefit from strategies in which power output and energy are distributed more evenly [1]. As the duration of the exercise event extends, an early peak power is of less consequence to the race outcome and so a fast starting strategy is less consequential to performance. That is, unless tactical/positional requirements enhance the specific relevance of a fast start [72].

Studies focusing on pacing strategies have tended to examine differences in performance during the first and second halves of a race (i.e. split times) [73]. However analysis of race split times is a relatively simple or gross analysis of one's overall pacing strategy and may miss more subtle variations of pace *within* a lap. The recent development of more accurate and reliable power and time meters has allowed scientists to specifically examine performance profiles during field competitions [74, 75]. Nevertheless, pacing strategies in response to athletic activities can be categorised according to common characteristics of power output or velocity profiles [1, 5, 12, 76, 77]: 1) positive, 2) negative 3) even, 4) all-out, 5) parabolic-shaped, and 6) variable pacing strategies (Figure 2.4).

A *positive* pacing strategy is one in which power output or velocity gradually declines throughout the duration of the event. Positive pacing could be referred to as a depletion-based pacing strategy in which energy gradually diminishes over the course of the event towards event completion. This type of power output or speed profile is consistent with the popular view of exercise physiology in which peripheral muscle or metabolic fuel variables are gradually exhausted.

An event is considered to have been performed with a *negative* pacing strategy when there is an increase in power output or velocity observed over the duration of the event. A negative-style pacing strategy is occasionally observed during middle distance events when power output and velocity are increased towards the end of the event. This final end spurt in exercise intensity commonly occurs when athletes are made aware of the remaining distance or duration.

During more prolonged events the starting pace has less of an effect on overall performance times because of the lower percentage of time spent in the acceleration phase [1]. As such, it has been suggested that an *even* paced strategy may be optimal for prolonged (>2min) locomotive events such as running, swimming, rowing, skiing, speed skating and cycling [78, 79].

All-out pacing strategies are those in which the athlete commences the exercise bout maximally and thereafter attempts to maintain maximal power output for the duration of the bout. This is perhaps the least cognitive strategy and could be construed as a non-paced strategy. However, even in a short duration exercise bout resources must be managed but are probably done so at a sub aware level rather than consciously. Although all-out exercise implies maximal work will be achieved for the duration of the bout, physical resources gradually decline over the bout.

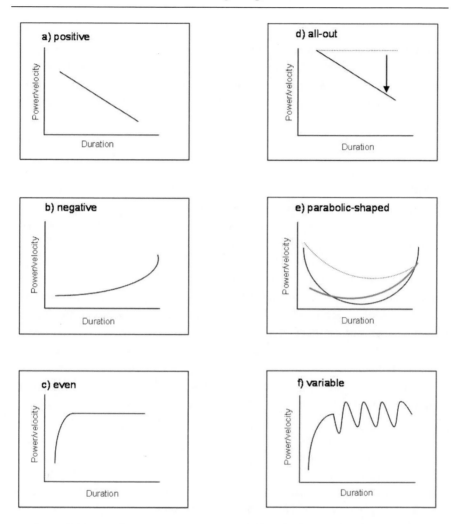

Figure 2.4. Six commonly observed pacing strategies. Note for panel d (all-out pacing), the aim (dotted line) may be to retain maximal power output/velocity but practical observations suggest this will deteriorate and produce a profile similar to positive pacing, albeit with a higher initial power output. The parabolic-shaped strategy (e) produces several variations of power/velocity as U, J or a reverse J shape.

Parabolic-shaped pacing is that which demonstrates a fast start followed by a progressive reduction in power or speed during the middle of an endurance trial but tends to increase during the latter portion of the event such as by the production of an end spurt. This tactic usually results in U, or J or reverse J-shaped pacing strategies.

Evidence for such a pacing strategy was shown by Garland [75] who examined the velocity of elite rowers during Olympic and World Championships. In each of these 2000m races, rowers completed the first 500m in the fastest time, slowed during the middle 1000m but increased speed during the final 500m of the race. This resulted in the adoption of a reverse J-shaped pacing strategy.

It is uncommon for athletes to experience constant external conditions during actual outdoor competition. Under the varying external conditions associated with field race conditions it has been suggested that a *variable* pacing strategy may be optimal in some cases which power output or speed frequently fluctuate [80]. These fluctuations may be influenced by a number of external factors including race duration, course geography and environmental conditions, such as wind and environmental temperature.

From a practical athletic perspective, pre-planning a race strategy using an appropriate situation-specific strategy may be a useful way to distribute effort and optimize performance for that event. However, this also pre-supposes that pacing is purely a pre-conceived (anticipatory) notion and this form of prior planning does not facilitate dynamic variations to strategy during an event, unless of course a variable (free) pacing strategy is selected. In consideration of this, Edwards and Noakes [81] devised an alternative pacing model specifically designed for team (invasion-style) game performances (see chapter seven) but which may also be applied elsewhere. In this model, pacing for an event (e.g. a soccer match) is considered at three levels: *macro*, *meso*, and *micro*. At the *macro* level, overall demands of the task (e.g. match) are appraised prior to the task and an appropriate level of energy expenditure is distributed over the course of the task by the player in accordance with both intrinsic and extrinsic considerations. At a *meso* level of pacing, major events may occur during the exercise task (e.g. match) such as a change in the score, tactical team alterations, positional change, or re-evaluation of strategy at half-time. *Meso*-pacing evaluations may therefore inform the overall *macro* pacing strategy and lead to adjustments of pacing if considered necessary. Instantaneous variations of pace during the task are considered at a *micro* pacing level in which the metabolic cost of a short sprint may be evaluated in relation to the higher order *macro* strategy. As such, an intense period of high energy sprinting may lead to subsequent rest or tactical behavioural changes such as tracking or passing the ball rather than the more demanding tasks such as tackling or dribbling until the player perceives sustainable metabolic demands have been re established and the immediate (*micro*) activity will not compromise the overall pacing plan i.e. a pre-set level of tolerable discomfort the individual is prepared to ensure for the specific event (match).

The circumstances, consequences and scientific basis of each pacing strategy will be considered in greater depth in subsequent chapters and in specific relation to the demands of different exercise situations. There is currently no evidence to suggest a single type of pacing strategy is common to all forms of exercise and situation-specific strategies are likely to be appropriate for most goals. However, for most race and time-trial activities, numerous studies have broadly identified a relatively fast starting strategy as preferential to most circumstances although there are several variations to this approach [5, 80].

CONCLUSION

- Pacing defined: *'The goal directed distribution and management of effort across the duration of an exercise bout.'*
- In sport, it is known that individuals perform less well in unfamiliar circumstances and this impairment occurs prior to the failure of any physiological system.
- In short duration exercise (e.g. vertical jump), strategy is pre-conceived prior to task execution. In these cases, all the necessary information is already held by the individual prior to the task. This situation is referred to as an open-loop control system as sensory information is either not required.
- Where the individual has sufficient time to consider the implications of sensory neural feedback and consequently modify action (e.g. a series of vertical jumps, or when running and so on), it is referred to as a closed-loop control system.
- The most logical way of viewing pacing is to consider it as a neural buffering process to prevent premature physical exhaustion.
- The abilities of efficient and effective locomotion are important to the survival of all species. Hunting, foraging, or avoiding predators are all achievement based outcomes and the more complex the organism, the greater the complexity of behaviour.
- Pacing strategies in response to athletic activities can be categorised according to common characteristics of power output or velocity profiles:

1) positive, 2) negative 3) even, 4) all-out, 5) parabolic-shaped, and 6) variable pacing strategies.

- To achieve a goal it is key that the individual is motivated. This motivation might come from within (intrinsic) because of the enjoyment or pleasure derived from the activity or from outside (extrinsic) sources such as rewards, threats or competition.

REFERENCES

[1]   Foster, C., et al., Pacing strategy and athletic performance. *Sports Medicine*, 1994. 17: p. 77-85.

[2]   St Clair Gibson, A. and T. Noakes, Evidence for complex system integration and dynamic neural regulation of skeletal muscle recruitment during exercise in humans. *British Journal of Sports Medicine*, 2004. 38: p. 797-806.

[3]   Noakes, T., A. St Clair Gibson, and E. Lambert, From catastrophe to complexity: a novel model of integrative central neural regulation of effort and fatigue during exercise in humans: summary and conclusions. *British Journal of Sports Medicine*, 2005. 39: p. 120-124.

[4]   St Clair Gibson, A., et al., The role of information processing between the brain and peripheral physiological systems in pacing and perception of effort. *Sports Medicine*, 2006. 36: p. 705-722.

[5]   Abbiss, C. and P. Laursen, Describing and understanding pacing strategies during athletic competition. *Sports Medicine*, 2008. 38(3): p. 239-252.

[6]   Wallechinksy, D., The complete book of the Olympics 2008: *Aurum Press Ltd.*

[7]   Miller, D., Sebastian Coe: born to run. 1992, London: *Pavillion Books Ltd.*

[8]   Foster, C., et al., Effect of pacing strategy on cycle time trial performance. *Medicine & Science in Sports & Exercise*, 1993. 25: p. 383-388.

[9]   Noakes, T., Time to move beyond a brainless exercise physiology: the evidence for complex regulation of human exercise performance. *Applied Physiology, Nutrition and Metabolism*, 2011. 36: p. 23-35.

[10]   Costill, D., H. Thomason, and E. Roberts, Fractional utilization of the aerobic capacity during distance running. *Medicine & Science in Sports*, 1973. 5: p. 248-252.

[11] Bassett, D. and E. Howley, Limiting factors for maximum oxygen uptake and determinants of endurance performance. *Medicine & Science in Sports & Exercise,* 2000. 32: p. 70-84.

[12] Tucker, R. and T. Noakes, The physiological regulation of pacing strategy during exercise: a critical review. *British Journal of Sports Medicine,* 2009. 43: p. 1-9.

[13] Paterson, S. and F. Marino, Effect of deception of distance on prolonged cycling performance. *Perceptual and Motor Skills,* 2004. 98: p. 1017-1026.

[14] Lambert, E., A. St Clair Gibson, and T. Noakes, Complex systems model of fatigue: integrative homoeostatic control of peripheral physiological systems during exercise in humans. *British Journal of Sports Medicine,* 2005. 39: p. 52-62.

[15] Dugas, J., et al., Rates of fluid ingestion alter pacing but not thermoregulatory responses during prolonged exercise in hot and humid conditions with appropriate convective cooling. *European Journal of Applied Physiology,* 2009. 105: p. 69-80.

[16] Rauch, H., A. St Clair Gibson, and E. Lambert, A signaling role for muscle glycogen in the regulation of pace during prolonged exercise. *British Journal of Sports Medicine,* 2005. 39: p. 34-38.

[17] Rauch, L., et al., Effects of carbohydrate loading on muscle glycogen content and cycling performance. *International Journal of Sport Nutrition,* 1995. 5: p. 25-36.

[18] Low, D., M. Gramlich, and B. Engram, Self paced exercise program for office workers: impact on productivity and health outcomes. *AAOHN Journal,* 2007. 55: p. 99-105.

[19] Day, M., et al., Monitoring exercise intensity during resistance training using the session RPE scale, *Journal of Strength and Conditioning Research,* 2004. 18: p. 353-358.

[20] Impellizzeri, F., et al., Use of RPE-based training load in soccer. *Medicine & Science in Sports & Exercise,* 2004. 36: p. 1042-1047.

[21] White, P., et al., Protocol for the PACE trial: A randomised controlled trial of adaptive pacing, cognitive behaviour therapy, and graded exercise as supplements to standardised specialist medical care versus standardised specialist medical care alone for patients with the chronic fatigue syndrome/myalgic encephalomyelitis or encephalopathy. *BMC Neurology,* 2007. 7: p. 1-20.

[22] Garland, T., Scaling the ecological cost of transport to body mass in terrestrial mammals. *The American Naturalist,* 1983. 121: p. 571-587.

[23] Garland, T., Physiological correlates of locomotory performance in a lizard: an allometric approach. *American Journal of Physiology,* 1984. 247: p. R806-R815.

[24] Christian, K. and C. Tracy, The effect of the thermal environment on the ability of hatchling Galapagos land iguanas to avoid predation during dispersal. *Oecologia,* 1981. 49: p. 218-223.

[25] Darwin, C., On the origin of species by natural selection. 5th Edition ed. 1872, New York: *Appleton.*

[26] Cloninger, C. and Gilligan, Neurogenetic mechanisms of learning: A phylogenetic perspective. *Journal of Psychiatric Research,* 1987. 21: p. 457-472.

[27] Pavlov, I., Conditioned reflexes, ed. T. G. V. *Anrep.* 1927, New York: Liveright.

[28] Jarvis, E. and e. al., Avian brains and a new understanding of vertebrate brain evolution. *Nature Reviews Neuroscience* 2005. 6: p. 151-159.

[29] Whittow, G., Sturkie's avian physiology. 5th Edition ed. 1999: *Academic Press.*

[30] Dawson, W., Physiological studies of desert birds: present and future consideration. *Journal of Arid Environments,* 1984. 7: p. 133-155.

[31] Thorpe, W., Learning and instinct in animals. 1956, Cambridge, Massachusetts: *Harvard University Press.*

[32] Kramer, D. and R. McLaughlin, The behavioural ecology of intermittent locomotion. *American Zoologist,* 2001. 41: p. 137-153.

[33] Taylor, C., et al., Effect of hyperthermia on heat balance during running in the African hunting dog. *American Journal of Physiology,* 1971. 220: p. 823-827.

[34] Garland, T., Scaling maximal running speed and maximal aerobic speed to body mass in mammals and lizards. *The Physiologist,* 1982. 25: p. 338.

[35] Blanchard, R. and D. Blanchard, Effects of hippocampal lesions on the rat's reaction to a cat. *Journal of Comparative and Physiological Psychology,* 1972. 78: p. 77-82.

[36] Gonyea, W., Adaptive differences in the body proportions of large felids. *Acta Anatomica,* 1976. 96: p. 81-96.

[37] Caro, T., Cheetah mothers' vigilance: looking out for prey or for predators? *Behavioural Ecology and Sociobiology,* 1987. 20: p. 351-361.

[38] Eaton, R., Hunting behaviour of the cheetah. *The Journal of Wildlife Management,* 1970. 34: p. 56-67.

[39] Cabanac, M., Exertion and pleasure from an evolutionary perspective, in *Psychobiology of Physical Activity* E.A.P. Ekkekakis, Editor. 2006, *Human Kinetics: Champaign IL.* p. 79-89.

[40] Borg, G., Psychophysiological bases of perceived exertion. *Medicine & Science in Sports & Exercise,* 1982. 14: p. 377-387.

[41] Ekkekakis, P., Let them roam free? Physiological and psychological evidence for the potential of self-selected exercise intensity in public health. *Sports Medicine,* 2009. 39: p. 857-888.

[42] Thayer, R., et al., Walking more each day elevates mood, especially energy, a central mood element, in *16th Annual Convention of the American Psychological Society.* 2004: Chicago.

[43] Polman, R., M. Kaiseler, and E. Borkoles, Effect of a single bout of exercise on the mood of pregnant women. *Journal of Sport Medicine and Physical Fitness,* 2007. 47: p. 103-111.

[44] Deci, E. and R. Ryan, Intrinsic motivation and self-determination in human behaviour. 1985, New York: *Plenum.*

[45] Nicholls, J., The competitive ethos and democratic education. 1989, Cambridge, MA: *Harvard University Press.*

[46] Nicholls, J., Conceptions of ability and achievement motivation, in Research on motivation in education: Student motivation R.A.C. Ames, Editor. 1984, *Academic Press:* New York.

[47] White, S. and J. Duda, The relationship of gender, level of sport involvement, and participation motivation to task and ego orientation. *International Journal of Sport Psychology,* 1994. 25: p. 4-18.

[48] Gernigon, C., et al., A dynamic system perspective on goal involvement states in sport. *Journal of Sport & Exercise Psychology,* 2004. 26: p. 572-596.

[49] Treasure, D. and G. Roberts, Relationship between female adolescents' achievement goal orientations, perceptions of the motivational climate, belief about success and sources of satisfaction in basketball. *International Journal of Sport Psychology,* 1998. 29: p. 211-230.

[50] Bandura, A., Self-efficacy: the exercise of control. 1997, San Francisco: *Freeman.*

[51] Moritz, S., et al., The relation of self-efficacy measures to sports performance: A meta-analytic review. *Research Quarterly for Exercise and Sport,* 2000. 71: p. 280-294.

[52] George, T. and D. Feltz, Motivation in sport from a collective efficacy perspective. *International Journal of Sport Psychology,* 1995. 26: p. 98-116.

[53] Spielberger, C., Theory and research on anxiety, in Anxiety and behaviour. *Spielberger,* Editor. 1966, Academic Press: New York. p. 3-20.

[54] Gould, D., C. Greenleaf, and V. Krane, Arousal-anxiety and sport, in Advances in sport psychology. 2002, *Human Kinetics: Champaign, IL.* p. 207-241.

[55] Moran, A., Sport and exercise psychology: a critical introduction. 2004, London: *Psychology Press.*

[56] Scanlan, T. and M. Passer, Factors related to competitive stress among male youth sport participants. *Medicine & Science in Sports,* 1978. 10: p. 103-108.

[57] Vealey, R. and M. Chase, Self-confidence in sport, in Advances in sport psychology, T. Horn, Editor. 2008, *Human Kinetics: Champaign, IL.*

[58] Gould, D., K. Dieffenback, and A. Moffett, Psychological characteristics and their development in Olympic champions. *Journal of Applied Sport Psychology,* 2002. 14: p. 172-204.

[59] Gould, D., et al., A survey of U.S. Olympic coaches; variables perceived to have influenced athlete performance and coach effectiveness. *Sport Psychologist,* 2002. 16: p. 229-250.

[60] Woodman, T. and L. Hardy, The relative impact of cognitive anxiety and self-confidence upon sport performance: a meta-analysis. *Journal of Sports Sciences,* 2003. 21: p. 443-457.

[61] Parkinson, B., et al., Changing moods: the psychology of mood and mood regulation. 1996, London: *Longman.*

[62] Lane, A., C. Beetie, and M. Stevens, Mood matters: a response to Mellalieu. *Journal of Applied Sport Psychology,* 2005. 17: p. 319-325.

[63] Beedie, C., P. Terry, and A. Lane, The profile of mood states and athletic performance: two meta-analyses. *Journal of Applied Sport Psychology,* 2000. 12: p. 49-68.

[64] Bird, A. and A. Horn, Cognitive anxiety and mental errors in sport. *Journal of Sport & Exercise Psychology,* 1990. 12: p. 211-216.

[65] Abernethy, B., Attention, in Handbook of sport psychology H.A.H. R.N. Singer, & C.M. Janelle Editor. 2001, *John Wiley:* New York.

[66] Frijda, N., The emotions. 1986, Cambridge: *Cambridge University Press.*

[67] St Clair Gibson, A., et al., The conscious perception of the sensation of fatigue. *Sports Medicine,* 2003. 33: p. 167-176.

[68] Micklewright, D., et al., Previous experience influences pacing during 20 km time trial cycling. *British Journal of Sports Medicine,* 2010. 44: p. 952-960.

[69] Foster, C., et al., Physiological responses during simulated competition. *Medicine & Science in Sports & Exercise,* 1993. 25: p. 877-882.

[70] Noakes, T., M. Lambert, and R. Hauman, Which lap is the slowest? An analysis of 32 world mile record performances. *British Journal of Sports Medicine,* 2009. 43: p. 760-764.

[71] Tucker, R., M. Lambert, and T. Noakes, An analysis of pacing strategies during men's world-record performances in track athletics. *International Journal of Sports Physiology and Performance,* 2006. 1: p. 233-245.

[72] Macdermid, P. and A. Edwards, Influence of crank length on cycle ergometry performance of well-trained female cross-country mountain bike athletes. *European Journal of Applied Physiology,* 2010. 108: p. 177-182.

[73] Ingen-Schenau, G. J.D. Koning, and G. Groot, The distribution of anaerobic energy in 1000 and 4000 metre cycling bouts. *International Journal of Sports Medicine,* 1992. 13: p. 447-451.

[74] Abbiss, C. and P. Laursen, Models to explain fatigue during prolonged endurance cycling. *Sports Medicine,* 2005. 35(10): p. 865-898.

[75] Garland, S., An analysis of the pacing strategy adopted by elite competitors in 2000 m rowing. *British Journal of Sports Medicine,* 2005. 39: p. 39-42.

[76] Davies, C. and M. Thompson, Aerobic performance of female marathon and male ultramarathon athletes. *European Journal of Applied Physiology,* 1979. 41: p. 233-245.

[77] Billat, V., et al., Effect of free versus constant pace on performance and oxygen kinetics in running. *Medicine & Science in Sports & Exercise,* 2001. 33: p. 2082-2088.

[78] Koning, J.d., M. Bobbert, and C. Foster, Determination of optimal pacing strategy in track cycling with an energy flow model. *Journal of Science and Medicine in Sport,* 1999. 2: p. 266-277.

[79] Thompson, K., et al., The effect of even, positive and negative pacing on metabolic, kinematic and temporal variables during breaststroke swimming. *European Journal of Applied Physiology,* 2003. 88: p. 438-443.

[80] Liedl, M., D. Swain, and D. Branch, Physiological effects of constant versus variable power during endurance cycling. *Medicine & Science in Sports & Exercise,* 1999. 31: p. 1472.

[81] Edwards, A. and T. Noakes, Dehydration: cause of fatigue or sign of pacing in elite soccer? *Sports Medicine,* 2009. 39: p. 1-13.

Chapter 3

LIMITATIONS TO PHYSICAL PERFORMANCE

3.1. ABSTRACT

The aim of this chapter is to investigate the circumstances and potential causes of performance limitations in response to exercise. Traditional theories have tended to present polar perspectives on this issue such as central (nervous system) vs. peripheral (muscle) limitations. However, neither hypothesis explains the occurrence of fatigue across all situations leading to the suggestion that an integrative control system may be influential. Different perspectives and interpretative models are discussed in this chapter and a new psychophysiological model presented, in which the conscious (aware and sub aware) brain regulates performance based on afferent sensory information received and via efferent instructions for muscle recruitment.

3.2. INTRODUCTION

Human performance is limited [1, 2]. It is not possible to endlessly sustain high intensity physical work as this is usually accompanied by increased severity of unpleasant physical sensations such as localised pain, nausea, and heat stress [3]. While there may be no argument that limits exist to which humans can perform physical tasks, the causes of such limitations remain fervently disputed [4].

The inability to voluntarily prevent a decline in work output despite our best efforts is generally referred to as fatigue [5]. Many complex physiological and psychological factors contribute to performance limitation and this chapter will consider these. However, it should be clear; the search for a single factor which causes fatigue and thus limits performance could be considered analogous to the search for the source of the Nile [6].

3.3. THE NERVOUS SYSTEM

The nervous system influences all physiological activity and is in many ways akin to a sophisticated computer network. In this system, the brain acts as the hub, integrating all sensory information received (via *afferent* pathways), selecting an appropriate response and then providing the motor stimulus (via *efferent* pathways) to initiate the process of voluntary muscle recruitment and subsequent physical action. This requires integrative communication and coordination between different regions of the brain, body and physiological systems [7] (Figure 3.1). Such conscious regulation occurs in the cerebral cortex as a consequence of either planned thought, or automaticity if the response is so familiar as to not warrant significant attention [8-10].

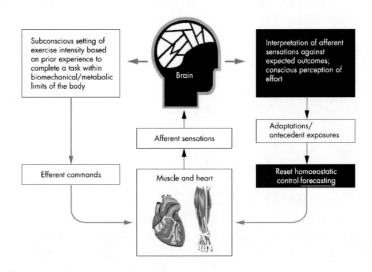

Figure 3.1. Brain regulation of human movement in response to afferent and efferent signals. Taken with permission [24].

The structural components of the brain that are most directly involved in control of movement are the cerebrum, diencephalon, cerebellum and brainstem (e.g. [11]). The cerebrum consists of two halves (right and left hemispheres) which are connected by a sheet of nerve fibres known as the corpus callosum. Both hemispheres are covered by an undulating, wrinkly, gray coloured surface called the cerebral cortex. This covering of thin tissue of nerve cell bodies has been referred to as the site of the conscious mind and intellect [12].

The frontal lobe of the cerebral cortex is the area anterior to the central sulcus (central lateral groove of the brain) and contains areas vital to the control of voluntary movement. The frontal lobe is involved in planning actions and movement, as well as abstract thought. This region of the cerebral cortex also hosts the primary motor cortex which contains motor neurons that send impulses to specific skeletal muscles throughout the body [9]. The parietal lobe is the area immediately posterior to the central sulcus and is the brain region primarily involved in the perception of sensory feedback. Specific types of sensory information are subsequently transmitted from the parietal region of the cortex via sensory nerves to the relevant areas of the brain for further processing. Inter-communication between cortical regions is crucial for the execution of voluntary movement [13].

The cerebral cortex is commonly described as comprising three main parts: sensory, motor, and association areas [9, 11]. The sensory areas are the regions that receive and process inputs from the thalamus and are called primary sensory areas. The supplementary motor areas and premotor cortex which select voluntary movements (association areas) lie anterior to the primary motor cortex. It is the primary motor cortex that executes voluntary movements in response to inputs from the motor association areas.

Subcortical brain regions also play important roles in the control of movement as for example the deep lying basal ganglia, receiving both descending information from the motor cortex and ascending information from the brainstem. This small region of nuclei is involved in the control of force, and initiation of movement [14]. The diencephalon contains the thalamus and hypothalamus and is a further deep region of the brain which lies between the cerebrum and the brainstem. The thalamus primarily acts as a relay centre, receiving and integrating most sensory inputs from the spinal cord and brainstem to higher brain regions (e.g. the cerebral cortex) for cognitive processing. The thalamus also plays an important role in the control of mood, attention, and the perception of pain [10]. The hypothalamus lies immediately beneath the thalamus and is the brain region for the control of the endocrine system, regulation of homeostasis, body temperature, hunger, thirst and physiological responses to stress.

Located directly under the cerebral hemispheres and connected to the spinal cord, the brainstem contains three main areas that are involved in involuntary human movement [9]. The pons is located at the top of the brain stem and acts as a bridge between the cerebral cortex and cerebellum. Various neural pathways either pass through the pons from the cortex on their way to the spinal cord or terminate as they come from the cortex. The pons region is involved in functions such as chewing, swallowing, salivating and breathing. The second area, the medulla [oblongata] is primarily an extension of the spinal cord and serves as a regulatory region for various autonomic physiologic processes such as respiration.

Although it appears everything starts and stops with the brain, there are specific reflex cases where physical action precedes brain activity. For example, when an impulse resulting from sensory stimulation of the skin is transmitted via sensory nerves to the spinal cord, it can trigger a local (immediate) reflex at that level, prior to travelling to the brain [11]. Such 'spinal' reflexes are immediate responses which act in a protective role. A common example is the withdrawal reflex. This may occur when a person touches a hot object and withdraws their hand from the hot object without thinking about it. This occurs as the heat stimulates temperature and pain receptors in the skin, triggering a sensory nerve impulse that travels to the spine. The sensory neuron then synapses with interneurons in the spine that connect to motor neurons. Some of these neurons send motor impulses directly to the flexor muscles of the arm to allow withdrawal; other motor neurons send inhibitory impulses to the extensor muscles so flexion is not inhibited (reciprocal innervation). This split-second action is evoked prior to brain involvement. Concurrently, interneurons relay the sensory information up to the brain so that the person becomes aware of the pain, what has occurred and will adopt a conscious behaviour (i.e. to stay away from the heat) so not repeat the action.

As the level of control moves from spinal cord to the motor cortex, the degree of possible movement complexity increases from simple reflex action to highly complicated movements. Thus, it is likely that all non-reflex exercise situations should be considered subject to neural regulation [15]. In summary, motor (neural) drive evokes muscular action and is the final result of communication between brain centres, collectively acting on the motor cortex. This process describes how sensory information stimulates a motor response.

3.4. LIMITATIONS: CENTRAL AND PERIPHERAL OBSERVATIONS

This section will examine the concepts and perspectives of performance limitation from central and peripheral neuromuscular control perspectives. Both mechanisms broadly predict the same outcome whereby reduced force generating capacity of the muscle is experienced, albeit with a different cause.

Peripheral fatigue has been defined as the loss of force caused by processes occurring at or distal to the neuromuscular junction [16]. It is generally considered as fatigue occurring within the muscle. Conversely, central fatigue is associated with instances where the central nervous system has a diminished neural (brain) drive to muscle [15]. If some loss of force occurs because of the failure of the central nervous system to maximally drive the muscle, it is known as central fatigue [16]. The debate is therefore broadly one of control mechanisms either within the central nervous system (brain and spine - central) or anywhere outside the central nervous system (e.g. muscle – peripheral) as the source of diminished force output/performance (fatigue) [17].

The common model used to describe the process and cause of fatigue among exercise physiologists has been the peripheral (muscle) explanation [18]. The general acceptance of this interpretation may be largely due to the early observations of Merton [17]. Merton addressed the issue of central vs. peripheral mechanisms by inducing fatigue in a muscle group in response to maximal voluntary contraction (MVC). He had the novel idea to additionally innervate the active muscles during the MVC with localized electrical stimulation utilising an interpolated twitch technique.

Merton reasoned it was possible to distinguish between fatigue components derived from the contracting muscle (peripheral fatigue) and components within the central nervous system (central fatigue). For example, an increase in muscle tension during MVC with the addition of electrical stimulation would support a central fatigue hypothesis (i.e. that greater stimulation from the brain could increase muscle tension and force). The production of greater force with stimulation would demonstrate that sustained maximal voluntary contractions do not result in the recruitment of all motor units, despite sustained maximal effort. Conversely, if muscle tension and force did not increase as a consequence of additional electrical stimulation, this would indicate a peripheral (muscle) source of fatigue. In Merton's study, a series of twitches evoked by stimulation of the ulnar nerve did not alter the fatigue pattern and consequently he logically concluded that the site of fatigue must have been within the muscle fibres.

> "Fatigue is peripheral, for when strength fails, electrical stimulation of the motor nerve cannot restore it." [17].

The study of Merton [17] provided compelling evidence for the primary role of peripheral (muscle) mechanisms in the limitation of maximal human performance. Nevertheless, it is possible that this classic study also influenced many scientists to automatically adhere to a model which is always peripheral in nature [19].

The twitch interpolation technique used by Merton is still utilised in modern investigations, but it is interesting to note that these studies have not confirmed the original findings of Merton that motor units are fully recruited and discharged at the onset of MVC. In contrast, it seems consistent that voluntary action recruits 85-90% of motor units during MVC [20]. Thus, further motor units seem to be kept in reserve for possible use in instances such as a final spurt of force if required in a race. An extreme example of the influence of central (stimulation) factors occurs when a task cannot be continued (task failure) but the muscles could still produce the required force when stimulated electrically [19].

The debate between central and peripheral mechanisms was reignited following Merton's work, when Bigland Ritchie [21] proposed three main regions as sites of fatigue 1) those which lie in the central nervous system (neural drive), 2) those concerned with the transmission from central nervous system to muscle, and 3) those within the individual muscle fibres. Nevertheless, although this study provided a welcome re-examination of fatigue it did not identify a primary site for limitation:

> "A major question yet to be answered is which of these events determine performance and which are simply incidental by-products." [21].

Evidence from various subsequent research studies suggests functional changes occur at each of the sites proposed by Bigland Ritchie [21, 22] and it is possible that they may work synergistically during exercise to control human performance [23]. However, an important shared characteristic of all central and peripheral fatigue models is the determination of researchers to search for a single site of catastrophic (limiting) system failure. In each model, individually nominated sites have been proposed as a source of performance limitation either centrally or peripherally. In this regard all models share the common goal of searching for a site (e.g. perhaps seeking the source of the Nile) [6]. The same study in which numerous (central and peripheral) causal sites were proposed [21] contains two interesting passages:

1) 'Everyone has experienced the sensations of fatigue and the increasing difficulty of continuing a given level of physical exercise.'
2) '...much evidence suggests that the physiological events underlying fatigue commence at the onset of activity, although they cannot always be readily detected.' [21]

The central nervous system plays a crucial role in the maintenance of the steady state of the internal environment (homeostasis) [24]. The motor cortex of the brain is responsible for the generation of the motor drive and recruitment of motor units during exercise [25]. We are conscious of this motor drive, but we are unaware of the concomitant motor control of muscles regulating our posture during exercise [5]. Furthermore, the brain is the centre of cognition and recognition of physical sensations experienced as fatigue develops. Sensations of fatigue caused by exercise are common and during exercise the work load may create such an intense sensation that it is perceived necessary to reduce force so to successfully complete the bout (pace), or even cease exercise if the sensations are too severe [3]. The sensations of fatigue and exhaustion may be considered psychological entities, which induce changes in behaviour. The physical and biochemical changes during exercise are physiological entities. When taken together as both being of importance in our ability to sustain exercise intensity, complete work as required, or simply successfully pace ourselves, it is perhaps useful to consider the possibility of integrated physiological and psychological models (psychophysiological) in which catastrophic system failure does not occur.

3.5. LIMITATIONS: CARDIOVASCULAR REGULATION

The cardiovascular system comprises the heart (pump), high pressure blood vessels (for distribution of arterial blood) and a low pressure collection and return system (venous blood returned to the heart and lungs). For many years, it has been widely considered that it is this system which regulates and limits sustained exercise [1, 26]. From this perspective, the cardiovascular system restricts performance via exercise induced deficiencies to the delivery of blood, nutrients and oxygen to the working muscles, by local muscle utilisation processes for the re-generation of ATP (energy currency), and by limitations to (pulmonary) blood circulation with the lungs for gas exchange [1, 18].

Cardiovascular limitation to physical performance is usually described by the *cardiovascular/anaerobic model* [27] (Figure 3.2). Professor Tim Noakes has previously identified several flaws with this model [2], such that it predicts fatigue develops as a consequence of the heart no longer being able to supply oxygen nor is the cardiovascular system able to remove waste products from the working muscles. According to this definition, limitations to 1) the pumping capabilities of the heart, 2) the density of capillaries supplying skeletal muscle with oxygenated blood and 3) the quantity of mitochondria with which to extract oxygen could all directly restrict performance.

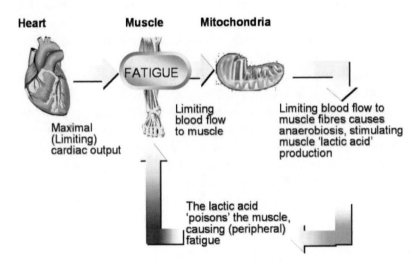

Figure 3.2. Mechanism of fatigue according to AV Hill's (Cardiovascular/Anaerobic) Model of Exercise Physiology. Taken from Noakes [74] with permission.

Numerous studies have confirmed maximal cardiac output improves as a consequence of training-induced changes to stroke volume [28]. Capillary density is also enhanced following training providing greater quantities of oxygenated blood to muscle, and mitochondrial density has also been reported to improve as a consequence of dedicated endurance training [18, 29]. These adaptations either singularly or collectively work to delay the onset of skeletal muscle anaerobiosis at exercise intensities above the anaerobic threshold, thereby reducing blood lactate concentrations in muscle and blood [27]. In a highly trained state, the delayed onset of blood lactate accumulation allows the exercising muscles to continue contracting for longer at higher intensities before the onset of fatigue and the eventual development of exhaustion. According to this model, exercise must cease as it is progressively driven towards the point of physical exhaustion, when physiological system failure occurs.

Variations to the cardiosvascular/anaerobic model have been proposed to incorporate factors such as *energy supply* and *energy depletion* (see [2] for review). Briefly, in the *energy supply* model, fatigue during high intensity exercise has been suggested to occur as a consequence of the inability to supply adenosine triphosphate (ATP) at rates sufficiently fast to sustain exercise [26]. In that model, training and dietary induced increases to (e.g. glycogen) storage capacity and improved ability to utilize metabolic substrates during exercise may provide a greater capability to produce ATP (i.e. supply energy).

The related *energy depletion* model is largely specific to endurance exercise situations lasting in excess of two hours. In that variation of the *cardiovascular/anaerobic* model, it has been argued that endogenous carbohydrate stores is a limiting (depleting) factor [26]. This is probably due to the observation that fatigue in prolonged exercise is associated with significant reductions in liver and muscle glycogen [18, 30]. In addition, correction of exercise-induced hypoglycaemia enables exercise to be continued [30] while supplementary carbohydrate ingestion during exercise appears to delay or slow the progression of fatigue [31]. Nevertheless neither *energy supply* and *energy depletion* models have universally received acceptance. For example, in the *energy supply* model, exercise ought to terminate when muscle ATP depletion occurs; however, that is only the case when muscle rigor develops (i.e. post death). ATP concentrations, even in muscles forced to contract under ischaemic conditions, do not drop below ~ 60% of resting values [18]. In the *energy depletion* model, pre-exercise carbohydrate loading ought to produce an ergogenic effect but this is not consistently the case [32]. Also, although carbohydrate supplementation may improve exercise outcomes in some cases, studies have also shown that post (endurance) exercise concentrations of muscle glycogen are similar between normal and supplementation conditions. This suggests that carbohydrate may be useful to exercise performance (i.e. the trajectory of performance may be different, but both are managed towards the same minimal reserve of glycogen) [31], it is still likely to be regulated and managed by a central (brain) process to avoid total depletion of muscle glycogen [33, 34]. The *cardiovascular/anaerobic* model and its variations has been the prevalent model in exercise physiology.

3.6. LIMITATIONS: BRAIN REGULATION

The *cardiovascular/anaerobic* model has received considerable criticism in recent years [2, 3, 15, 35] as it does not explain the occurrence of fatigue across all situations where it would be expected [36]. That model ignores the role of neural control over all physiological systems. Regulatory command from the brain operates both during the pre exercise anticipatory period and also in response to exercise where motor cortex stimulation of the medulla (brainstem) oscillates in accordance with the size of the muscle mass required to be activated during exercise. Since the conscious brain expresses a voluntary desire (impulse) to the motor cortex to initiate and continually regulate muscle recruitment during exercise [9], it is surprising that brain regulation of performance is considered a contentious or new concept.

Examples of neural regulation of performance can easily be discerned in hot conditions, where athletes are well known to self-regulate (pace) performance from the initial stages of the bout [37, 38], well in advance of the failure of heat dissipation mechanisms such as sweating [39]. According to the traditional *cardiovascular/anaerobic model*, fatigue should be a gradual involuntary process of a declining force generating capacity of muscle as it approaches depletion of a substrate or other physiological factor [1, 26]. Fatigue would therefore be consequent to a failing physiological system. Eventually the system would fail (a depleted/empty state) at which time the individual is no longer fatiguing, but exhausted. However, this perspective is not compatible with sport or exercise observations in which athletes are free to choose how to pace themselves. Athletes display behaviour similar to our animal counterparts and pace in accordance to the environment and the demands of the task [40]. The consequence of this behaviour is a voluntary redistribution of effort when tired so to avoid excessive fatigue sensations [15]. This action is adopted in response to continual and progressively stronger afferent sensations (signals) received by the brain [7]. It is a sensory feedback system which becomes more intense and persuasive if the intensity of exercise continues to increase towards its endpoint. The decision to either slow down or cease exercise therefore precedes the development of physiological system failure. The cardiovascular system provides powerful afferent feedback to the brain which informs the decision to slow down or cease exercise, but is unlikely to directly limit performance.

Further evidence for the presence of a behavioural mechanism controlling physical performance is present in both 1) tests of maximal aerobic power ($\dot{V}O_2$ max) and 2) during exercise performed at moderate to high altitude [3]. In response to $\dot{V}O_2$ max testing, the cardiovascular/anaerobic model predicts that individuals will reach a maximal level of oxygen uptake at which point oxygen uptake will plateau as the cardiovascular system reaches capacity. The observation of a plateau in oxygen uptake has been a central tenet of $\dot{V}O_2$ max testing for many years and yet ~60% of individuals undertaking this test show no sign of attaining such a plateau [41]. A substantial proportion of individuals reach a maximal level of tolerable discomfort at which point they voluntarily decide to cease exercise without exhibiting a plateau in $\dot{V}O_2$. This questions whether maximal performance is truly experienced, or simply whether a maximal level of tolerable discomfort (or effort) is reached in advance of physiological system capacity. If more muscle were able to be voluntarily recruited at maximal effort, more oxygen would be consumed and $\dot{V}O_2$ would continue to increase. The $\dot{V}O_2$ max should perhaps more correctly be labelled the '*maximum of voluntary effort*' (Figure 3.3).

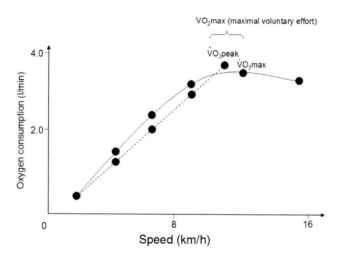

Figure 3.3. Example of oxygen uptake ($\dot{V}O_2$) responses to two maximal incremental exercise challenges. The dotted line represents a progressive increase in $\dot{V}O_2$ towards a maximal (peak) value without evidence of a plateau. The solid line represents a similar maximal value but with evidence of a plateau. Each are examples of maximal voluntary performance, restricted by the limits of tolerable discomfort.

At moderate to high altitude, physiological responses to exercise have also been cited as clear contrary evidence to the cardiovascular/anaerobic model [41]. For example, the reductions of O_2 partial pressure at altitudes above sea level inevitably restrict the amount of O_2 that can be taken up by muscles and used to provide aerobic energy. This should mean exercise will require greater anaerobically sourced energy at an earlier stage than experienced at sea level due to the reduced availability of O_2. As a consequence, continuation of exercise would have to be powered to a greater extent by anaerobic energy in which lactic acid is a by-product. The fact that maximal blood lactate at altitude remains either unchanged or, more frequently, is lower than at sea level has been termed the *lactate paradox* [42].

Importantly for the *cardiovascular/anaerobic, energy supply*, and *energy depletion* models, each predicts physiological system failure at the point of physical exhaustion. In all cases, fatigue is a developing feature in the gradual progression towards a final (terminal) exhaustion (e.g. running to empty) where it is a physical imperative to immediately cease exercise. However, as skeletal muscle is never fully recruited during exercise, muscle ATP never falls below 60% of resting levels, glycogen concentration declines but is not depleted during exercise [34], and fatigue in many circumstances occurs prior to high concentrations of metabolites such as lactate and hydrogen ions [2].

In 1996, Ulmer proposed that exercise performance might be regulated by a control centre located somewhere in the central nervous system [43]. In this model, it was suggested alterations in exercise intensity were continuously regulated by a feedback system where afferent information (such as muscular metabolism or force) are received by the central controller via afferent pathways. The controller would then be able to use this information from the muscles, as well as feedback from other organs to optimise and regulate performance.

Professor Tim Noakes and his group have since expanded Ulmer's theory by suggesting that central skeletal muscle activation is controlled by a regulator, probably located in the brain which acts to protect vital organs from injury or damage [15]. This system has been termed the *central governor model* of metabolic control [3, 44]. It is proposed in this model that exercise performance is continuously manipulated in response to the interaction of numerous physiological systems monitored by a central controller via constant feedforward and feedback loops between peripheral systems and the brain [7]. In this system, the endpoint of the bout represents a known variable by which the central governor continually manipulates pace [45, 46] (Figure 3.4). In this sense, the brain controls (and oscillates) motor unit recruitment so that the athlete can complete the known duration of the task without experiencing intolerable physical discomfort which might necessitate immediate cessation of exercise. In this model, fatigue is a subconscious process, representing an underlying neural integrative process [15, 24, 47]. Therefore, according to Noakes and co-workers the central controller subconsciously oscillates and regulates muscle recruitment so to avoid unsustainable and, eventually, intolerable conscious physical sensations [45, 46].

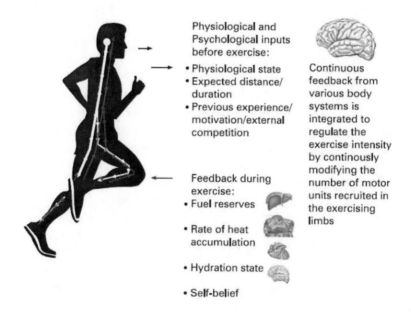

Figure 3.4. Brain regulation of performance based on feedback (afferent) signals from different physiological systems and feedforward (efferent) signals to muscle. Regulation by the brain is in accordance with the willingness to tolerate discomfort across the exercise bout in knowledge of the known demands of the task, prior experience, and motivation. Taken with permission from Noakes [41].

An interesting recent perspective to the brain regulation model was proposed by Marcora who, while appearing to accept the brain regulates muscle recruitment and limits performance, also questioned whether there is a need for a central regulatory governor [48]. This perspective suggests that the search for a central governor in the subconscious brain could be similar to that currently pursued by reductionists searching for a singular cause of fatigue.

Another simpler perspective which we propose, is that the conscious brain is the central governor. A single neural (controller) region which regulates exercise performance within the subconscious is most unlikely as the brain is the summation of a vast neural network and each region is tasked with contributory functions towards overall system (brain) operation. Millions of nuclei ensure inter-region neural communication within the circuitry of the brain without the need for a single 'master' or 'governor', other than perhaps regulation by our consciousness. In many ways the idea of a single intelligent regulatory governor within the subconscious mind is akin to the homunculus theory of a 'little man' operating the body from within the brain [49]. Clearly such a concept would also require the homunculus to have decision making intelligence; however; this would require conscious awareness within the subconscious brain. Therefore the homunculus would require a homunculus of its own (and so on). After all, a bird is capable of thought and conscious awareness [50], yet does not possess a neocortex (outer layer of the cerebral cortex) where thoughts occur in the mammalian brain. Neural circuitry adapts among our avian contemporaries to counteract this anatomical omission and so still facilitates conscious thought. Admittedly, the avian brain is not capable of sophisticated thought processes, but conscious behavioural decisions such as seeking shade in hot weather are not beyond the average bird. It might therefore make greater practical sense to consider the brain as a complex system of neural communications, regulated by consciousness.

It is well known that sensory (afferent) information is received by the thalamus [10] and communicated to the primary sensory cortex within the parietal lobe. Visual information is processed in the occipital lobes (visual cortex) and temporal lobes process auditory information (auditory cortex). These sources of information interact with considerations such as planning and problem solving (prefrontal regions of the cerebral cortex). Additionally, the cerebellum provides coordinative information while deep brain regions such as the hippocampus process memories of past experiences and nuclei within the hypothalamus receive and pass on important information from the brainstem such as body temperature, hunger, and thirst [9]. These factors all interact, and collectively act upon the motor cortex to stimulate voluntary muscle recruitment. Nevertheless, this does not explain how we slow down, or speed up during exercise without consciously deciding to do so. Hence, this leads to the current search for an unlikely regulatory control centre in the subconscious brain [15].

We propose that it is possible to alternatively explain neural regulation of exercise performance by re-examining the way in which the subconscious brain is interpreted. For example, if the subconsciousness is considered as a state of 'sub awareness' within a conscious state [12], then the potential for neural regulatory control becomes more compelling. The subconscious logically operates to keep the brain active while in either a state of rest (i.e. sleeping) or for automating processes which require skeletal muscle activity but are considered so routine as to not require our conscious awareness. We are capable of executing many physical tasks without dedicating much of our 'aware' consciousness to them (such as changing gear at the appropriate time in a car) and these tasks all require motor unit recruitment which is still regulated by the same neural processes, but without awareness from the conscious mind [10]. As we become more consciously aware of an exercise situation it is usually consequent to sensory information bombarding the brain with increasingly negative cues such as developing sensations of thirst, nausea, and over heating [3, 51]. In the continuance of high intensity exercise, the severity of these sensory cues eventually reaches such intensity as to trigger conscious awareness. Until that time, such as at low levels of physical effort, regulatory control can be accomplished with minimal conscious awareness. This regulation would therefore still be maintained by the conscious brain, albeit at a level of automated sub awareness (Figure 3.5). This process is not merely limited by physiological sensations but could also be triggered by psychological stress. Hence, one of the characteristics of increased stress is switching from an implicit or sub aware mode of task execution to a consciously aware attempt to regulate behaviour [52].

Such an interpretation of brain regulatory control remains largely consistent with the models proposed by Noakes [15] and also Marcora [48] but removes the requirement for a single intelligent, decision making homunculus in the subconscious brain. It is therefore a regulatory process of the brain which operates at relative levels of our conscious awareness. This is a subtle difference, but it explains regulatory control of exercise performance as a gross function of the cerebral cortex. Individual neural activities may predominate in isolated brain regions (e.g. planning within the prefrontal cortex) but are not limited to specific neural sites. Regulatory afferent information is constantly passed to the thalamus from the peripheral nervous system and upwards to different parts of the cerebral cortex for attention.

It seems likely that while that regulatory information is within parameters considered to be of automaticity, it does not receive our significant conscious attention. Where acceptable limits of automaticity (i.e. based on prior experience or expectations of the task demands) are encroached, the stimulus gains intensity (e.g. increasing sensations of nausea, or developing a thirst) and thus reaches a level of awareness that requires significant attention and a gross behaviour. A behaviour (e.g. to take a drink) is therefore a gross response to a developing state of awareness at a time of significant need. This response is less subtle than the minor manipulations and control of performance that we make without significant awareness or apparent thought.

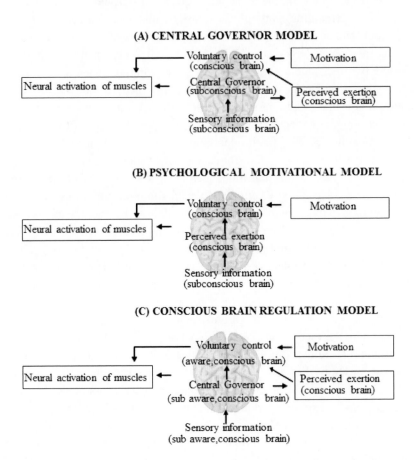

Figure 3.5. A comparison of brain regulation models of human movement. The Central Governor Model (A) and Psychological-Motivational Model (B) conceptualize the brain as comprising conscious and subconscious. Our Conscious Brain Regulation model (C) suggests the brain is continually in a conscious state, thus regulating muscle activation at different levels of awareness. At low intensity of effort (minimal physical discomfort), the brain regulates (oscillates) muscle activity via automaticity and minimal conscious awareness. As sensations become increasingly severe, they reach conscious awareness, requiring a less subtle (gross) behaviour to redress discomfort.

In situations where maximal effort is sustained towards the end of an exercise bout and yet power output/force still declines, this represents a conscious desire to override the overwhelming sensations of fatigue, but also represents a voluntary failure to do so. At this point, conscious attention may be focused on achieving the best possible outcome, but this desire is also tempered by the realisation of the physical consequences and projected (apprehensive) sensations of system failure. It is difficult to separate these considerations when determining maximal voluntary effort. In summary, the brain is the sum of many parts, each communicating via complex neural circuits. Therefore, maybe the question should not be where in the brain is the central governor? Perhaps the brain is the central governor.

3.7. LIMITATIONS: PSYCHOLOGICAL CONSIDERATIONS

Researchers have tried on many occasions to identify those psychological factors or skills which limit or enhance athletic performance. There is some tentative evidence that the psychological profile of successful athletes is different from those who are less successful. Using questionnaires (e.g. Psychological Skill Inventory for Sport [53]) to assess differences in psychological factors between athletes who have been more or less successful it has been found that successful athletes are more self-confident, use more imagery, are better in controlling levels of anxiety, prepare better mentally, use positive self-talk, set clear goals, are more committed, competitive, and motivated to do well, and have better concentration or are better at re-focussing (e.g. [54, 55]). Qualitative studies have supported most of these quantitative findings but have also uncovered a number of additional psychological attributes. These include a positive attitude, distraction control strategies, use of competitive simulation, emphasis on quality rather than quantity of practice; post-competition evaluation and continual refinement of their mental approach (e.g. [56]). Failure or poor performance has been associated with poor arousal control, negative thoughts, concerns about losing, not being able to concentrate, feeling listless and lack of coping [57, 58]. What seems clear is that psychological factors influence the way we behave in sport and exercise settings. These psychological factors can enhance and help the way an athlete trains-competes or worsen and impede performance.

Stress is an important factor which might limit athletic performance [59]. Although the sport psychology literature is awash with descriptions of sources of sport specific stressors few studies have reported pacing to be a stressor. For example, in a recent study using concept maps, 18 stressors were identified by athletes from different sports and of different achievement levels [60]. Although keeping pace was not identified as a stressor, there were a number of stressors which were related to this including fitness, performance and training. However, Lazarus [61] indicated that stressors are situation specific and there have been differences in the stressors experienced by athletes competing in different sports [62]. The demands of the sport or activity appear to influence the type of stressors experienced by athletes or exercisers. For example, in a study of international cross-country runners, fatigue was the most reported stressor (21.4%) during training [63]. However, this was less important during competition (3.6%). This is a common finding. That is, athletes tend to experience more, but less intense stressors, during training than competition. This suggests that intervention should be tailored to both the training and competition context.

The process by which an athlete or exerciser attempts to reduce the unpleasant feelings and emotions following stress is called coping [59]. It seems logical to assume that pacing is associated with coping. Hence, athletes need to be able to deal with the pain and negative emotions associated with high intensity training loads. Adopting the stress and coping model proposed by Lazarus [59] it is important to distinguish a number of phases. This model depicts stress and coping to be a dynamic process which involves transactions between environmental and personal variables. Primary appraisal refers to the process of assessing the impact of the event on an individual's physical and psychological well-being. An important distinction is whether an event is perceived as a challenge/benefit or threat/loss. Hence, if a situation is perceived as a challenge or benefit the athlete or exerciser is likely to experience less stress, experience positive emotions, and be more committed to achieve their goals. A threat/harm appraisal on the other hand is likely to result in higher levels of stress, experience of negative emotions and failure to achieve goals [64].

Secondary appraisal involves the assessment of the possible coping options to deal with the specific situation whilst trying to maximize gains and favourable outcomes and reducing harm [59]. This includes judgments of the resources available by the athlete or exerciser to deal with the event including coping strategies and perceptions of control over the event [65]. Following the appraisal process athletes will invoke coping strategies to deal with the stress. Having an extensive coping repertoire will help athletes to cope more effectively with the stress they experience and the emotions experienced. Hence, if coping was successful then the individual is likely to experience positive emotions, whereas a failure to cope effectively will result in negative emotions. The emotional state in turn will have a significant influence how the next stressful encounter is appraised.

Coping always takes place within an emotional environment. It is important to recognize that the intensity at which we exercise influences the emotions we experience [66]. Higher levels of exercise intensity (above the anaerobic threshold) results in experiencing adverse or unpleasant emotions or a lack or pleasurable emotions (reduced pleasure or increased displeasure) whereas exercise intensities below the anaerobic threshold are associated with positive emotions. This suggests that the anaerobic threshold could perhaps be viewed as a pleasure/pain point (Figure 3.6). Consequently when exercising at high intensities stress experienced is likely to be augmented by the negative emotions induced by the exercise itself. This would require the individual to first utilize coping strategies which down regulate the negative emotional state which are stressful in themselves. Also, the negative emotions can interfere with more active and adaptive ways of coping. Of course coping only refers to a strategy used to deal with a stressful encounter and does not guarantee a reduction in unpleasant emotions [67].

The ability to pace an exercise bout is an important skill. However, this is likely a very difficult thing to do for those about to embark on a new exercise programme and who have little experience in engagement in physical activity or exercise. This might be particularly the case for individuals who are obese or have chronic conditions which might make it more difficult to pace themselves. Experience with different exercise regimes is therefore an important variable which influences self-regulation of pacing. Although lack of experience appears to be an obvious factor which influences exercise behaviour there are also differences in performance at the elite level which might to some extent be attributed to familiarity or learning factors. The 'home advantage' phenomenon suggests that teams and individual athletes at all levels are more likely to perform well and succeed on their home ground [68]. Although it is unclear what causes these differences in performance, it could be due to a number of factors such as learning, environmental familiarity, and critical psychological, physiological and behavioural states.

Although the evidence is equivocal, another explanation for differences in selection of pacing strategy in general and tolerance for exercise intensity in particular is personality. For example, there is evidence to suggest that extraverts perceive lower levels of RPE and better mood than introverts after a high intensity exercise bout [69]. Extraverts have also been found to show higher persistence in a static leg contraction task [70] and cycling against a constant load than introverts [71]. Extraversion is also positively related to exercise participation and adherence. In particular, extraverts engage in more demanding physical activities and are more likely to participate in endurance sports requiring pacing skills, than introverts [72] .

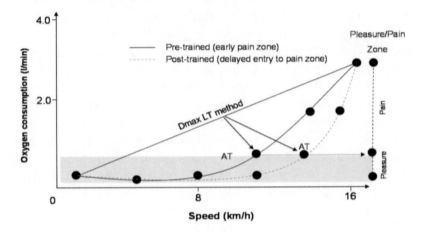

Figure 3.6. Negative sensations such as metabolic acidosis develop in severity as exercise becomes progressively challenging. Exercise performed at low intensity or where the cost of the muscle action is metabolically minimal, could be considered pleasurable as the stimulus of outcome satisfaction outweighs physical discomfort. It is possible to conceptualize the anaerobic threshold therefore as a pleasure/pain threshold.

It has recently been suggested [73] that preference for exercise and tolerance for exercise intensity are relatively stable predispositions or traits which influence the exercise intensity an individual will select if given the freedom to do so (intensity-preference) and their ability to continue an exercise bout with an imposed intensity (intensity-tolerance). Ekkekakis et al. (2005) developed the Preference for and Tolerance of the Intensity of Exercise Questionnaire (PRETIE-Q) and provided some support for the predictive validity of this instrument. Although the research in this area is still in its infancy this provides a promising avenue to explain the large inter-individual differences in the selection and tolerance of exercise intensities (pacing) by individuals.[24]

A number of psychological constructs are likely to positively or negatively shape the way we pace our exercise. This includes levels of trait and state anxiety, self-confidence, self-efficacy believes, mood, motivational orientation of the individual, the environment and personality. All these psychological variables will to some extent influence how the individual will appraise the upcoming training session or competition and the decision on the amount of effort to be exerted. The way the exercise or competition is progressing will also influence the individual's appraisal of the situation and determine whether to continue, put in more or less effort, or terminate the activity altogether.

CONCLUSION

- While there may be no argument that limits exist to which humans can physically perform tasks, the causes of such limitations remain fervently disputed.
- Peripheral fatigue has been defined as the loss of force caused by processes occurring at or distal to the neuromuscular junction. It is generally considered as fatigue occurring within the muscle.
- Central fatigue is associated with instances where the central nervous system has a diminished neural (brain) drive to muscle.
- The traditional model used to explain the occurrence of exercise –induced fatigue holds that the cardiovascular system limits performance via exercise induced deficiencies to the delivery of blood, nutrients and oxygen to the working muscles, by local muscle utilisation processes for the re-generation of ATP (energy currency), and by limitations to (pulmonary) blood circulation with the lungs for gas exchange.
- A new theory suggests that skeletal muscle activation is continually managed by a subconscious/conscious regulator in the brain which acts to protect vital organs from injury or damage. This system has been termed the central governor model of metabolic control.
- Psychological factors interact to contribute to negative afferent information received by the brain and thus limit performance. Overriding negative sensations is fundamental to extending exercise capabilities from a psychophysiological perspective.
- It is possible to explain brain regulation of exercise performance by considering that the brain remains in relative states of consciousness (e.g. aware and sub aware). In this new conscious awareness model of regulatory control, there is no requirement for an elusive and perhaps implausible intelligent central regulator within the subconscious.

REFERENCES

[1]   Bassett, D. and E. Howley, Limiting factors for maximum oxygen uptake and determinants of endurance performance. *Medicine & Science in Sports & Exercise,* 2000. 32: p. 70-84.

[2]   Noakes, T., Physiological models to understand exercise fatigue and the adaptations that predict or enhance athletic performance. *Scandinavian Journal of Medicine & Science in Sports,* 2000. 10: p. 123-145.

[3]   Noakes, T., Time to move beyond a brainless exercise physiology: the evidence for complex regulation of human exercise performance. *Applied Physiology, Nutrition and Metabolism,* 2011. 36: p. 23-35.

[4]   Gandevia, S., Spinal and supraspinal factors in human muscle fatigue. *Physiological Reviews,* 2001. 81: p. 1725-1789.

[5]   St Clair Gibson, A., et al., The conscious perception of the sensation of fatigue. *Sports Medicine,* 2003. 33: p. 167-176.

[6]   Bruce, J., Travels to discover the source of the Nile, in the years 1768-1773. 1804: *General Books Club* (2010).

[7]   St Clair Gibson, A., et al., The role of information processing between the brain and peripheral physiological systems in pacing and perception of effort. *Sports Medicine,* 2006. 36: p. 705-722.

[8]   Abernethy, B., Attention, in Handbook of sport psychology H.A.H. R.N. Singer, & C.M. Janelle Editor. 2001, John Wiley: New York.

[9]   Magill, R., Motor learning and control: concepts and applications. 9th ed. 2011, New York: McGraw Hill.

[10] Portas, C., et al., A specific role for the thalamus in mediating the interaction of attention and arousal in humans. *The Journal of Neuroscience,* 1998. 18: p. 8979-8989.

[11] Rolls, E. and A. Treves, Neural networks and brain function. 1998, Oxford: Oxford University Press.

[12] DeYoung, C., J. Peterson, and D. Higgins, Sources of openness/intellect: cognitive and neuropsychological correlates of the fifth factor of personality. *Journal of Personality,* 2005. 73: p. 825-858.

[13] Windhorst, U. and G. Boorman, Overview: potential role of segmental motor circuitry in muscle fatigue., in Fatigue, S. Gandevia, Editor. 1995, Plenum Press: New York. p. 241-258.

[14] Alexander, G. and M. Crutcher, Functional architecture of basal ganglia circuits: neural substrates of parallel processing. *Trends in Neurosciences,* 1990. 13: p. 266-271.

[15] Noakes, T., A. St Clair Gibson, and E. Lambert, From catastrophe to complexity: a novel model of integrative central neural regulation of effort and fatigue during exercise in humans: summary and conclusions. *British Journal of Sports Medicine,* 2005. 39: p. 120-124.

[16] Taylor, J., G. Todd, and S. Gandevia, evidence for a supraspinal contribution to human muscle fatigue. *Clinical and Experimental Pharmacology and Physiology,* 2006. 33: p. 400-405.

[17] Merton, P., Voluntary strength and fatigue. *Journal of Physiology,* 1954. 123: p. 553-564.

[18] Fitts, R., Cellular mechanisms of muscle fatigue. *Physiological Reviews,* 1994. 74: p. 49-94.

[19] Laurent, C. and J. Green, Multiple models can concurrently explain fatigue during human performance. *International Journal of Exercise Science,* 2009. 2: p. 280-293.

[20] Herbert, R. and S. Gandevia, Muscle activation in unilateral and bilateral efforts assessed by motor nerve and cortical stimulation. *Journal of Applied Physiology,* 1996. 80: p. 1351-1356.

[21] Bigland-Ritchie, B. and J. Woods, Changes in muscle contractile properties and neural control during human muscular fatigue. *Muscle and Nerve,* 1984. 7: p. 691-699.

[22] Bigland-Ritchie, B., et al., Changes in motorneurone firing rates during sustained maximal voluntary contractions. *Journal of Physiology,* 1983. 340: p. 335-346.

[23] Kent-Braun, J., Central and peripheral contributions to muscle fatigue in humans during sustained maximal effort. *European Journal of Applied Physiology,* 1999. 80: p. 57-63.

[24] Lambert, E., A. St Clair Gibson, and T. Noakes, Complex systems model of fatigue: integrative homoeostatic control of peripheral physiological systems during exercise in humans. *British Journal of Sports Medicine,* 2005. 39: p. 52-62.

[25] St Clair Gibson, A., M. Lambert, and T. Noakes, Neural control of force output during maximal and submaximal exercise. Sports Medicine, 2001. 31: p. 637-650.

[26] Costill, D., H. Thomason, and E. Roberts, Fractional utilization of the aerobic capacity during distance running. *Medicine & Science in Sports,* 1973. 5: p. 248-252.

[27] Bassett, D. and E. Howley, Oxygen uptake: "classical" vs. "contemporary" viewpoints. *Medicine & Science in Sports & Exercise,* 1997. 29: p. 591-603.

[28] Mier, M., et al., Cardiovascular adaptations to 10 days of cycle exercise. *Journal of Applied Physiology*, 1997. 83: p. 1900-1906.

[29] Coyle, E., et al., Physiological and biomechanical factors associated with elite endurance cycling performance. *Medicine & Science in Sports & Exercise*, 1991. 23: p. 93-107.

[30] Coggan, A. and E. Coyle, Reversal of fatigue during prolonged exercise by carbohydrate infusion or ingestion. *Journal of Applied Physiology*, 1987. 63: p. 2388-2395.

[31] Coyle, E., et al., Muscle glycogen utilization during prolonged strenuous exercise when fed carbohydrate. *Journal of Applied Physiology*, 1986. 61: p. 165-172.

[32] Hawley, J., E. Schabort, and T. Noakes, Carbohydrate loading and exercise performance: *An update. Sports Medicine*, 1997. 24: p. 73-81.

[33] Rauch, L., et al., Effects of carbohydrate loading on muscle glycogen content and cycling performance. *International Journal of Sport Nutrition*, 1995. 5: p. 25-36.

[34] Rauch, H., A. St Clair Gibson, and E. Lambert, A signalling role for muscle glycogen in the regulation of pace during prolonged exercise. *British Journal of Sports Medicine*, 2005. 39: p. 34-38.

[35] Edwards, A. and T. Noakes, Dehydration: cause of fatigue or sign of pacing in elite soccer? *Sports Medicine*, 2009. 39: p. 1-13.

[36] Hargreaves, M., Fatigue mechanisms determining exercise performance: integrative physiology is systems biology. *Journal of Applied Physiology*, 2008. 104: p. 1541-1542.

[37] Tucker, R. and T. Noakes, The physiological regulation of pacing strategy during exercise: a critical review. *British Journal of Sports Medicine*, 2009. 43: p. 1-9.

[38] Tucker, R., The anticipatory regulation of performance: the physiological basis for pacing strategies and the development of a perception-based model for exercise performance. *British Journal of Sports Medicine*, 2009. 43: p. 392-400.

[39] Saunders, A., et al., The effects of different air velocities on heat storage and body temperature in humans cycling in a hot, humid environment. *Acta Physiologica Scandinavica*, 2005. 183: p. 241-255.

[40] Noakes, T., Lore of Running. 2002: *Human Kinetics*.

[41] Noakes, T., Testing for maximum oxygen consumption has produced a brainless model of human exercise performance. *British Journal of Sports Medicine*, 2008. 42: p. 551-555.

[42] Hochachka, P., The lactate paradox: analysis of underlying mechanisms. *Annals of Sports Medicine*, 1988. 4: p. 184-188.

[43] Ulmer, H., Concept of an extracellular regulation of muscular metabolic rate during heavy exercise in humans by psychophysiological feedback. *Experimentia*, 1996. 52: p. 416-420.

[44] Noakes, T., The central governor model of exercise regulation applied to the marathon. *Sports Medicine*, 2007. 37: p. 374-377.

[45] Tucker, R., et al., Non-random fluctuations in power output during self-paced exercise. *British Journal of Sports Medicine*, 2006. 40: p. 912-917.

[46] Lander, P., R. Butterly, and A. Edwards, Self-paced exercise is less physically challenging than enforced constant pace exercise of the same intensity: influence of complex central metabolic control. *British Journal of Sports Medicine*, 2009. 43: p. 789-795.

[47] St Clair Gibson, A. and T. Noakes, Evidence for complex system integration and dynamic neural regulation of skeletal muscle recruitment during exercise in humans. *British Journal of Sports Medicine*, 2004. 38: p. 797-806.

[48] Marcora, S., Do we really need a central governor to explain brain regulation of exercise performance? *European Journal of Applied Physiology*, 2008. 104: p. 929-931.

[49] Impellizzeri, F., et al., Use of RPE-based training load in soccer. *Medicine & Science in Sports & Exercise*, 2004. 36: p. 1042-1047.

[50] Whittow, G., Sturkie's Avian Physiology. 5th Edition ed. 1999: Academic Press.

[51] Edwards, A., et al., Influence of moderate dehydration on soccer performance: physiological responses to 45 min of outdoor match-play and the immediate subsequent performance of sport-specific and mental concentration tests. *British Journal of Sports Medicine*, 2007. 41: p. 385-391.

[52] Masters, R., R. Polman, and H. Hammond, "Reinvestment": A dimension of personality implicated in skill breakdown under pressure. *Personality and Individual Differences*, 1993. 14: p. 655-666.

[53] Mahoney, M., T. Gabriel, and T. Perkins, Psychological skills and exceptional athletic performance. *The Sport Psychologist*, 1987. 1: p. 181-199.

[54] Meyers, M., A. LeUnes, and A. Bourgeois, Psychological skill assessments and athletic performance in collegiate rodeo athletes. *Journal of Sport Behaviour*, 1996. 19: p. 132-146.

[55] St Clair Gibson, A. and C. Foster, The role of self-talk in the awareness of physiological state and physical performance. *Sports Medicine*, 2007. 37: p. 1029-1044.

[56] Krane, V. and J. Williams, Psychological characteristics of peak performance, in *Applied sport psychology: Personal growth to peak performance*, J. Williams, Editor. 2010, McGraw Hill: New York. p. 169-188.

[57] Eklund, R., A season long investigation of competitive cognition in collegiate wrestlers, *Research Quarterly for Exercise and Sport*, 1994. 65: p. 169-183.

[58] Nicholls, A., N. Holt, and R. Polman, A phenomenological analysis of coping effectiveness in golf. *The Sport Psychologist*, 2005. 19: p. 111-130.

[59] Lazarus, R., Stress, appraisal and coping. 1984, New York: Springer.

[60] Nicholls, A., et al., Stressors, coping, and coping effectiveness: Gender, sport type, and ability differences. *Journal of Sports Sciences*, 2007. 25(1521-1530).

[61] Lazarus, R., Stress and emotion: A new synthesis. 1999, *Springer:* New York.

[62] Polman, R., Elite athletes' experiences of coping with stress, in Coping and emotions in sport, M.J. J. Thatcher, & D. Lavallee Editor. 2011, Routledge.

[63] Nicholls, A., et al., Stress appraisals, coping, and coping effectiveness among international cross-country runners during training and competition. *European Journal of Sports Science*, 2009. 9: p. 285-293.

[64] Nicholls, A., et al., An exploration of the two-factor schematization of relation meaning and emotions among professional rugby union players. *International Journal of Sport and Exercise Psychology*, 2011. 9: p. 1-14.

[65] Zakowski, S., et al., Appraisal control, coping, and stress in a community sample: A test of the Goodness-of-Fit hypothesis. *Annals of Behavioural Medicine*, 2001. 23: p. 158-165.

[66] Ekkekakis, P., E. Lind, and S. Vazou, Affective responses to increasing levels of exercise intensity in normal-weight, overweight, and obese middle-aged women. *Obesity*, 2009. 18: p. 79-85.

[67] Compass, B., Coping and stress during childhood and adolescence. *Psychological Bulletin*, 1987. 101: p. 393-403.

[68] Pollard, R. and G. Pollard, Long-term trends in home advantage in professional team sports in North America and England. *Journal of Sports Sciences,* 2005. 23: p. 337-350.

[69] Koller, M., M. Haider, and H. Recher, Metabolic stress during different work loads as personality-related risk factor. *Activitas Nervosa Superior,* 1984. 26: p. 134-137.

[70] Costello, C. and H. Eysenck, Persistence, personality, and motivation. *Perceptual and Motor Skills,* 1961. 12: p. 169-170.

[71] Shiomi, K., Performance differences between extraverts and introverts on exercise using an ergometer. *Perceptual and Motor Skills,* 1980. 50: p. 356-358.

[72] Courneya, K. and L. Hellsten, Personality correlates of exercise behaviour, motives, barriers and preferences: An application of the five factor model. *Personality and Individual Differences,* 1998. 24: p. 625-633.

[73] Ekkekakis, P., E. Hall, and S. Petruzzello, Some like it vigorous: measuring individual differences in the preference for and tolerance of exercise intensity. *Journal of Sport & Exercise Psychology,* 2005. 27: p. 350-374.

[74] Noakes, T., How did A V Hill understand the $\dot{V}O_2$ max and the "plateau phenomenon"? Still no clarity? *British Journal of Sports Medicine,* 2008. 42: p. 574-580.

Chapter 4

MONITORING AND SELF-REGULATING TRAINING

4.1. ABSTRACT

The aim of this chapter is to examine the basis of generic and self-regulatory systems for monitoring training and to identify skills which may assist in optimising training outcomes. Numerous systems have been developed for monitoring training responses such as by heart rate or other metabolic variables. However, such systems are unlikely to be suitable to all exercise situations where physical conditioning, type of exercise, or the environment can change from day to day. A rating of perceived exertion system for monitoring training is discussed, as are specific self-regulatory skills which may assist in the development of an optimal training strategy.

4.2. INTRODUCTION

The ancient Greek *tetrad* (see chapter one) demonstrated an early appreciation of the need to vary the intensity and focus of training from day to day towards a specific goal (e.g. the Olympics) [1]. It seems clear that thorough planning and implementation of an appropriate training programme are vital considerations for preparing athletes for competition or for individuals aiming to achieve a specific personal target (e.g. weight loss or improved fitness).

The content of a training programme is highly specific to the needs of the individual and consequently task-specific considerations for training in different contexts are addressed in subsequent chapters of this book. However, the usefulness of a training programme extends beyond simply performing physical tasks in the anticipation that these will lead to the achievement of goals. A systematic method of tracking performance outcomes in response to the training stimulus (e.g. load) is vital [2, 3]. This is the means of identifying whether or not the stimulus is appropriate for the individual and that key targets are regularly attained. If the training stimulus is inadequate, physiological adaptation will not be optimal while over zealous training can lead to sustained overreaching and eventually to overtraining [4]. It is therefore of considerable importance that training is regularly checked via a systematic approach to monitoring both tangible outcomes (e.g. performance) and some form of feedback as to whether or not the prescribed stimulus (training load) is appropriate for the individual [5, 6].

4.3. METHODS TO MONITOR TRAINING OUTCOMES

Monitoring training requires the assembly of relevant, usable information. Gathering information for no specific purpose is pointless and can lead to situations where unreliable, inconsistent data are acted upon simply because these have been collected. It is therefore important to determine how the monitoring of training will be helpful, what information is useful, and how to best obtain reliable data.

Modern training methods usually adopt the principles of either linear or non-linear periodization [7], thereby focusing on or emphasizing different qualities at various stages of the training programme. Therefore, the objective indices used to monitor training may also need to differ, depending on the activities undertaken. This can prove problematic if, for example, a physiological variable (e.g. heart rate) is used to gauge the training response and that variable is not relevant or overtly stressed for all components of the programme (such as when resistance training) [5, 8, 9].

The simplest, most common and probably effective tool of monitoring training outcomes is for an athlete to maintain a training log [10]. Although obvious, a training log containing performance outcomes and details of the training load is not always maintained. This log is a personal monitoring tool for an individual and should represent a record of session-to-session performance outcomes and thoughts or feelings about the session. The training log often can also reflect factors peripheral to training such as sleep, diet, and other stressors which may all indirectly impact on training and performance. In addition to the individual's log, the trainer/coach should also maintain a training log of outcomes for each athlete in their squad as this can be useful to identifying areas of concern or explanatory observations for good or poor performance. It can also act as a data source for future development of performance targets and improved session design. Perhaps most importantly, it can be used to summarise planned vs. actual work completed, compare the perceived rating of the athlete in response to the intended intensity of the work, and contain the detailed description of performance outcomes.

Monitoring training should address the issue of session-to-session exercise intensity for individuals [2, 3]. This has acute implication to whether or not each session is of a meaningful intensity for different athletes. For example, two athletes might complete the same training session, achieve the same training performance, and yet experience different adaptive responses [11]. This is most often due to differences in their maximal performance capabilities whereby a more advanced performer may achieve the same result as their training partner but with a lower effort and reduced physiological strain [5]. This would clearly represent a lower relative training load for the more advanced athlete and therefore present a reduced stimulus for potential adaptation which might impede further progress [12]. Therefore, performance should be monitored not just simply in terms of performance outcome (e.g. performance time) but also in terms of physiological and psychological responses to the imposed training stimulus [3]. This will enable the coach to determine whether or not the stimulus from an individual session or even the overall programme is appropriate. Such a systematic approach also minimizes the potential for issues of overreaching and overtraining which may occur if the stimulus is too severe or is generalized to a group.

Numerous systems have been proposed for monitoring training responses (e.g. [3, 13]) using a variety of metabolic and performance variables. Several of the most common systems are discussed in the following chapter.

4.3.1. Metabolic and Performance Outcome Variables

The measurement of heart rate during a training session is commonly used as a biofeedback marker to estimate physiological response, or to directly set the intensity of exercise (i.e. running at a level of effort to produce a target heart rate) [13]. Increases to heart rate during aerobic exercise are well known to be directly related to the intensity of work performed and, as a consequence, this measurement may provide useful explanatory information to supplement performance outcomes.

Cardiac output (CO) is well known to increase to match the demand of exercise [14] and this is accomplished by increases to both stroke volume (SV) and heart rate (HR) (CO = SV x HR). Stroke volume may increase from ~100 to 160 mL (approx. 50% increase) during exercise but not in direct relation to exercise intensity; however, heart rate increases gradually in response to exercise, from ~ 60 b/min at rest to maximal levels ~185 b/min during strenuous exercise (approx 200% increase). Therefore, increases to heart rate accounts for a larger proportion of the increase in cardiac output [15] and, as such, this easily measured variable has gained considerable popularity as a means of quantifying physiological stress in response to exercise.

Heart rates can provide useful feedback of progressive cardiovascular changes to standardised exercise sessions. Also, numerous studies have shown that aerobic capabilities improve if the sustained exercise intensity is broadly maintained within a heart rate zone of 55-70% of maximum age predicted heart rate (e.g. 220 − age) [14]. This knowledge can provide reassurance to novice athletes that the training session has provoked an appropriate physiologic response, or they can alternatively directly pace an exercise bout to achieve a target heart rate in the required target zone.

Monitoring, or pre-setting, training intensity via heart rate methods can yield useful biofeedback information for athletes and their coaches, but it is difficult to use these data beyond simple identification of the required training zone for a single session. To extrapolate this information for the purpose of monitoring training outcomes, a system called the TRaining IMPulse (TRIMP) was developed [13]. The TRIMP is a practical technique for monitoring the intensity of prescribed physical work across sessions and estimates a training impulse based on session duration and the average heart rate in response to it:

Heart Rate TRIMP = training session duration x average session heart rate.

The TRIMP therefore, represents a basic dose of aerobic training such that a 30 min exercise session completed with an average heart rate of 160 b/min results in a TRIMP of 4800 (30 min x 160 b/min = 4800). A longer training session (e.g. 40 min) completed at the same heart rate (intensity) (160 b/min) represent a greater sustained metabolic challenge and so derives a higher TRIMP. Table 4.1 demonstrates a comparison of TRIMP outcomes for three different training sessions. The accumulation of session to session TRIMP scores within a cycle of training (e.g. microcycle) can therefore be used to quantify a basic training load.

Table 4.1. A comparison of heart rate TRIMP outcomes for three training sessions and their accumulated score as an indicator of cyclic training load

Session	Time (min)	Average Heart rate (b/min)	TRIMP (duration x HR)
High intensity continuous run	25	192	4800
Continuous steady run	30	160	4800
Continuous steady run	40	160	6400
Aerobic circuit training	60	150	9000
Total TRIMP load (accumulation of selected scores)			25000

The TRIMP method enables coaches and athletes to plan and monitor a range of aerobic activities using both expected heart rates (applying the TRIMP to *plan* sessions if using a target heart rate) and subsequently the actual heart rate responses achieved (applying TRIMP to *monitor* session responses). At a basic level, it facilitates practical organisation of aerobic training and broadly ensures week-to-week (or cycle-to-cycle) balance of training load can be planned and achieved.

Although this system is intuitively attractive and simple to implement, a significant flaw is that it does not accurately distinguish between different levels of activity. As identified, the example of a 30 min exercise bout at an average heart rate of 160 b/min provides a TRIMP of 4800 (Table 4.1). However, it is also evident that 25 minutes of exercise at an average heart rate of 192 b/min also results in a TRIMP of 4800. These two sessions are likely to produce quite different metabolic outcomes, utilise different energy systems and require differential recovery periods despite being TRIMP being matched. Quite obviously, twenty five minutes of exercise at an average heart rate of 192 b/min is a much harder training session than 30 min at 160 b/min.

To overcome this limitation, the basic TRIMP concept was modified (e.g. Foster et al. 2001) to incorporate weighting for intensity of exercise in the calculation. In this revision, a heart rate zone number (1-5) replaces the average heart rate from the original TRIMP calculation to quantify training intensity (Table 4.2).

The revised heart rate zone TRIMP is therefore calculated as the total time spent in each zone. For example, 30 min of aerobic exercise completed at an average heart rate of 160 b/min by an athlete with a maximum heart rate of 200 b/min (80% of max heart rate) would place that individual in zone 4. The calculation of duration (30 min) x heart rate zone (4) produces a revised TRIMP of 120. Using our previous comparison with a harder session, 25 min at an average heart rate of 192 b/min by the same athlete places the session in zone 5 (96% of maximum) and multiplied by exercise duration (25 min) produces a TRIMP of 125. This method now distinguishes between the two sessions where the intensity of sustained physical effort is different. It is only a subtle difference but potentially meaningful.

Table 4.2. Heart rate zone TRIMP [3]. This system allocates average heart rates into zones for subsequence TRIMP calculation (duration x zone)

Heart Rate Zone	% of maximum heart rate
1	50-59
2	60-69
3	70-79
4	80-89
5	90-100

There are, of course, limitations to using any single physiologic variable (e.g. heart rate, or blood lactate concentrations) for the purpose of planning and/or monitoring training. The particular limitation of both the TRIMP heart rate methods is that they are only suited to endurance-based exercise. Strength, speed, anaerobic and technical sessions, which do not evoke high heart rates or where heart rate does not accurately reflect overall effort, cannot be calculated accurately by these means.

A further limitation to the use of heart rate methods is the impact of environmental conditions on the cardiovascular system. For example, it is well known that the heart must beat faster than normal to maintain the required cardiac output in hot conditions due to peripheral redistribution of blood to the skin [16]. Consequently, in hot conditions, power output is lower than for the same heart rate as in cool conditions [8]. This has implications for assigning or evaluating training sessions to heart rate zones when the environmental conditions differ between sessions.

As indicated earlier in this section, heart rate is a metabolic response to the exercise performed and as such it also takes time to reflect the work already being performed. For example, at the start of a running interval, heart rate takes seconds, or even minutes in some cases to accurately reflect the task [17]. During a short sprint heart rate increases, yet simply reflects a cardiodynamic, general increase in frequency which does not accurately reflect the task requirements and thus cannot give an accurate measurement of the applied effort in that context.

Although heart rate methods are generally well suited to endurance events, these may also not be reliable for ultra-endurance activities such as Ironman triathlon events [18]. During these events, most competitors are able to sustain a constant heart rate, but due to physiological changes such as dehydration (inducing changes to blood viscosity), cardiovascular drift occurs. The term cardiovascular drift describes the gradual time-dependent 'drift' in factors such as stroke volume (which declines as blood viscosity increases) [19]. This means that heart rate must increase during such prolonged exercise to sustain a constant cardiac output and consequently the effort required to sustain a constant target heart rate increases over the course of the event. Therefore, it can be misleading to use this as an external indicator of exercise intensity for the purpose of pacing.

The relatively recent development of reliable telemetry systems (such as power meters and Global Positioning Systems: GPS) for the measurement of power output and distances covered can be useful for sports such as cycling, rowing and team sports [2]. These can provide useful feedback for estimations of accumulative work achieved in a session, movement patterns and other outcome driven data. However, day to day fluctuations of health/wellbeing /soreness and so on also affect the ability to attain a given power output, as does the environmental conditions, surface conditions and terrain. Examination of power output or GPS data does not provide any physiological explanation for changes to performance, but if coupled with perceptual feedback (i.e. RPE evaluations) this could be a useful means of quantifying training. For example, the power output attained at key stages of an exercise bout can be coupled with other sensory information to determine regulatory check points of physical and mental wellbeing in comparison to previous bouts of exercise over the same course or in response to the same task. If, for example, a cyclist climbed to the top of a steep hill it would represent considerable physical work. The work required to reach to the top of that hill will be the same regardless of how fast or slow it was climbed; however, if the climb was twice as fast as the time before, the cyclist would have exerted twice the amount of average power, utilized different energy systems and worked at quite a different intensity. Therefore, this information is useful, but should be coupled with additional sensory data to properly assess the extent of physical challenge.

4.3.2. Self-Regulated Management of Training

The principles of self-regulation suggest that suitably constructed RPE methods of monitoring training are likely to be effective across all types of exercise.

The American College of Sports Medicine position statement recognizes RPE as a valid and reliable indicator of level of physical exertion during endurance exercise [20]. This psychophysiological approach to monitoring training requires athletes to rate on a numerical scale their perceived feelings relative to an exertion level [21]. RPE represents a conscious perception of effort experienced during exercise and consequently has considerable practical value to the athlete. In addition, exercise corresponding to higher levels of energy expenditure and physiologic strain consistently produce higher RPE ratings [22] and individuals appear to learn quite quickly to exercise at a specific RPE [17]. Exercise paced at an RPE of 13-14 (somewhat hard; 6-20 RPE scale) consistently coincides with approx 70% HRmax during cycle ergometer and treadmill exercise, while other research has shown RPE to be related to the percentage of heart rate during running and to the time spent at different intensities corresponding to heart rate at lactate thresholds [22]. Consequently, exercising according to RPE provides an effective way to prescribe exercise based on individual's perception of effort that coincides with individualised metabolic strain (e.g. %HR max, % $\dot{V}O_2$ max, blood lactate concentration).

The practical usefulness of RPE has also been suggested to extend beyond simply self-regulating or monitoring the intensity of training, to actually replacing heart rate in the calculation of TRIMP for the assessment of training load. As RPE relates to all types of exercise and not merely aerobic sessions [3, 5] it means the same monitoring system can be applied to all types of sessions and is thus highly attractive to coaches seeking to quickly and effectively monitor all training sessions.

The session rating of perceived exertion (RPE) TRIMP model is a simple system for coaches to monitor the load of ALL different training modalities (technical, tactical, endurance, speed and strength). With this system, individuals are required to provide an RPE based on the 10-point (CR10) scale [21] (Figure 4.1) for each exercise session which is then multiplied by the training session duration (min) to determine training load. Weekly or otherwise periodically summed training load (i.e. microcycle) can then offer a tangible representation of the training experience and offer a rapid, effective and meaningful method for monitoring the training experiences across most sport and exercise contexts. This makes it a very powerful monitoring tool for many different types of training sessions and/or sports.

Rating	Descriptor
0	Rest
1	Very, very easy
2	Easy
3	Moderate
4	Somewhat hard
5	Hard
6	–
7	Very hard
8	–
9	–
10	Maximal

Figure 4.1. the CR10 Borg Rating of Perceived Exertion scale [21].

To calculate the RPE TRIMP, the session duration is multiplied by the RPE evaluation. For example, for 60 minutes of training, rated as very hard (RPE = 7), TRIMP = 60 x 7 = 420.

Using the RPE TRIMP system, the individual provides a 'global' rating of the session and so enables comparisons between different types of training (Figure 4.2). This system has also been shown to be useful for resistance training, further demonstrating considerable diversity of its application [5]. It is also potentially useful for athletes in sports that involve a variety of training modes, especially anaerobic and technical training, e.g. team games and power sports. Athletes in these sports may train for long periods of time, while their average heart rate for the session may be low. Using heart rate TRIMP methods, the overall training load may appear of lower stress than actually experienced by factors such as local muscle soreness, mental fatigue and dehydration. RPE evaluations capture the afferent sensations received by the brain and can thus represent a holistic view of metabolic challenge across all physiologic systems when either devising a training load, or examining its impact on the individual.

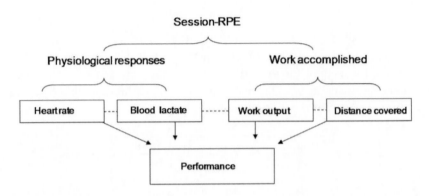

Figure 4.2. An RPE-based system for monitoring responses and performance outcomes from a training programme. As the brain regulates all physiologic systems and perceived sensations, it is possible for this system to provide a quick and effective means of determining training load and response across all exercise types.

In summary, there are numerous methods for objectively evaluating the intensity and load of training. The basic heart rate TRIMP method may be suited in some cases to those training for general health benefits; however, it contains several inaccuracies which are to some extent addressed by the TRIMP heart rate zone method. This is a simple modification for monitoring all aerobic training and is generally well suited for endurance athletes. There are several confounding variables relating to differences in environmental conditions, dehydration and training where sustained high heart rates do not properly reflect the demands of the task. The use of variables such as blood lactate concentrations as a gauge of training intensity or training adaptation are largely impractical, except to those with access to portable blood testing equipment. It could not be used practically to quantify responses to training. Monitoring power output or performance data provides a useful index of objective outcomes from training, but this would best be coupled with a system of biofeedback (such as RPE) to properly explain the basis behind performance. The final method, session RPE, is the most versatile and practical since it can be used to *ex post facto* rate the load of any kind of training and also can be used *ante eventum* to pre set a level of effort to perform exercise i.e. perform the session at a prescribed RPE. Coupled with performance outcome data, session RPE provides a powerful and practical tool for both setting the exercise intensity and also for monitoring training via self-regulation (Figure 4.2). However, the ability to use a self-regulatory system in sport and exercise may take some training and skill [23].

4.4. SELF-REGULATORY TRAINING SKILLS

'Good judgment is the result of experience. Experience is the result of bad judgment.'

Mark Twain

Inexperienced athletes are unable to pace themselves effectively compared to experienced athletes [24]. This is largely due to the intricacies of performing such a complex skill [25] and specific self-regulatory training is likely to assist in the capacity to improve the execution of a pacing strategy. This is a concept implicitly based on the integration of mind and body in regulating performance [26].

As active muscles and the cardiovascular system approach their limits during sustained exercise, the brain has to overcome increasingly negative stimuli suggesting it might be a good idea to reduce motor drive and slow down. This is not usually desirable in a competitive situation and so the brain must resist increasingly potent negative stimuli in the effort to sustain the required pace. This inevitably drives the perception of effort ever upwards until such time as negative (afferent) sensations can no longer be tolerated and the athlete feels compelled to either slow down, stop, or, if well-judged, cross a finish line in a physical state considered to be of maximal manageable discomfort [27]. As discussed previously though, this does not represent a state of catastrophic exhaustion at which time a physiological system has failed [28]. It is a physical state determined by the individual's appraisal, based on the physical limits of tolerability the individual is able to endure in response to that activity. It is a matter of pain/discomfort management and once accepted that this is THE limitation to exercise performance, it is trainable.

In 2007, 'Brain Training for Runners', Matt Fitzgerald [23] presented a practical interpretation of how to integrate mind-body for the purpose of optimising training by feel rather than external instruction. The concept of training the brain may seem unusual to many coaches and athletes, but the concept strongly relates to overriding central regulatory (brain) control of performance. If the brain limits our physical efforts, perhaps with systematic and dedicated training we can get closer to our true physical limits. Of course this does not mean ignore all physical training and merely concentrate on training the mind; the brain is the limitation to physical effort and so releasing some of our natural inhibition may facilitate greater physical training and performance outcomes. Therefore, physical training remains vital to athletic success, but specific (brain) self-regulatory training skills may be useful to aid this process.

> 'The body does not want you to do this. As you run, it tells you to stop but the mind must be strong. You always go too far for your body. You must handle the pain with strategy...It is not age; it is not diet. It is the will to succeed.'
>
> Jacqueline Gareau (Boston Marathon winner, 1980)

4.4.1. Coping Strategies

Participation in sport and exercise is almost inevitably associated with encountering stressors and these can include making technical or tactical mistakes, officials making wrong decisions and bodily feedback associated with the physical work performed (e.g., pain or fatigue). The development of appropriate coping strategies may help athletes to perceive stressful events positively as challenges rather than negatively as threats.

Athletes can be taught coping strategies. Prior to implementing a coping intervention it is useful to first assess the stressors athletes regularly encounter in their training and competition as well as the coping strategies they use to deal with these situations and their perceived effectiveness. Hence, athletes are frequently not aware of which situations cause stress to them and often do not invoke adequate coping strategies when experiencing a stressful event [29]. Not coping with a stressful event is related to frustration [30] and performance decrements [31].

Evidence appears to suggest that athletes improve performance by developing coping strategies to make the exercise situation better. For example, one study of competitive rowers induced pain by occluding specific limbs during training and observed that the rowers showed both greater tolerance to pain and also reported using a range of their own coping strategies to manage the pain. These coping strategies were reported to be the same as used in competition thus suggesting their sporting experience had prepared them to tolerate considerable pain and also to develop their own methods for dealing with it; certainly more so than untrained subjects [32].

4.4.2. Mental Toughness

'Sport is not about being wrapped up in cotton wool. Sport is about adapting to the unexpected and being able to modify plans at the last minute. Sport, like all life, is about taking risks.'

Sir Roger Bannister

Clough, Earle and Sewell [33] suggest that mental toughness consists of 4 inter-related but independent factors: (1) Commitment (stickability, ability to execute tasks successfully despite any problems or obstacles that arise); (2) Challenge (regard challenges as opportunities for self development); (3) Control (in control of environment, emotions and life); and (4) Confidence (self-belief to successfully complete tasks). Although operationalised as a personality construct these four factors which make-up mental toughness each relate to potentially trainable characteristics. Mental toughness training would therefore be a gateway to influence exercise behaviour in athletes and help the athlete to buffer against stress [29].

The way an athlete appraises a stressful encounter has consequences for the amount of stress experienced and the selection of coping strategies. For example, if significant stress is experienced it will be difficult for the athlete to make rational and accurate judgments. In such a situation it would be advisable for the athlete to first down-regulate their emotional state before trying to solve the problem. Athletes with more mental toughness have been shown to appraise stressful events as less stressful, more controllable [34], view the stressor as a challenge rather than threat [35], tolerate pain better, and have lower levels of perceived exertion. Additionally, mental toughness has been found to be related to the use of more adaptive coping strategies and greater use of some performance strategies in competition, namely activation, relaxation, self-talk, emotional control, and goal setting [36]. Taken together, these findings might explain why being mentally tough is often associated with success in sport.

Increasing an athlete's mental toughness could be accomplished by teaching athletes psychological skills which are akin to stress management and include thinking optimistically (see the challenge rather than the threat), development of structured approaches to competition and training (e.g. pre-performance routines), learning to deal with nervousness (e.g. progressive muscular relaxation, breathing), learning not to worry about what can't be controlled, learning from failure or mistakes, use of positive self-talk, keeping perspective and not dwelling on mistakes.

Baron and co-workers [37] recently suggested that athletes select optimal pacing strategies by associating a level of emotion with the ability to maintain a particular pace. At the high end of exercise intensities, this is likely to be a negative emotion driven by unwillingness to incur significant physical discomfort unless it is absolutely necessary. To resist the urge to slow down requires considerable mental toughness and, intuitively, most athletes will know that fighting the temptation to ease off in training is a significant battle. This is a battle that can be easily lost by intermittently attending training sessions and/or simply completing work directed by a coach with no regard to personal investment of significant effort. There are many occasions in training where other commitments mean it is difficult to attend sessions, when it is too cold or too hot to apply the necessary effort during training, when external factors have meant athletes were mentally fatigued prior to training and so were unable to fully commit, or simply when the athlete did not apply themselves each day with the same dedication. Training is a constant battle for most individuals and mental toughness is required to both tolerate the discomfort of training and to withstand the desire to simply put it off to another day.

As Sir Roger Bannister identifies: 'Sport is not about being wrapped in cotton wool.' It takes dedication, commitment and the confidence to succeed. Such characteristics of mental toughness apply to all physical activity situations. We are not all likely to win an Olympic medal or even win a race, but we do need mental toughness to stick to a task and achieve our aims.

4.4.3. Improvisational Training

This form of training does not mean an athlete should simply turn up to an athletics track and commence exercise without consciously considering, or adhering to, a training plan. What it means is that the athlete should consider, be given, and explore new innovative options in training. Options when placed in the hands of inexperienced athletes can lead to poor choices, but self-regulatory exercise is simply a process of listening to the body and should not be confused as a process of ignoring the advice of experienced coaches. Devising a training schedule means working to an overall plan, while also facilitating flexibility. The ancient Greek *tetrad* was criticised by many at that time for being inflexible to individual differences and it is important we recognise the need to amend training according where required. A method to develop flexibility in response to training is simply to have options and to use them. For more experienced athletes with greater understanding of their limitations, this may involve greater autonomy and more choice. For less experienced athletes or general exercise enthusiasts, the options would therefore be more limited. For example a coach may determine a particular style of session which on a given day fits within the overall plan. There is nothing wrong with this and that style of session could still include variety encompassing choices of low, medium and high intensity variations. To make a properly informed choice, the athlete needs to consider their feelings on the day in relation to the session requirement, its place in the week's schedule and other factors such as suitability of the session to the environmental conditions. The coach can certainly guide the athlete to ensure the required training load remains on track, but flexibility and inclusion in the decision-making process will lead to positive psychological associations, greater engagement, enjoyment and hopefully improved performance [17].

A further example of improvisational training is to perform some exercise sessions by tempo. Completing sustained periods of training at competitive pace enables the athlete to improve task familiarity and respond to the exercise challenge confidently when required to do so in a race. However, exercise in accordance with tempo refers to the skill of listening to the body's optimal rhythm and determining a self-selected preference for work intensity. This does not necessarily mean choosing a low intensity of effort because it feels easy, it is the voluntary desire to explore different tempos (e.g. occasionally over tempo) of performance and experience different (e.g. heightened) physical sensations in largely familiar/routine training circumstances.

In competition, the rhythm of performance and level of tolerable physical discomfort are invariably increased and this makes tempo work an important feature of training. For example, what may seem over-tempo in training may coincide with race pace in competition. To simply work at a 'race pace' in training based on prior race performance times can lead to disappointment, anxiety and an inability to sustain the required level of work. Augmented race-day motivation often leads to minor increases in pace for the same level of perceived effort, but enabling the athlete to work at their naturally perceived race (high) tempo pace rather than externally forcing a pace upon them is more consistent with self-regulatory processes. A recent study [38] for example clearly demonstrated that when athletes are forced to adopt an externally paced intensity it is more physically demanding and leads to premature fatigue more than self-pacing a bout, even though the power output is exactly the same. Therefore, varying the tempo work according to the athlete's perception of their own relative intensities is the best mix.

Central regulation infers that the brain controls performance and, as mentioned previously, part of that process is to pace a session (or bout) based on prior experience and other available knowledge of the task demands (e.g. distance or time) [39, 40]. Occasionally surprising an athlete with an unexpected change in the stimulus such as by extending the distance or time can lead to an augmented exercise challenge if the aim of that session (e.g. a preconceived high intensity workout) is to override central regulatory control [41]. If the athlete has paced the bout or session to finish in a particular physical condition, an acute (late in the session) change to the stimulus can increase the level of physical discomfort beyond that anticipated by the athlete. Of course, if this type of surprise is over-used, it can mean anticipation of surprise will be factored into the pacing plan by the athlete which will leads to more conservative, slower performances in training.

4.4.4. Self-Confidence

Being confident in oneself and one's ability are crucial to success. Commitment to training requires dedication, tolerance to significant physical discomfort, and substantial self-sacrifice. Each of these attributes can, and are, displayed to a greater or lesser extent by all individuals; but without high levels of self-efficacy beliefs and self-confidence none are likely to be meaningful. If an individual is not confident in his ability to succeed in the task (low self-efficacy belief), compromise is inevitable and most likely will be evident by poor effort and adherence to exercise. Compromise is also likely for both (diminished) tolerable level of physical discomfort the athlete is prepared to endure, and the sacrifices he is prepared to make.

Confidence underpins all training and this is where a coach can be invaluable. The coach must not only tell the athlete he believes in him, he must actually believe in him and encourage the athlete to believe in himself. Although nearly all athletes and coaches must work with a sense of perspective and, to some extent disappointment, that can be managed with realistic expectations and goal setting.

Young athletes experiencing rapid improvements tend to believe they will one day represent their country, appear at the Olympics, score the winning goal in a World Cup match or break a world record. The coach's role in confidence building and goal setting doesn't mean the shattering of childhood dreams, but it should be a matter of setting short and long term targets that can be attained, are appropriate to the athlete and can be objectively assessed and measured. Appropriate goal setting is the cornerstone of confidence building and it is important the coach provides athletes or exerciser with successful experiences. This can be done by setting short-term challenging, but realistic, goals which when achieved will increase perceptions of competence. Similarly, providing athletes or exercisers with vicarious experiences or helpful verbal encouragements will enhance self-efficacy beliefs which in turn will result in enhanced athletic performance.

It is important that individuals have the confidence to manage an exercise session, gained from prior experience in similar circumstances. This could include the knowledge of safe practice of lifting weights or executing a complex fine motor skill. Alternatively it could be managing effort across a series of repetition runs so that the entire series is completed or having the confidence to set off at a good pace and self-regulate a time-trial, finishing with enough, but not too much energy intact. Knowing the task, the demands of it, whether and how it can be optimally completed are consequent to experience.

Finally, a more recent development in influencing particular exercise behaviour is to tap into unconscious processes. There is now some agreement that many behaviours can be guided by both explicit (conscious, aware) or implicit (conscious, sub aware) processes. In particular, through implicit priming tasks it is possible to manipulate and activate an individual's motivation. This has resulted in exercisers improving the effort and duration of the exercise bout as well as future exercise frequency. In addition, the behavioural differences were accompanied by higher ratings in enjoyment and lower ratings of perceived exertion [42]. The underlying mechanisms which accompany implicit or unconscious priming of exercise behaviour are unclear; however, such mechanisms could have a significant influence on pacing strategies used by athletes and exercisers.

In summary, the skills identified in this section are not exhaustive, but do identify a number of factors which affect training behaviour (Table 4.3). Although there is more empirical evidence for the efficacy of these psychological factors in relation to athletic performance it is easy to see that these are also of benefit to the regular exerciser. It is an important aspect that all these psychological factors are trainable and would help the athlete or exerciser to better self-regulate their behaviour. As with physical skills, mental or psychological skills need to be trained in a systematic way to be effective. To this end it is important that individuals learn a variety of psychological skills. This will allow them to cope more effectively with stressors they encounter to circumvent the negative effects on performance and satisfaction.

Table 4.3. Summary of selected self-regulatory training skills. Many of these skills inter-relate. Gains in mental toughness, improvisation, self-confidence and self-efficacy could each be considered a strategy with which to self manage exercise. These strategies should be considered additions to existing training practices and not replacements

	Description	Example
Coping strategies	Practiced mechanisms to deal with stressful situations. Often classified as problem-focused, emotion-focused or avoidance coping strategies.	Problem-focused: Planning, goal-setting, increasing effort or concentration. Emotion-focussed: Breathing, imagery, self-talk. Avoidance: Block or stop thinking about stressful event.
Mental toughness	Personality trait which helps to deal with negative sensations during exercise and helps to cope more effectively	Training to sustain effort in the presence of considerable negative sensations. Interpreting stressful stimuli as a challenge rather than a threat.
Improvisation	Poor performance is associated with unfamiliar situations. Improvisation of training intentionally places the individual in different and unfamiliar situations.	Occasionally varying pace during an exercise bout to adopt different tempos of performance. This may assist coping with the unpredictable demands of racing and competition.
Self-confidence	Believe that you can perform a desired behaviour (e.g. to execute physical, perceptual, or psychological skill)	Confidence comes from practice, familiarity, experience and appropriate goal setting.
Self-efficacy	Perception that you can perform a specific task successfully (situation specific self-confidence)	Have successful performance accomplishments; see others completing the task successfully; receiving verbal acknowledgement that you are capable of executing the task.

CONCLUSION

- Monitoring training requires the assembly of relevant, usable information. Gathering information for no specific purpose can lead to situations where unreliable, inconsistent data are acted upon simply because these have been collected.

- The simplest, most common and effective tool of monitoring training outcomes is for an athlete to maintain a training log. The training log often can also reflect factors peripheral to training such as sleep, diet, and other stressors which may all indirectly impact on training and performance.

- Monitoring training should address the issue of session-to-session exercise intensity for individuals. This has acute implication to whether or not each session is of a meaningful intensity for different athletes.

- The limitation of heart rate or other metabolic variables for monitoring training is that they are task specific. For example, strength, speed, anaerobic and technical training sessions do not evoke high heart rates and thus heart rates cannot be used to accurately represent the metabolic challenge of these activities.

- The principles of self-regulation suggest that suitably constructed RPE methods of monitoring training are likely to be effective across all types of exercise.

- Important self-regulatory training skills include mental toughness, self-confidence, improvisational training and coping strategies to counteract the many obstacles blocking the path to success.

REFERENCES

[1]   Crowther, N., Athlete and state: qualifying for the Olympic Games in ancient Greece. *Journal of Sport History,* 1996. 23: p. 34-43.

[2]   Impellizzeri, F., et al., Use of RPE-based training load in soccer. *Medicine & Science in Sports & Exercise,* 2004. 36: p. 1042-1047.

[3]   Flouhaug, C.F.J., et al., A new approach to monitoring training. *Journal of Strength and Conditioning Research,* 2001. 15: p. 109-115.

[4]   Fleck, S., Periodized strength training: a critical review. *Journal of Strength and Conditioning Research,* 1999. 13: p. 82-89.

[5]   Day, M., et al., Monitoring exercise intensity during resistance training using the session RPE scale, *Journal of Strength and Conditioning Research,* 2004. 18: p. 353-358.

[6]   White, P., et al., Protocol for the PACE trial: a randomised controlled trial of adaptive pacing, cognitive behaviour therapy, and graded exercise as supplements to standardised specialist medical care versus standardised specialist medical care alone for patients with the chronic fatigue syndrome/myalgic encephalomyelitis or encephalopathy. *BMC Neurology,* 2007. 7: p. 1-20.

[7]   Fleck, S. and W. Kraemer, The ultimate training system: periodization breakthrough. 1996, New York: Advanced Research Press.

[8]   Stannard, S. and M. Thompson, Heart rate monitors: coaches' friend or foe? *Sports Coach,* 1998. 21: p. 36-37.

[9]   Glass, S. and D. Stanton, Self-selected resistance training intensity in novice weightlifters. *Journal of Strength and Conditioning Research,* 2004. 18: p. 324-327.

[10]   Mazzetti, S., et al., The influence of direct supervision of resistance training on strength performance. *Medicine & Science in Sports & Exercise,* 2000. 32: p. 1175-1184.

[11]   Gamble, P., Periodization of training for team sports athletes. *Strength and Conditioning Journal,* 2006. 28: p. 56-66.

[12]   Ratamess, N., et al., Self-selected resistance training intensity in healthy women: the influence of a personal trainer. *Journal of Strength and Conditioning Research,* 2008. 22: p. 103-111.

[13]   Bannister, E. and T. Calvert, A systems model of training for athletic performance. *Australian Journal of Sports Medicine,* 1975. 7: p. 57-61.

[14]   McArdle, W., F. Katch, and V. Katch, Exercise physiology: nutrition, energy and human performance. 7 ed. 2010: *Lippincott Williams & Wilkins.*

[15]   Leff, A., Cardiopulmonary exercise testing. 1986, London: *Grune & Stratton.*

[16]   Edwards, A. and T. Noakes, Dehydration: cause of fatigue or sign of pacing in elite soccer? *Sports Medicine,* 2009. 39: p. 1-13.

[17]   Edwards, A., et al., Self-pacing in interval training: a teleoanticipatory approach. *Psychophysiology,* 2011. 48: p. 136-141.

[18]   Davies, C. and M. Thompson, Aerobic performance of female marathon and male ultramarathon athletes. *European Journal of Applied Physiology,* 1979. 41: p. 233-245.

[19] Coyle, E. and J. Gonzalez-Alonzo, Cardiovascular drift during prolonged exercise: new perspectives. *Exercise and Sports Science Reviews*, 2001. 29: p. 88-92.

[20] Whaley, M., et al., ACSM's guidelines for exercise testing and prescription. 7th ed. 2006, Philadelphia: *Lippincott Williams & Wilkins*.

[21] Borg, G., Psychophysiological bases of perceived exertion. *Medicine & Science in Sports & Exercise*, 1982. 14: p. 377-387.

[22] Chen, M., X. Fan, and S. Moe, Criterion-related validity of the Borg ratings of perceived exertion scale in healthy individuals: a meta-analysis. *Journal of Sports Sciences*, 2002. 20: p. 873-899.

[23] Fitzgerald, M., Brain training for runners. 2007, New York: New American Library.

[24] Eston, R. and J. Williams, Reliability of ratings of perceived effort regulation of exercise intensity. *British Journal of Sports Medicine*, 1988. 22: p. 153-155.

[25] St Clair Gibson, A., et al., The role of information processing between the brain and peripheral physiological systems in pacing and perception of effort. *Sports Medicine*, 2006. 36: p. 705-722.

[26] Fitzgerald, M., Run: The mind-body method of running by feel. 2010, Boulder, Colorado: Velopress.

[27] Noakes, T., The central governor model of exercise regulation applied to the marathon. *Sports Medicine*, 2007. 37: p. 374-377.

[28] Noakes, T., A. St Clair Gibson, and E. Lambert, From catastrophe to complexity: a novel model of integrative central neural regulation of effort and fatigue during exercise in humans: summary and conclusions. *British Journal of Sports Medicine*, 2005. 39: p. 120-124.

[29] Polman, R., Elite athletes' experiences of coping with stress, in Coping and emotions in sport, M.J. J. Thatcher, & D. Lavallee Editor. 2011, Routledge.

[30] Nicholls, A., et al., Stress and coping among international adolescent golfers. *Journal of Applied Sport Psychology*, 2005. 17: p. 333-340.

[31] Haney, C. and B. Long, Coping effectiveness: a path analysis of self-efficacy, control, coping and performance in sport competitions. *Journal of Applied Social Psychology*, 1995. 25: p. 1726-1746.

[32] Ord, P. and K. Gijsbers, Pain thresholds and tolerances of competitive rowers and their use of spontaneous self-generated pain-coping strategies. *Perceptual and Motor Skills*, 2003. 97: p. 1219-1222.

[33] Clough, P., K. Earle, and D. Sewell, Mental toughness: the concept and its measurement, in Solutions in sport psychology I. Cockeril, Editor. 2002, Thompson Publishing: London. p. 32-43.

[34] Kaiseler, M., R. Polman, and A. Nicholls, Mental toughness, stress, stress appraisal, coping and coping effectiveness in sport. *Personality and Individual Differences*, 2009. 47: p. 728-733.

[35] Polman, R., P. Clough, and A. Levy, Personality and coping in sport: the big five and mental toughness 2010, Nova Science Publishers. p. 141-157.

[36] Crust, L. and K. Azadi, Mental toughness and athletes' use of psychological strategies. *European Journal of Sport Science*, 2010. 10: p. 43-51.

[37] Baron, B., et al., The role of emotions on pacing strategies and performance in middle and long duration sport events. *British Journal of Sports Medicine*, 2011. 45: p. 511-517.

[38] Lander, P., R. Butterly, and A. Edwards, Self-paced exercise is less physically challenging than enforced constant pace exercise of the same intensity: influence of complex central metabolic control, *British Journal of Sports Medicine*, 2009. 43: p. 789-795.

[39] Albertus, Y., et al., Effect of distance feedback on pacing strategy and perceived exertion during cycling. *Medicine & Science in Sports & Exercise*, 2005. 37: p. 461-468.

[40] Nikolopoulos, V., M. Arkinstall, and J. Hawley, Pacing strategy in simulated cycle time-trials is based on perceived rather than actual distance. *Journal of Science and Medicine in Sport*, 2001. 4: p. 212-219.

[41] Paterson, S. and F. Marino, Effect of deception of distance on prolonged cycling performance. *Perceptual and Motor Skills*, 2004. 98: p. 1017-1026.

[42] Banting, L., J. Dimmock, and J. Grove, The impact of automatically activated motivation on exercise-related outcomes. *Journal of Sport & Exercise Psychology*, 2011. 33: p. 569-585.

Chapter 5

PACING FOR ENDURANCE

5.1. ABSTRACT

The aim of this chapter is to examine the issue of pacing specifically in relation to endurance. The chapter identifies and discusses physiological and psychological demands of activities such as marathon running, cycling, triathlon and rowing. Regular training for these activities produces specifically adaptive responses with which to improve performance. These factors are discussed in addition to evidence-based observations of successful pacing strategies in endurance events. Common pacing strategies for endurance events suggest front loaded, fast start approaches are optimal for most endurance events, other than those of extreme duration as, in the early stages of a performance, there is relatively minor metabolic disturbance. Increasing the pace of an exercise bout in the presence of accumulating negative sensations of fatigue requires considerable motivation. Therefore, psychological coping strategies for endurance activities are identified. Finally, a practical model for devising and monitoring training via a self-paced programme is presented and explained. This can be adapted to the specific requirements of the endurance performer.

5.2. INTRODUCTION

The ability to sustain physical work for prolonged periods underpins successful performance in many sports, most of which have been deliberately designed to maximally tax the physical limits of the participants. In endurance activities, the ability to tolerate physical discomfort for prolonged periods is vital to success and as such, we have suggested in previous chapters of this book that this may be accomplished through the development of self-regulatory training skills (see chapter four).

Many nutritional, physical, psychological, or technical interventions can also aid performance and each may be broadly grouped as 1) augmenting the physical attributes of the performer (e.g. by direct physical training or using a technical innovation), 2) improving the performer's mental state (e.g. psychological skills training), or 3) improving regulatory physiological processes (e.g. nutritional supplementation). Viewing the human from a psychophysiological perspective, it is possible to see how these factors inter-relate [1]. For example, it has been suggested that conducting training in a state of carbohydrate depletion may produce positive performance outcomes [2, 3] despite intuitively sounding like a very bad idea. Performing endurance training with minimal muscle glycogen is unlikely to lead to quality performance outcomes and if over-used could lead to a detraining effect; however, if adopted as an occasional training practice it may be useful from both psychological and physiological perspectives.

The voluntary denial or debilitation of a metabolic substrate such as carbohydrate would reduce residual muscle glycogen stores and require a mental coping response as a means to improve factors such as mental toughness (see chapter four). Additionally, voluntarily performing endurance exercise in a state of glycogen depletion not only develops mental toughness, but also encourages the body to up regulate fat metabolism while glycogen stores are diminished [2]. Consequently, the responses of the human body to endurance exercise are multi-dimensional and this chapter considers factors pertinent to both physiological and psychological perspectives before combining into a practical psychophysiological training model specifically for the development of endurance capabilities.

5.3. PHYSIOLOGY OF ENDURANCE

The critical determinant of success for all endurance-based activities is the ability to sustain a high rate of work for prolonged periods [4]. Endurance trained athletes are better able to sustain high levels of physical effort powered from aerobic energy pathways than non-athletes and consequently [5] place less demand on the body's limited body stores of muscle glycogen. Metabolism of glycogen facilitates more rapid ATP regeneration than from lipid [6] and the preservation of glycogen for times of need is of prime importance as a conserving/protecting mechanism [7]. An overview of energy metabolism from carbohydrate and lipid sources is shown in Figure 5.1.

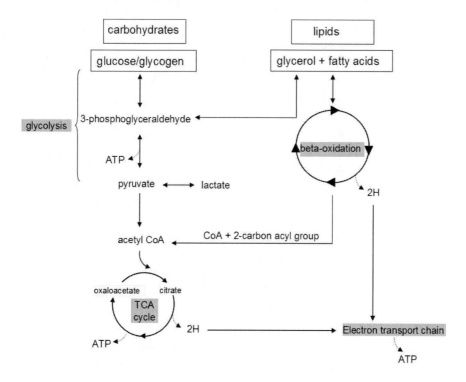

Figure 5.1. Summary of the main pathways of energy metabolism using carbohydrate and lipids as energy sources. Through the reactions of glycolysis, carbohydrates are broken down to pyruvate under aerobic conditions and lactate under anaerobic conditions. The anaerobic process of glycolysis produces limited ATP, but does so rapidly. In response to slower demand for energy (aerobic exercise), carbohydrate converted to pyruvate is further converted to acetyl CoA and then completely oxidized in the tricarboxylic acid (TCA or Krebs') cycle within mitochondria. Lipids are hydrolysed to fatty acids and glycerol. Glycerol can enter the glycolytic pathway, while fatty acids are converted via beta-oxidation to acetyl CoA and subsequently enter the TCA cycle. The TCA cycle produces ATP, as does the electron transport chain which removes electrons from hydrogen. In this process, oxygen accepts hydrogen to form water.

It would be easy to conclude that carbohydrate availability simply limits performance by facilitating higher power outputs until muscles are completely depleted of glycogen. Thereafter, the athlete would be forced to slow down to facilitate resynthesis of ATP from the slower energy producing substrate of fat

[6]. Such an observation is analogous to running a car until the fuel tank is empty. However, most people are able to look at the fuel gauge of their car and behaviourally avoid this occurring. Brain regulation of exercise suggests we are able to prevent running on empty by listening to afferent sensory information (whether or not we are consciously aware of this) and thus avoid the potential catastrophe of running out of fuel [8].

According to the principles of conscious brain regulation, the body stores of glycogen should never fully deplete during exercise. This has shown to be the case in several studies whereby individuals pace themselves in receipt of afferent sensory feedback alerting them to reductions in metabolic stores [9, 10]. The brain therefore adjusts pace to properly manage the fuel stores across the exercise bout so they are not maximally depleted. This can be seen in practical operation during endurance time trial performances as carbohydrate loading has frequently been demonstrated to result in greater pace compared to a placebo condition. However, at the conclusion of exercise, the residual stores of glycogen are not different between loading and placebo condition, neither of which results in maximal muscle glycogen depletion [10]. The trajectory of power output reflects the available substrates, such that the condition with greater initial intra-muscular stores of higher energy fuel usually results in a better performance. This simply reflects effective pacing via muscle-neural communication in the sub aware knowledge of greater metabolic fuel [7]. Sensations of fatigue (i.e. metabolic warning signs) occur prior to glycogen depletion. This tends to support the theory of a conserving mechanism by which sensory feedback informs the brain of glycogen availability amongst other variables.

All successful endurance trained athletes obviously possess good aerobic fitness. An individual's oxygen uptake response to a graded, incremental exercise test is a reasonable predictor of endurance performance [4] and this is commonly referred to as a test of maximal aerobic power ($\dot{V}O_2$ max) [11]. The capacity of the individual for energy transfer requires the integration of the respiratory, cardiovascular, and neuromuscular systems for the purpose of 1) up take, 2) transport and 3) utilization of O_2. This facilitates improved oxygen uptake (O_2) at the lungs, greater transport of O_2 in the blood to the working muscles, and more effective O_2 extraction from the blood as it reaches muscle [6].

Improvements to $\dot{V}O_2$ max can be observed in the cardiovascular system by means of increased cardiac output during exercise [12, 13]. Cardiac output is the product of heart rate and stroke volume and as the maximal achievable heart rate does not change with training [13], the potential to improve maximal

cardiac output is consequent to increases in beat-to-beat efficiency via stroke volume augmentation. This occurs as a long term adaptation to endurance training, by which the heart becomes more efficient to pump greater quantities of oxygenated blood around the body with each beat. Therefore, to achieve a given cardiac output, the trained heart grows in efficiency and no longer needs to beat with the same high frequency of an untrained heart which pumps lower volumes of oxygen carrying blood with each beat [6].

The concept of $\dot{V}O_2$ max has been studied extensively to gauge its importance to performance and a high $\dot{V}O_2$ max (e.g. >70 ml/kg/min) is commonly associated with success in endurance events [5]. However, this measurement does not have a high correlation among homogenous populations of endurance athletes. For example, several studies have demonstrated a wide range of endurance performances among populations with similar $\dot{V}O_2$ max or alternatively, equivalent performances with dissimilar $\dot{V}O_2$ max (e.g. 50-80 ml/kg/min) [14]. This is largely to be expected as the aim of endurance sports performance is to win a race, competition or complete a specific task. The aim is not to improve $\dot{V}O_2$ max and although this is a by-product of enhanced endurance capabilities, numerous studies have shown that $\dot{V}O_2$ max does not vary to a large extent with training [15]. As discussed in chapter three, it is also perhaps naive to assume that $\dot{V}O_2$ max represents a true physiologic maximum as we have seen previously that performers do not fully tax physiological systems [16, 17]. Therefore it is more suitable to refer to $\dot{V}O_2$ max as either $\dot{V}O_2$ peak or $\dot{V}O_2$ max (maximum voluntary effort). As a consequence, although the maximal ability to take up and use oxygen during exercise ($\dot{V}O_2$ max) is one of the parameters explaining successful performance in prolonged exercise, performance is most likely dependent upon a complex blend of contributions from a number of physiological factors, all subject to regulation by the brain.

Metabolic changes occur with endurance training in the muscles to allow for the efficient use of available oxygen. These adaptations include: increased number and size of mitochondria [18], increased ATP production, decreased amounts of lactic acid, increased triglyceride content, increased energy derived from fatty acid, lower glycogen usage in the muscles during exercise, increased enzyme activity for energy turnover, and improved efficiency in utilising oxygen from the blood supply [19].

Endurance training increases the number and size of the mitochondria within muscle fibres for aerobic production of ATP and this is accompanied by greater concentrations of oxidative enzymes to up regulate metabolic reactions, and increases to the density of capillaries supplying oxygenated blood to muscle [6, 20]. There is also an association in the time course between the changes in oxidative enzyme activities and improvement in $\dot{V}O_2$ max [4, 21].

The efficiency with which the chemical energy of ATP hydrolysis is converted to physical work depends greatly on muscle factors. Type I (slow twitch) fibres have been shown to display greater mechanical efficiency. Elite endurance athletes typically possess a predominance of type I muscle fibres and these are more mechanically efficient at the velocities of distance running [18, 22]. It is therefore not surprising that elite endurance athletes typically possess a higher percentage of type I muscle fibres, given that they are more efficient. Although type I muscle fibres in untrained humans possess higher mitochondrial density compared with type II fibres (fast twitch), it is important to note that with intense, sustained cardiovascular training, mitochondrial activity can be increased in both fibre types [23]. Thus, with endurance training over many years, the main functional advantages of type I fibres appears to be efficiency and a greater ability to oxidize fat.

Mechanical efficiency does not occur spontaneously, it is acquired through prior experience and dedicated practice to improve neuromuscular coordination. A natural tendency to favour genetic dispositions for exercise is evident in the events or sports individuals tend to select for participation. Equally, while performing activities, movements reflect individuals' inherent abilities although it is difficult to discern whether this is consequent to unique morphological characteristics, or whether characteristics become consequent to movements through specific training [24]. An interesting study by Hansen et al. [18] sought to investigate whether athletes display a natural preference for movement strategy based on their muscle characteristics. In that investigation, subjects were requested to self select an optimal cycling pedal rate so to attain at power output equivalent to 70% of their maximal aerobic power. Perhaps unsurprisingly, subjects with higher levels of type II (fast twitch) muscle fibres self selected faster pedal rates to attain the target power output while those with greater type I (more O_2 efficient) muscle fibres selected slower rates. This study neatly demonstrated that athletes tend to self select movement patterns closely related to their natural disposition for exercise.

Other factors that influence the metabolic responses to exercise include training status, diet, environmental temperature, and gender [4, 21, 25-27]. These all combine to produce improvements in exercise efficiency, attenuation of lactate and H+ concentrations during exercise, diminishing the reliance on limited body fuels such as glycogen and reducing the need for aggressive sweating to evoke evaporative cooling as a means of counteracting excessive heat production.

5.4. PSYCHOLOGY OF ENDURANCE

At the elite level, long distance runners complete training loads in excess of 150 km each week which not only place significant physical and psychological demands on the athlete but may also place strain on their personal lives. Since the 1980s, participation in marathon running by recreational athletes has also increased dramatically[28]. The motives for this group of runners are associated to some extent with winning but more generally with the achievement of personal goals, health, self-esteem and affiliation [29]. Accumulative running time means that athletes have a significant amount of thinking time (more than 2 hours during a marathon event) and during this period, athletes process internal and external information while also maintaining concentration for racing. In the marathon, it is generally assumed that athletes have to be aware of their own physical limitations to pace their race correctly.

As alluded to in chapter two, differences in personality have been reported between athletes. Much of this research started with long distance runners [30] and there is evidence that successful athletes have certain desirable psychological characteristics. For example, long distance runners have been found to be more emotionally stable, less introverted and neurotic and have a more desirable mental health profile (so called 'iceberg' profile; [30]). They have also been reported to have lower levels of depression and anxiety, with concomitant higher levels of vigour [31, 32]. Finally, marathon runners score higher in achievement motivation and are more intrinsically motivated [33]. Since personality traits are assumed to be relatively stable over time this would indicate that these psychological factors would at least, to some extent, be predictors to both running participation and success. With regard to the latter, the desirable psychological characteristics are more evident in successful athletes in comparison to less successful athletes [34] and they are more likely to allow athletes to cope with the physical and psychological stressors innate to endurance activities.

Although some of the psychological factors outlined above are modifiable, there are other ways to help athletes with the stress associated with endurance activities. A number of studies have examined the cognitions of endurance athletes during their training and competition. These studies have generally investigated how the athletes cope with the extreme physical (pain and discomfort) and psychological demands of their events (e.g. [35, 36]. Successful athletes, in this respect, will use either *association* or *dissociation* as coping strategies during endurance events [30, 35, 37]. *Association* is the monitoring of physical or bodily sensations related to running (e.g. body awareness and breathing) and tactics (including running pace). *Dissociation* is the diversion of attention away from unpleasant physical sensations. A number of sub-categories have been identified for dissociation. Goode and Roth [37], in the development of the Thoughts During Running Scale (TDRS), distinguished between external surrounding, interpersonal relationships, daily events, and spiritual reflection. It has also been suggested that associative (task-relevant) and dissociative (task-irrelevant) cognitions have both an internal and external dimension [38]. Examples of internal associative cognitions would be related to breathing, perspiration and other bodily functions. Internal dissociative cognitions could include daydreams, fantasies and philosophical musing. Alternatively, external associative cognitions may be related to strategies or split times, while external dissociation cognitions could involve thoughts on the environment, scenery or attention to other athletes.

The suggestion has been made that the term dissociation in a sports context would be inappropriate because of its use in clinical settings. Although both clinical patients and athletes use dissociation to escape unpleasant stimuli in the environment, athletes generally have control over this cognitive strategy and some have suggested that the terms internal versus external cognitive strategies should be used (see [39] for a review).

In his article *'the mind of the marathoner'*, Morgan [35] outlined that successful marathon runners are more likely to use associative coping strategies. Based on the examination of 24 United States of America world class runners he found that these elite athletes were in tune with their bodies and monitored physiological sensations of exertion such as respiration, temperature, heaviness in their legs, hydration, muscular pain, and abdominal sensations whilst running. On the whole the literature supports the notion that associative coping strategies result in faster running performance.

Associative coping strategies can be used to optimize efficiency and determine pace and there is some evidence that associative coping strategies are related to running economy. In a study of 18 competitive male distance runners it was found that running economy was related ($r = -.50$) to self attention. That is runners who habitually directed attention inwards had the

most economical running style [40]. An inward focus would allow the runner to be more sensitive and deal appropriately with muscular tension which might interfere with performance or engage the use of other associative cognitive strategies aimed at improving running economy.

Running speed is a factor which moderates the relationship between running performance and the use of associative coping strategies. Tammen [41] in a study of eight elite runners required to run at different speeds, showed that as running pace increased the athletes reported more use of associative rather than dissociative coping strategies. The runners in the study found it difficult to use internal cues to regulate their pace at lower speeds because they were not used to running at such low running velocities. In these situations they relied on external feedback to regulate their pace (e.g. listening to experimenter). At maximum pace, which was close to training or race pace, the runners used their bodily sensations, breathing and cadence to determine their performance.

The stage of a running event might also be a factor which influences the use of associative or dissociative coping strategies. Dissociation coping strategies are used early in a race and associative strategies towards the end of a race [36]. At the end of a race the runner will suffer from reduced energy resources and at this stage, associative coping would allow for better monitoring and regulation of pace and therefore optimize performance.

Non-elite runners have been found to use a number of psychological strategies which intentionally distract them from the often uncomfortable sensations associated with intense physical exertion. Such strategies include listening to music, adhering to pre-race strategy, conducting complicated mathematical calculations, or imaging pleasant past experiences. Morgan [35] in his classic paper considered dissociative strategies to be dangerous with athletes more likely to hit the proverbial 'wall' and increase the probability of injury by ignoring important afferent (warning) signals. However, although elite marathon athletes appear mainly to use associative coping strategies during competition, many use and prefer dissociative coping strategies during training runs [39]. A possible explanation for the preference of dissociation during training runs is that these tend to be conducted at lower pace.

The 'wall' (often called 'bonk' by cyclists and triathletes) is a particular psychological phenomenon in endurance sports which is perhaps best explained as a neural anticipatory (protective) response preceding a necessary change of the dominant energy supply from glycogen to lipid. This occurs after approximately 30 km of running. Up to 50% of runners experience the wall (e.g. [28]) with a higher prevalence in males in comparison to females.

The use of associative coping strategies has been shown to protect athletes from experiencing the wall [30]. In a more recent study by Buman et al. [28] the cognitive, behavioural, and affective characteristics as well as the coping responses of hitting the wall were examined qualitatively in a sample of 52 marathon runners of different abilities. This study highlighted the notion that the wall is a multi-facetted phenomenon that consists of the interaction between physiological (cramping, diet/hydration, generalized fatigue, illness, pain, leg-related fatigue, cardio-respiratory, sensory distortions), behavioural (loss of running form, pace disruption, running difficulty, tunnel vision), cognitive (anxiety, changing goals, confusion, mental battle, trouble focussing), affective (crying, discouragement, frustration, irritability, shame) and motivational (decreased motivation, desire to quit or walk) characteristics. Although the runners used associative and dissociative coping strategies, not all their coping responses could be classified under this higher order distinction. Surprisingly a significant number of participants (30%) had no strategies to cope with hitting the wall (not sure what to do; nothing works; just let it happen). Also, the runners used mental reframing (race segmentation; performance justification) and willpower (e.g. just keep running; tough it out; push through it) to cope with it. An important practical implication from this research is that runners need a large repertoire of coping strategies to deal effectively with the different interacting elements associated with hitting the wall. For example, to deal with the physical stressors could be through the use of associative strategies whereas the cognitive or motivational aspects might be best dealt with through self-regulatory strategies like dissociation, mental reframing and self-talk [28, 42].

A very common dissociative technique used by endurance athletes is music. Findings suggest that in particular synchronous music has ergogenic properties and that individuals feel less tired whilst running or cycling to music and workout times are increased up to 20% [43]. This is also true for clinical populations. Chronic obstructive pulmonary disease (COPD) patients do more work on the treadmill when listening to music and reported lower maximal RPE levels [44]. This would suggest that music diverts attention from fatigue as well as altering perception of how hard an individual is working. Music can also increase positive mood and decrease negative mood and alter psychomotor arousal. As such, it can be used as a stimulant or psyching-up strategy, or even as a relaxation tool prior to and during physical exercise depending on the characteristics of the music [43, 45]. Musical preferences are very individual and selection of the right stimulus may take prior planning to ensure that the music chosen works as intended. A good example is the

Ethiopian Olympic long distance winner Haile Gebreselassie. He enjoys music and has previously indicated it gives him energy, while providing him with a rhythm to fit with his record pace. Alternatively, music can also hinder performance; the English former Olympic decathlon winner Daly Thompson apparently found music an unwanted distraction.

5.5. PACING AND STRATEGY FOR ENDURANCE

The ability to accurately self-pace an endurance exercise bout is an important feature of race and time trial performances [27, 46]. However, self-paced exercise bouts are known to demonstrate considerable intra-trial fluctuations of power output, [47] and this may have led to a misconception that they are unreliable. It is perhaps due to the variability of power output in self-paced exercise that scientists have tended to develop laboratory exercise protocols in which participants are required to respond to externally imposed/fixed work rates. This is of course a completely alien form of exercise compared to racing and is probably the most obvious reason why protocols such as those used to test $\dot{V}O_2$ max do not accurately reflect the determinants of endurance race performances.

In race situations, competitors anticipate and decide how best to approach the race in the knowledge of the race duration, the circumstances of the event and their own capabilities. To some extent, athletes respond (dynamically) to the race circumstances as these unravel around them, while still adhering to an overall performance strategy [48]. Interestingly, a recent study identified that pacing in response to an externally imposed protocol is considerably harder than conducting exactly the same activity when self-paced [47]. Consequently, fluctuations in work output during exercise probably represent meaningful changes of pace, mediated by the transient sensations of well being (i.e. feeling good or bad from moment to moment). Nevertheless, variable pacing strategies have not always been shown to be augment performance among well-trained endurance runners, probably because their well established and intrinsic sense of pacing [49, 50]. This is less likely to occur in less automated activities such as race or competitive situations. In most solo competition time-trials, fluctuations of pace may be driven by sensations of wellness (or absence of negative emotions), while in a race with fellow competitors, they may represent unexpected and externally forced work rate changes with additional self-mediated changes (such as down-regulating effort as a coping mechanism) in response to significant metabolic disturbance where, when, or if possible [51].

External paced exercise does not facilitate deviation from a prescribed work output and simply drives all physiological systems to a state of discomfort which at some point will develop into a level of intolerance which in turn will provoke the athlete to decide to stop the exercise bout [17]. This of course does not occur in a race, because races are self-paced and the competitors are able to decide how to properly pace themselves to get the best out of their performance. Racing and competitive situations are therefore prime examples of brain regulation controlling performance. Consequently, a number of psychological factors, like pre-race state anxiety or self-confidence will impinge on determining pacing. A race, in this respect, is usually judged on the final performance outcome, not on the length of time taken to reach a maximal plateau in a measured physiological variable and displayed on a computer screen. That would be a very dull race.

The outcome of all Olympic endurance events has been estimated to occur at intensities above 85% $\dot{V}O_2$ max [20] which means each event requires a high level of energy metabolism and considerable motivation to sustain exercise intensity. Of course, participation at events such as the Olympics is a motivating factor in itself, but data trends have emerged in recent years which enable comparisons of how high performance athletes determine pacing plans for particular events. In chapter two, numerous categories of pacing strategies were identified which may be adopted by athletes to optimize performance. There is no 'one-size fits all' model of pacing for endurance events as each model requires specific physical attributes, could be affected by the race circumstances, and of course, be influenced by the duration of the event. However, outcomes from most endurance based activities generally demonstrate success is consistent with utilizing front loaded strategies and/or 'U' shaped pacing i.e. a relatively fast start and a final end spurt [52-54]. This makes practical racing sense as the accumulated negative sensations of fatigue in the middle-latter stages of a race diminish the desire to propel the body towards a state of greater physical discomfort, unless the event is of particularly meaningful importance. In the early stages of a race, high work outputs can be attained while negative afferent sensory information is relatively minor. These sensations of course accumulate during a race, but by that stage considerable work has been accomplished.

An example of pacing strategies in practical operation during endurance events may be observed in Triathlon [55]. Triathlon races vary in distance with

1) 'Sprint' events (750 m swim, 20 km bike, 5 km run), 2) the 'Short Course' commonly referred to as "Olympic" (1.5 km swim, 40 km ride, 10 km run), 3) the 'Long Course' commonly referred to as the Half Ironman (1.9 km swim, 90 km ride, 21.1 km run, and 4) the Ultra Distance (3.8 km swim, 180 km ride, and a marathon: 42.2 km run), known as the Ironman distance.

Le Meur et al. [56] identified that all of the 136 triathletes competing in an international Olympic distance event adopted a "positive pacing strategy" through the running phase. During this race, the first of the four laps was run 10.0% faster than the three remaining laps. However, it is not always possible to discern from these data whether or not a final end spurt exists as triathlon laps are long and end spurts relatively brief. Nevertheless, Le Meur's observations are broadly similar to those of Vleck et al. [57] who neatly demonstrated triathlon pacing across the different stages of Olympic distance racing among elite ITU competitors. The swimming stage of triathlon (Figure 5.2) demonstrates a substantially faster pace for the first 200m compared to all other sectors of that stage. This could suggest that the athletes are seeking to maximize their physiologic performance while fresh; however, a much more likely explanation lies in seeking optimal race position and strategy. In triathlon, the swimming stage commences as one large cohort and the first 200m is largely a scramble as athletes seek clear water and separation from other racers.

Field-based research has shown that well-trained triathletes perform the cycle phase of the Ironman triathlon at approx 80—83% of maximum heart rate and 55% of peak power output [58]. However, cycling pace is largely consequent to the 'pack' pace and an even pacing strategy is commonly observed in this stage of triathlon (Figure 5.3). Each of the three stages in triathlon are obviously part of the same race performance and although there may be occasional deviations of pace due to tactical considerations i.e. seeking to quickly transit from bike to running, pacing is performed in relation to completing the collective event (triathlon) and not simply each stage. The running stage is the final element for the triathlon and Vleck demonstrated a common reverse 'J' shape triathlon running where a final end spurt is clearly observable as the competitors accelerate towards the finish despite considerable physical sensations of fatigue (Figure 5.4).

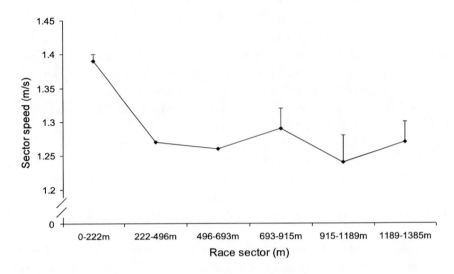

Figure 5.2. Average speeds (m/s) (± SD) for swimming stage of the Lausanne 2002 ITU World Cup triathlons (n=68 males). Original drawing from previously published data [57].

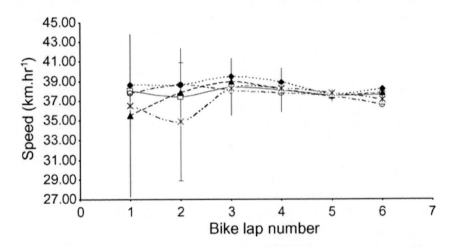

Figure 5.3. Speed (average ±S.E. (km/h) over each bike lap of ITU male Triathlon by pack number to which the athletes belonged (5 packs). All packs except pack 5 (*) adopted an even pace strategy. Pack 5 dropped from the pace at lap 2 and worked to rejoin the even pacing strategy of the whole group from laps 3-6. Taken with permission [57].

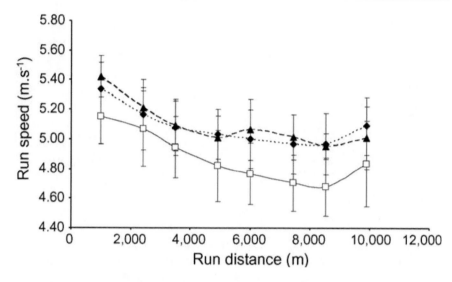

Figure 5.4. Run speed (±S.E) for three packs of ITU World Cup male triathlon competitors. Although the running stage is the final phase of the triathlon, a fast start and final end spurt of speed is evident. This would not occur if athletes simply ran to exhaustion without a means of self-regulating performance. It is a pacing response to manage effort effectively across the entire triathlon, thus retaining energy for the final stage. Taken with permission [57].

In other endurance events such as rowing, elite competitive 2000 m races take 330–460 seconds to complete [53]. In these events, it is tactically and psychologically advantageous to gain placement at the front of the race by increasing effort at the start (Figure 5.5). This allows the rowers to look backwards down the course, so to strategically monitor the position of other boats and react to any sudden advances from other crews, while also allowing them to avoid the wake (water disruption) of other boats. Inexperienced rowing crews occasionally overestimate their physical conditioning and set off at a pace that is too fast, but the consequences of this miscalculation are rarely repeated with gained experience [53, 54]. Interestingly, positive pacing strategies in rowing are also evident in dry land ergometer training (admittedly to a lesser extent) suggesting that 1) rowers train to race and 2) that this is probably due to the advantages of working harder when negative afferent sensations are less severe in the early stages of the bout (Figure 5.5).

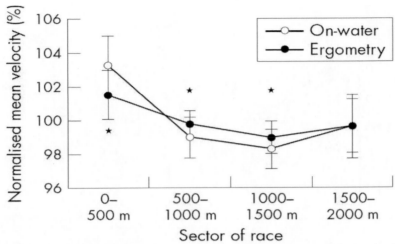

*Significant differences between the two groups (p<0.05). Taken with permission [53].

Figure 5.5. Race pace profiles comparing on-water (n = 948) and ergometry (n = 170) trials. Both on water and dry land ergometer performances demonstrate fast start techniques, with a propensity for a final end spurt of power (reverse J shaped pacing).

5.6. SELF-REGULATORY TRAINING FOR ENDURANCE

The planning and development required to methodically organize a training programme can appear daunting if starting from a blank canvas. Coaches are well aware of the technical and physical demands of the events or sports they coach, and can easily devise any number of individual training sessions for their athletes. However, designing and blending training sessions with a plan to optimize performance takes considerable care, attention to detail and an appreciation of the individual needs of the athlete. This is a complex process. Devising a training programme is therefore probably not a process that should be exclusively performed by the coach, yet that is overwhelming the common case. One strategy to involve the athlete and share ownership of training is in the design of the programme through a technique called performance profiling [59]. This technique allows the identification and construction of a profile of desirable variables (physical, biomechanical or psychological) for high-level performance. The attractiveness of prior performance profiling is to elicit information from the athlete in what they find important rather than responding to pre-determined measures or externally controlled training programmes. As such, performance profiling encourages athletes to become aware of their own perceptions of the importance of various elements in their sport, assess their own abilities, and illuminate potential discrepancies between the two. Performance profiling therefore will increase self-determination or self-motivation and adherence to training programmes.

Coaches often prescribe a target speed, distance covered, or power output of the session as a useful means of quantifying the training load. Clearly though, these are training outcomes which do not consider the variability of day-to-day changes in conditioning, muscle soreness, health or environmental conditions. Some coaches may prescribe the training load according to a target heart rate or other physiologic variable subsequently seeking biofeedback information to confirm the pre-set training intensity. The coach might additionally estimate the athlete's likely RPE to a session when prescribing the load and, by pairing coach-athlete RPE evaluations, be able to identify any mismatches of training intensity. This is a well-intentioned perspective but it misses the point of training with RPE.

A training intensity set by a coach, based on an external factor such as work output (or a target performance time), with subsequent confirmation of intensity via RPE can only identify mismatches and cannot correct them, except by modifying future action. It could be argued it is important for the athlete to simply adapt to a pre-determined, fixed training load set by an experienced and knowledgeable coach, as this is a blueprint for success. However, Fitzgerald [60, 61] recently introduced the concept of 'running by feel' and is not the first, or only, coach to recognize the limitations of fixed-inflexible training schedules (see Greek *tetrad* in chapter one) [62].

The recognition of individual differences in training raises an important question in the development of training programmes. Instead of imposing an externally devised training intensity (e.g. to achieve a pre-set performance time) and then evaluating RPE *ex post facto*, why not simply perform the session at an intensity based on the RPE where possible? If athletes learn to associate a given level of effort based on the RPE (0-10) as pre-determined and agreed by the coach, then the only difference between athlete and coach would be any conceptual difference between them on what constitutes 5/10 or 7/10 effort and so on. There would be no difference in the RPE levels between coach and athlete as they would be using the same RPE scale. It will take some practice for the coach and athlete to determine their agreed interpretation and expectations of effort corresponding to the scale but this should not be an insurmountable task. It will, of course, facilitate pacing-based training on sensations rather than externally imposed, pre-set work outputs. Work outputs would remain important outcomes for the purpose of evaluating training progression, but would not force the athlete to adapt to an external load that is either insufficient, or excessive, depending on their stage of training, accumulative muscle soreness or other factors.

As stated earlier, choice, options and engagement with the athlete are important considerations when devising training programmes. Performance profiling allows for the development of clear goals and serves as a monitoring device. However, the trajectory to achieving these goals, yearly, monthly, weekly and daily plans need to be developed.

During individual training sessions, some athletes may routinely choose either an easier or more difficult option and therefore choice should not be confused with free choice. There is an important difference; in a training programme facilitating individualized pacing (via RPE), it is also possible to facilitate some elements of choice but also to manage the overall training experience by amending load from week-to-week and changing sessions as required. Such an approach to training is not a freeform (or free-for-all) style, it is a system requiring time-investment by coach AND athlete in determining a battery of training sessions that may be called upon and organized in such way that balance is achieved. Time dedicated to the planning and sourcing of appropriate sessions is time well-spent and applies to all levels of athletes and general-exercisers across their sports or physical activity interests.

To systematically devise an endurance training programme using RPE, types of sessions can be grouped according to their style and general aim as they can all be equally quantified in establishing an overall training load (e.g. interval, steady state runs, resistance training). This adds considerable choice and options to help sustain athlete interest and engagement.

For the purposes of this chapter, a theoretical example of a 5000m endurance running schedule has been selected for an advanced, club-level, athlete (Tables 5.1-5.6). Training sessions have been divided into five categories: 1) interval training (sets of repetitive bouts), 2) tempo running (self selecting to vary pace at different tempos) 3) steady state running (sustained pace endurance runs) 4) recovery running (low intensity active recovery) and 5) weighted circuits (light intensity resistance training). Each of these categories includes different choices of session for the coach and athlete to call upon when devising the programme. This process facilitates choice and interest and, as each session is designed to be performed via self-pacing, (using RPE) it is possible to have multiple options for most styles of session. Sessions could therefore contain high or low level effort options in some cases. This may be useful when considering the specific session in relation to the overall training load. Session selection depends on the place of session in the programme and whether or not different intensities of that session are meaningful. That is an issue for the coach and athlete to consider.

The interval training sessions provided in the example 5000m programme (Table 5.1) have been included for the purpose of 'over-speed' training, whereby the effort applied to each run is anticipated to be at a self-regulated intensity corresponding to the desired RPE where RPE is specific to that session. For example, pacing a session with an RPE of 7/10 (very hard) for an interval session of 3 x 400m would be expected to produce faster performance times than for a 7/10 (very hard) session of 5 x 400m with the same inter-repetition recovery periods. The individual therefore considers 7/10 (very hard) in relation to completing the specific task.

For interval training, inter-repetition recovery periods facilitate greater accumulations of high-speed distance than is possible at usual pace. This can be useful for generating local muscle and metabolic responses not normally experienced in response to lower intensity continuous exercise. This metabolic disturbance creates negative conscious sensations and repeated exposure to this condition may avoid an immediate, precautionary down-regulation of effort in the presence of an unfamiliar sensation.

To obtain optimal outcomes from interval training, an endurance athlete may consider the amount of energy they would be prepared to maximally commit to an interval session and then consider the RPE at which they are requested to perform each bout. A previous study [14] indicated that athletes can also optimally self-determine their minimum necessary inter-repetition recovery periods with no compromise to session outcomes (e.g. performance times) by simply perceiving the minimum time to recommence exercise as the trigger to start the next bout. This technique is based on responding to sensations of perceived readiness to recommence exercise [14]. However, for situations where athletes train as a group, it remains preferable to operate the session by using common recovery durations for all athletes so to facilitate athlete motivation and optimal time management of the session. In that case, performance time is self-regulated in the knowledge of the known demands of the session which includes the known duration of each recovery period.

Tempo running sessions have been included in the continuous running category (Table 5.2) in this example programme as a means of facilitating variable self-pacing in response to sustained exercise. In these sessions, runners are expected to naturally pace themselves at an underlying RPE based on the known duration of the activity.

Table 5.1. Preliminary profiling of interval (Int) training sessions for endurance athletes (duration x RPE). The sessions can thereafter be allocated into the training programme as appropriate when determining overall training load

Session			Intensity option (Low)			Intensity option (High)	
Name	Detail	Duration	RPE (L)	Session-RPE (L)		RPE (H)	Session-RPE (H)
Int_1	6 x 200m	35min	5	175		8	280
Int_2	3 x 400m	35min	5	175		8	280
Int_3	5 x 400m	40min	5	200		8	320
Int_4	10 x 200m	40min	5	200		8	320
Int_5	8 x 400m	50min	5	250		8	400
Int_6	4 x 800m	50min	5	250		8	400
Int_7	7 x 800m	60min	5	300		8	480

For endurance-based interval training performed individually, it is possible to self-regulate inter-repetition recovery using the minimum time (perceived readiness) self-regulation method i.e. restart exercise as soon as perceived ready [14]. For group training, it is more convenient and manageable to use single standardised inter-repetition recovery durations for all athletes so that this becomes a fixed variable and the flexible variable for manipulation by the athlete is the run performance in relation to the known demands of the session and recovery duration. The coach and athlete should consider durations of inter-repetition recovery in accordance with the session aims/needs i.e. a shorter recovery will dampen down the performance times.

Table 5.2. Preliminary profiling of all continuous-run session options

Category	Type	Detail	Duration	Intensity option (Low) RPE (L)	Session-RPE (L)	Intensity option (High) RPE (H)	Session-RPE (H)
Tempo run	T_1	Variable pace	30min	4	120	7	210
Tempo run	T_2	Variable pace	35min	4	140	7	245
Tempo run	T_3	Variable pace	40min	4	160	7	280
Recovery run	RR_1	Easy run	20min	3	60	-	-
Recovery run	RR_2	Easy run	25min	3	75	-	-
Recovery run	RR_3	Easy run	30min	3	90	-	-
Steady state	SS_1	Constant pace	60min	2	120	4	240
Steady state	SS_2	Constant pace	70min	2	140	4	280
Steady state	SS_3	Constant pace	80min	2	160	4	320

Table 5.3. Preliminary profiling of all resistance training sessions

Category	Type	Detail	Duration	Intensity option (Low) RPE (L)	Session-RPE (L)	Intensity option (High) RPE (H)	Session-RPE (H)
Weighted circuit	W_1	Light weight repetitions	50min	6	300	7.5	375
Weighted circuit	W_2	Moderate weight repetitions	50min	6	300	7.5	375

They are required to periodically pace up or down from the main tempo across the bout as agreed or discussed with the coach, but conclude the run having achieved the overall RPE for the session. Again, this is determined by the athletes basing the session on how they feel (level of discomfort throughout the bout) rather than achieving a strict performance time.

The steady-state runs (Table 5.2) are listed as long duration constant pace bouts of continuous exercise are intended to be paced at sub-race effort. The recovery runs (Table 5.2) are relatively short duration bouts designed for instances where the athlete is moderately activating and working major leg muscles but is essentially on an active rest day. The weighted circuit (Table 5.3) is a means of moderate cross-training to improve local muscle strength and power in response to aerobic-session stimulation. Once all sessions have been listed, and categorized into the tables (Tables 5.1-5.3) it is possible to consider how/where/when these might fit with the training programme (Table 5.4).

The prior calculation of session-RPE TRIMP (session duration x session RPE) for each type of training session offers a quick comparison score among all sessions. Thus it facilitates a quick, easy and manageable view of setting a training load. An estimated session-duration has been allocated to each activity based on prior experience but which could easily be varied by the coach. To directly calculate all exercise and rest durations, the coach would need to place a stopwatch on all intervals and all recovery periods, or at the beginning and end of every weight lifted in a resistance training session. It makes no practical sense to do so and this would be a fairly meaningless exercise for resistance or any stop/start training. It is more sensible to simply estimate overall session duration based on typical experiences.

The example provided demonstrates two weeks of training in a 'preparation' mesocycle of a training programme where the emphasis is to sustain a high workload from week-to-week. The individual session-RPE scores are summed as an RPE-Load for each week (Table 5.4) which enables the coach to select options from the training battery that are either consistent with previous weeks, or could be graduated, progressively becoming more intense in accordance with week to week objective (outcome/performance) data and the aim of the programme. The weekly summed RPE training load can therefore be compared with low-high (1-5) categories (Table 5.5), based on relative percentages of a maximal achievable score from the sessions in the lists (Tables 5.1-5.3).

Table 5.4. The example of a training schedule drawing on sessions identified from Tables 1-3 by the coach for implementation. The weekly training load represents the accumulative score of all session-RPE results

Training phase	Week	Monday	Tuesday	Wednesday	Thursday	Friday	Saturday	Sunday	Session-RPE Weekly load
Mesocycle 1 (Race preparation)	1 Session-RPE	$SS_{2(L)}$ & $W_{1(L)}$ 140 &300	$Int_{3(H)}$ 320	$SS_{1(L)}$ 120	$T_{1(L)}$ & $W_{2(L)}$ 120 & 300	Rest	$SS_{3(H)}$ 320	RR_3 90	**1710**
	2 Session-RPE	$SS_{3(H)}$ & $W_{1(H)}$ 320 & 375	$Int_{5(L)}$ 250	RR_2 75	T_2 & $W_{1(L)}$ 140 & 300	Rest	RR_3 90	$SS_{2(L)}$ 140	**1690**
Mesocycle 2 (Race tapering)	7 Session-RPE	$SS_{1(L)}$ 120	$Int_{3(H)}$ 320	Rest	$W_{1(H)}$ 375	Rest	T_2 140	$SS_{2(L)}$ 140	**1095**
	8 (Race) Session-RPE	RR_3 90	$Int_{1(H)}$ 280	RR_1 60	$T_{2(H)}$ 245	Rest	Rest	**Race**	**675**

Only weeks 1-2 and 7-8 are included in this schematic view of how to schedule and monitor a training programme for a 5000m runner. Training should be individualised and the use of session descriptors, options and weekly assessments of weekly RPE loads enables comparison of overall in training. Balance of training load can therefore be maintained using a simple monitoring technique.

Table 5.5. Benchmarked descriptors and evaluation of training load. The coach determines a maximal achievable weekly score as a benchmarked criterion (e.g. the hardest possible week he/she would ever realistically prescribe). In this example case 1800 has been estimated as the maximal load likely to be prescribed in any one week of training. Thereafter, zones (%) similar to those of the heart rate zone TRIMP method can be applied (see Table 4.2, chapter four). Note the values provided in this example are purely for academic purposes and are not meant as a prescription for all 5000m runners

Weekly RPE-Load	% of maximum	Load Descriptor	Score
1620 - 1800	90-100	High	5
1440 - 1619	80-89	Moderate – high	4
1260 - 1439	70-79	Moderate	3
1080 - 1259	60-69	Low – moderate	2
< 1079	50-59	Low	1

Table 5.6. Athlete's weekly self evaluation and coping self assessments in relation to training load

Training week	Weekly RPE-Load	Load Descriptor	Athlete evaluation (1-5: Low-High)	Athlete self coping (0-10)
Week 1	1710	High		
Week 2	1690	High		
Week 7	1095	Low-moderate		
Week 8	675	Low		

The weekly accumulative score for training load can be compared against the zone descriptors for low-high loads. The athlete should also score the weekly load according to their self perception of low-high (1-5) and their ability to cope with that load (0-10: none to maximum).

The coach should estimate a maximal achievable weekly (accumulative) session-RPE from the list of options that could be prescribed and this would represent a 100% load. In this way, training zones (e.g. 90-100% and so on) based on RPE-Load can be used to easily identify if the weekly training stimulus is low-high according to the zone descriptors (Table 5.5). For the purpose of the example in this chapter, a maximal weekly (session-RPE) load has been estimated as 1800.

In this session-RPE system, the athlete can also provide end of week (microcycle) feedback as to how he/she perceived their ability to cope with the cyclic (e.g. weekly) load by self rating the intensity of the weekly training load (1-5) to see whether their perception of low-high load is consistent with the aims of the prescribed stimulus (Table 5.6). For example, this would be of assistance in instances where athletes perceive a week designed as a moderate load stimulus (3/5) to be a high load (5/5) (Table 5.6). The identification of mismatch between intent and athlete perception, can additionally be accompanied by an athlete coping rating (0-10) as a rapid form of feedback for the coach. This would indicate to the coach/trainer that the athlete is not coping well (e.g. perhaps in the presence of illness) and subsequent loads may be adjusted until the athlete returns to health or is coping better with the stimulus. This process helps to inform the coach's practice and in cases such as tapering for a race (e.g. in weeks 7-8 of the example in Table 5.4), the summed RPE weekly training load can easily be seen to progressively reduce while still focusing on several key preparatory high performance sessions. The aim at this stage might be to augment characteristics important to success such as high quality race-like sessions with increased inter-session recovery. Although session-RPE is not perfect, it is a system which enables objectivity, management and monitoring of training and is recommended by these authors.

5.7. ATHLETE COMMENT: ENDURANCE

No matter how well your training programme is designed, there are times when you simply cannot manage your goal pace. This has happened to me on many occasions, usually after I've been ill, had a disturbed night's sleep or stressful day at work, if it's blowing a gale, or I can't find a flat stretch of road/track to carve out 1km reps. That's not to say I (or you) should forgo the training session in the face of such adversity. I'd feel worse if I didn't get out there and attempt my planned run. However, running is often a battle between pleasure and pain and in my opinion knowing how your body overcomes adversity is vital to distance running. Using RPE helps you get the pacing right, and coupling this with heart rate and other measures lets you track progress over time. You simply can't account for all day-to-day factors and negative sensations affecting training unless you build how you 'feel' into your training. After all, the hardest part is often to resist the temptation to stay on the couch!

Maria Bentley, New Zealand Half Marathon Champion (2010).

CONCLUSION

- The critical determinant of success for all endurance-based activities is the ability to sustain a high rate of work output for prolonged periods.
- A high maximal oxygen uptake ($\dot{V}O_2$ max) is commonly associated with success in endurance events. However, several studies have also demonstrated a wide range of endurance performances among populations with similar $\dot{V}O_2$ max.
- The aim of endurance training is to improve performance, not $\dot{V}O_2$ max.
- Metabolic changes occur with endurance training to allow for the efficient use of available oxygen. These adaptations include: increased number and size of mitrochondria, increased ATP production, decreased amounts of lactic acid, increased triglyceride content, increased energy derived from fatty acid, lower glycogen usage in the muscles during exercise, increased enzyme activity for energy turnover, and improved efficiency in utilising oxygen from the blood supply.
- Endurance athletes have been found to be more emotionally stable, less introverted, with lower levels of depression and anxiety than the general population.
- Successful athletes commonly use either association (e.g. body awareness) or disassociation (e.g. diverting attention from unpleasant sensations) as coping strategies depending on the specific circumstances. Non-elite athletes tend to use disassociation to a greater extent.
- Practice-based evidence of pacing strategies in endurance events suggests front loaded (positive/fast start) pacing strategies are generally optimal.
- RPE-based training facilitates an individualised approach to determining training load and monitoring responses.

REFERENCES

[1]   Lind, E., A. Welch, and P. Ekkekakis, Do 'mind over muscle' strategies work? Examining the effects of attentional association and dissociation on exertional, affective and physiological responses to exercise. *Sports Medicine,* 2009. 39: P. 743-764.

[2]   Proeyen, K.V., et al., Beneficial metabolic adaptations due to endurance exercise training in the fasted state. *Journal of Applied Physiology,* 2011. 110: P. 236-245.

[3]   Yeo, W., et al., Skeletal muscle adaptation and performance responses to once a day versus twice every second day endurance training regimens. *Journal of Applied Physiology,* 2008. 105: P. 1462-1470.

[4]   Coyle, E., et al., Physiological and biomechanical factors associated with elite endurance cycling performance. *Medicine & Science in Sports & Exercise,* 1991. 23: P. 93-107.

[5]   Costill, D., H. Thomason, and E. Roberts, Fractional utilization of the aerobic capacity during distance running. *Medicine & Science in Sports,* 1973. 5: P. 248-252.

[6]   McArdle, W., F. Katch, and V. Katch, Exercise physiology: nutrition, energy and human performance. 7 Ed. 2010: Lippincott Williams & Wilkins.

[7]   Rauch, H., A. St Clair Gibson, and E. Lambert, A signalling role for muscle glycogen in the regulation of pace during prolonged exercise. *British Journal of Sports Medicine,* 2005. 39: P. 34-38.

[8]   Noakes, T., Time to move beyond a brainless exercise physiology: the evidence for complex regulation of human exercise performance. *Applied Physiology, Nutrition and Metabolism,* 2011. 36: P. 23-35.

[9]   Baldwin, J., et al., Glycogen availability does not affect the TCA cycle or tan pools during prolonged, fatiguing exercise. *Journal of Applied Physiology,* 2003. 94: P. 2181-2187.

[10]   Rauch, L., et al., Effects of carbohydrate loading on muscle glycogen content and cycling performance. *International Journal of Sport Nutrition,* 1995. 5: P. 25-36.

[11]   Mitchell, J., B. Sproule, and C. Chapman, The physiological meaning of the maximal oxygen intake test. *The Journal of Clinical Investigation,* 1958. 37: P. 538-547.

[12]   Karvonen, M., E. Kentala, and O. Mustala, The effects of training on heart rate; a longitudinal study. *Annales Medicinae Experimentalis Et Biologiae Fenniae,* 1957. 35: P. 307-315.

[13] Gledhill, N., D. Cox, and R. Jaminak, Endurance athletes' stroke volume does not plateau: major advantage is diastolic function. *Medicine & Science in Sports & Exercise,* 1994. 26: P. 1116-1121.

[14] Edwards, A., et al., Self-Pacing in interval training: A teleoanticipatory approach. *Psychophysiology,* 2011. 48: P. 136-141.

[15] Edwards, A., N. Clark, and A. Macfadyen, Lactate and ventilatory thresholds reflect the training status of professional soccer players where maximum aerobic power is unchanged. *Journal of Sports Science And Medicine,* 2003. 2: P. 23-29.

[16] Noakes, T., How did a v hill understand the $\dot{V}$ O₂ max and the "plateau phenomenon"? Still no clarity? *British Journal of Sports Medicine,* 2008. 42: P. 574-580.

[17] Noakes, T., Testing for maximum oxygen consumption has produced a brainless model of human exercise performance. *British Journal of Sports Medicine,* 2008. 42: P. 551-555.

[18] Hansen, E., et al., Muscle fibre type, efficiency, and mechanical optima affect freely chosen pedal rate during cycling. *Acta Physiologica Scandinavica,* 2002. 176: P. 185-194.

[19] Taylor, J., G. Todd, and S. Gandevia, Evidence for a supraspinal contribution to human muscle fatigue. *Clinical and Experimental Pharmacology And Physiology,* 2006. 33: P. 400-405.

[20] Joyner, M. And E. Coyle, Endurance exercise performance: The physiology of champions. *Journal of Physiology,* 2008. 586.1: P. 35-44.

[21] Coyle, E., et al., Determinants of endurance in well-trained cyclists. *Journal of Applied Physiology,* 1988. 64: P. 2622-2630.

[22] Sharp, R., et al., Effects of eight weeks of bicycle ergometer sprint training on human muscle buffer capacity. International Journal of Sports Medicine, 1986. 7: P. 13-17.

[23] Chi, M., et al., Effects of detraining on enzymes of energy metabolism in individual human muscle fibers. *American Journal of Physiology,* 1983. 244: P. C276-C287.

[24] Edwards, A. and P. Lander, Physiological responses to self-paced exercise: effort matched comparisons across running and rowing modalities. *Journal of Sports Medicine and Physical Fitness,* In Press.

[25] Bassett, D. and E. Howley, Limiting factors for maximum oxygen uptake and determinants of endurance performance. *Medicine & Science in Sports & Exercise,* 2000. 32: P. 70-84.

[26] Kubukeli, Z., T. Noakes, and S. Dennis, Training techniques to improve endurance exercise performances. *Sports Medicine,* 2002. 32: P. 489-509.

[27] Billat, V., et al., Physical and training characteristics of top-class marathon runners. *Medicine & Science in Sports & Exercise,* 2001. 33: P. 2089-2097.

[28] Buman, M., et al., Experiences and coping responses of 'hitting the wall' for recreational marathon runners. *Journal of Applied Sport Psychology,* 2008. 20: P. 282-300.

[29] Masters, K., B. Ogles, and J. Jolton, The development of an instrument to measure motivation for marathon running: The motivations of marathoners scales (Moms). *Research Quarterly for Exercise and Sport,* 1993. 64: P. 134-143.

[30] Morgan, W. and M. Pollock, Psychological characterization of the elite distance runner. *Annals of the New York Academy of Sciences,* 1977. 301: P. 382-403.

[31] Morgan, W., Selected psychological factors limiting performance: A mental health model, In *Limits of human performance,* D.H. Clarke, H.M. Eckert Editors. 1985, Human Kinetics: Champaign, Il.

[32] Raglin, J., Psychological factors in sport performance: The mental health model revisited. *Sports Medicine,* 2001. 31: P. 875-890.

[33] Morgan, W., Mind games: The Psychology of sport, In *Optimizing sport performance: Perspectives in exercise and sports medicine* D.R. Lamb & R. Murray, Editors. 1997, Cooper: Carmel, Il. P. 1-54.

[34] Raglin, J., The psychology of the marathoner: Of one mind and many. *Sports Medicine,* 2007. 37: P. 404-407.

[35] Morgan, W., The mind of the marathoner. *Psychology Today,* 1978. 11: P. 38-49.

[36] Schomer, H., Mental Strategy training programme for marathon runners. *International Journal of Sport Psychology,* 1987. 18: P. 133-151.

[37] Goode, K. and D. Roth, Factor analysis of cognitions during running: Association with mood change. *Journal of Sport & Exercise Psychology,* 1993. 15: P. 375-389.

[38] Stevinson, C. and S. Biddle, Cognitive strategies in running: A response to masters and ogles (1998). *The Sport Psychologist,* 1999. 13: P. 235-236.

[39] Masters, K. and B. Ogles, Associative And dissociative cognitive strategies in exercise and running: 20 years later, what do we know? *The Sport Psychologist,* 1998. 12: P. 253-270.

[40] Martin, J., M. Craib, and V. Mitchell, Relationship of anxiety and self-attention to running economy in competitive male distance runners. *Journal of Sports Sciences,* 1995. 13: P. 371-376.

[41] Tammen, V., Elite middle and long distance runners associative /dissociative coping. *Journal of Applied Sport Psychology,* 1996. 8: P. 1-8.

[42] St Clair Gibson, A. and C. Foster, The role of self-talk in the awareness of physiological state and physical performance. *Sports Medicine,* 2007. 37: P. 1029-1044.

[43] Karageorghis, C. and P. Terry, Inside sport psychology. 2011, Champaign, Il: Human Kinetics.

[44] Thornby, M., F. Haas, And K. Axen, Effect of distractive auditory stimuli on exercise tolerance in patients with copd. *Chest,* 1995. 107: P. 1213-1217.

[45] Elliot, D., R. Polman, And R. Mcgregor, Journal of music therapy. *Journal of Music Therapy,* 2011. 48: P. 263-287.

[46] Abbiss, C. and P. Laursen, Describing and understanding pacing strategies during athletic competition. *Sports Medicine,* 2008. 38(3): P. 239-252.

[47] Lander, P., R. Butterly, and A. Edwards, Self-Paced exercise is less physically challenging than enforced constant pace exercise of the same intensity: Influence of complex central metabolic control, *British Journal of Sports Medicine,* 2009. 43: P. 789-795.

[48] Edwards, A. and T. Noakes, Dehydration: Cause of fatigue or sign of pacing in elite soccer? *Sports Medicine,* 2009. 39: P. 1-13.

[49] Billat, V., et al., Effect of free versus constant pace on performance and oxygen kinetics in running, *Medicine & Science in Sports & Exercise,* 2001. 33: P. 2082-2088.

[50] Garcin, M., M. Danel, and V. Billat, Perceptual responses in free vs. constant pace exercise. *International Journal of Sports Medicine,* 2008. 29: P. 453-459.

[51] Noakes, T., The central governor model of exercise regulation applied to the marathon. *Sports Medicine,* 2007. 37: P. 374-377.

[52] Foster, C., et al., Effect of pacing strategy on cycle time trial performance. *Medicine & Science in Sports & Exercise,* 1993. 25: P. 383-388.

[53] Garland, S., An analysis of the pacing strategy adopted by elite competitors in 2000 m rowing. *British Journal of Sports Medicine,* 2005. 39: P. 39-42.

[54] Muehlbauer, T. and T. Melges, Pacing patterns in competitive rowing adopted in different race categories. *International Journal of Performance Analysis in Sport,* 2011. 11: P. 239-253.

[55] Hausswirth, C., et al., Pacing strategy during the initial phase of the run in triathlon: Influence on overall performance. *European Journal of Applied Physiology,* 2010. 108: P. 1115-1123.

[56] Meur, Y.L., et al., Influence of gender on pacing adopted by elite triathletes during a competition. *European Journal of Applied Physiology,* 2009. 106: P. 535-545.

[57] Vleck, V., et al., Pacing during an elite olympic distance triathlon: Comparison between male and female competitors. *Journal of Science and Medicine in Sport,* 2008. 11: P. 424-432.

[58] Abbiss, C., et al., Dynamic pacing strategies during the cycle phase of an ironman triathlon. *Medicine & Science in Sports & Exercise,* 2006. 38: P. 726-734.

[59] Jones, G., The role of performance profiling in cognitive behavioural interventions in sport. *The Sport Psychologist,* 1993. 7: P. 160-172.

[60] Fitzgerald, M., Run: The mind-body method of running by feel. 2010, Boulder, Colorado: Velopress.

[61] Fitzgerald, M., Brain training for runners. 2007, New York: New American Library.

[62] Philostratus, F., Concerning gymnastics (Translated), In *The research quarterly,* T. Woody, Editor. 1936, Ann Arbor: Mi.

Chapter 6

PACING FOR POWER, STRENGTH AND SPEED

6.1. ABSTRACT

The aim of this chapter is to examine whether or not pacing is of importance to the performance of anaerobic activities requiring power, strength and speed. Intuitively, it might be expected that short duration maximal performances do not require pacing, but evidence presented in this chapter indicates this may not be the case. In very short duration activities (e.g. a vertical jump) it is not possible or necessary to receive feedback with which to modify performance; however, this applies to relatively few activities and is still an example of a (all-out) paced activity. Anaerobic activities such as resistance training, sprint events, or even repetitive vertical jumps should be considered consequent to feedback-driven pacing strategies. Pacing strategies of short duration athletic events are presented and discussed. Additionally, the practical application of a self-paced approach to training for a power, strength, and speed athlete is proposed on the basis of principles discussed here and in previous chapters.

6.2. INTRODUCTION

It is apparent (see chapter five) that pacing is a fundamental component of endurance performance, acting as a protective mechanism to individually manage effort across an exercise bout. However, the principles of pacing are less obvious for anaerobic activities. Nevertheless, we shall investigate in this chapter whether or not there is evidence of pacing in short duration activities. For example, other than trying to attain top speed in the shortest possible time and thereafter sustain it, pacing seems to be a limited feature of events such as the Olympic 100m race. Although this might initially appear to suggest pacing is not important for sprinting or a sprinter, that may not be the case. Sprinters are required to train to enhance their physiological efficiency, while also enhancing maximal strength and power. Training for sprinters requires the completion of multiple, repetitive actions, most of which are performed at high intensity. High intensity exercise utilises anaerobic energy systems such as glycolysis and this produces lactic acid. The production of lactic acid leads to sensations of nausea which influences behaviour. Therefore, pacing may not directly influence the performance of very short duration maximal events to a great extent, but it is likely to be highly influential in the training for these events. Also, we cannot all run the 100m in 9.58s like the current world record holder Usain Bolt. Taking longer (e.g. 14-20s) to run the 100m may require direct pacing of the race due to extended duration and consequent energy provision from different metabolic pathways. These factors and the influences of pacing on anaerobic performance will be discussed in greater depth during this chapter.

6.3. PHYSIOLOGY OF ANAEROBIC EXERCISE (POWER, STRENGTH AND SPEED)

The energy requirements for high or maximal force production are largely met by the intramuscular high-energy phosphate sources, adenosine triphosphate (ATP) and phosphocreatine (PCr)[1]. ATP is the body's 'energy currency'[2] and must be continually resynthesised for muscular work to continue. The body retains only small quantities of ATP (approx 3-8 mmol/kg) and must, therefore, resynthesise ATP from other sources such as PCr, stored glycogen or lipids. The interchange between ATP and PCr (ATP-PCr system) represents the most rapid means of gaining the necessary energy for maximal muscle tension in power and strength activities. As intramuscular PCr levels are also limited (approx 15-40 mmol/kg), this system can only support maximal power outputs for a few seconds (approx 6s) [3]. Supplementary energy for resynthesising ATP during high intensity exercise is provided by the breakdown of stored muscle glycogen, by anaerobic glycolysis. Therefore, for very short duration maximal voluntary contractions, the primary source of energy for peak force output is from the ATP-PCr system, supplemented by energy derived from glycolysis.

Physiological adaptations to glycolytic energy metabolism have been observed in response to training regimes utilising short duration exercise bouts [1]. This effect has been observed by increased activities (~20%) of several key glycolytic enzymes such as phosphorylase, phosphofructokinase and lactate dehydrogenase in response to exercise of durations greater than 6 s. Phosphofructokinase is considered a rate limiting enzyme for glycolysis and consequently increased concentrations of this enzyme up regulate glycolysis.

Exposure to sustained anaerobic training also enhance muscles' capabilities to function in the presence of accumulating metabolic acidosis [4]. The accumulation of lactate and hydrogen ions (H^+) are generally considered to interfere with muscle contractile processes, reduce physiologic pH and, via afferent feedback, trigger a conscious awareness of negative sensory information (e.g. nausea and pain) [5]. However, buffering of metabolic acidosis has been shown to improve by up to 50% in response to eight weeks of specific anaerobic training [6]. Augmented buffering capabilities enable experienced athletes to produce more lactate in muscles and thus sustain higher muscle tension for longer periods. Additionally, as a consequence of buffering, negative afferent sensory information takes longer to reach such severity in the brain as to warrant conscious attention and a behaviour change (i.e. to slow down or stop exercising).

The time-course of physiological adaptations in response to training, range from those that occur early, to those that take place through years of dedicated practice. It is apparent that neuromuscular adaptations to anaerobic training precede structural change in skeletal muscles and occur within the early days and weeks of training [7]. An increase in neural drive is critical to maximising strength and power and this is thought to occur via increases to the firing rate, timing and pattern of coordinated impulse discharge to the major muscles [8]. It is therefore a change to the potency, coordination and timing of electrical impulse from brain to muscle rather than structural changes within the muscle which leads to initial gains of strength [7].

Untrained individuals usually display suboptimal motor unit recruitment, until coordinative patterns of motor unit recruitment are well established [8]. For example, Adams et al. [9] demonstrated that only 71% of muscle tissue was activated during maximal effort in untrained subjects, while other studies have demonstrated training can increase muscle activation (~ 91% of muscle tissue), although not to the extent of full motor unit recruitment [10]. Following specific training, muscle does not require as much neural activation to generate adequate tension for a given force output due to improvements in coordinated muscle firing and efficiency. It is likely that synchronization of firing rates is crucial to the timing and management of optimal force production [7, 8, 11].

Skeletal muscle adapts to anaerobic training primarily by increasing its size and enhancing its biochemical and ultra-structural components (i.e. architecture, enzyme activity, and substrate concentrations) [1]. Collectively these factors result in enhanced muscular strength, power, and endurance which are all crucial to athletic success. Muscle hypertrophy is the enlargement of muscle resulting from training and this occurs as a consequence of an increase to the cross-sectional area of the muscle fibres. This can take several weeks to become evident in response to resistance training. With the initiation of a training programme, muscle proteins such as fast myosin heavy chains display early adaptation, while muscle fibre hypertrophy appears to require longer (approx 4 weeks or 16 training sessions) [12].

Heavy resistance training does not appear to significantly affect aerobic capacity. The exception is in untrained individuals who have been shown to increase $\dot{V}O_2$ max (5-8%) as a result of resistance training. Circuit training of high volume exercise with short rest periods have also been shown to improve $\dot{V}O_2$ max in untrained subjects [13] but the impact on anaerobic training on aerobic capability is negligible.

Hormones also play a multitude of important regulatory roles in adaptation to anaerobic training. Anabolic hormones such as testosterone, insulin, insulin-like growth factors, and the growth hormones all influence the development of muscle, bone, and connective tissue [14]. Hormones are involved in a wide variety of homeostatic mechanisms that are dedicated to keeping the body functions with a normal range [1, 13]. Anaerobic exercise and, in particular, resistance training has been shown to result in elevated testosterone, growth hormone and cortisol immediately post exercise [2]. Consequently, regular resistance training stimulates an acute hormonal response so that muscular adaptations occur and the individual is gradually able to exert more effort in response to successive training sessions.

6.4. PSYCHOLOGICAL ASPECTS OF PACING FOR POWER, STRENGTH AND SPEED

Activities which require high intensity effort from the start (e.g. weight lifting, sprinting) benefit from psychological preparatory strategies. In particular, strategies which psych-up the athlete by increasing arousal levels, or strategies which increase expectancies, have been shown to enhance performance levels [15]. Surprisingly the sport psychology literature does not provide much empirical support and advice on strategies to increase arousal levels. This is probably due to the notion that most athletes have problems with over arousal. Athletes who use some form of psych-up as part of their pre-performance routine generally combine a number of strategies which include a combination of arousal manipulation, positive self-talk, attention control, and imagery [16].

Arousal manipulation can be achieved through a number of ways. Intense breathing and in particular several hard exhales can increase intensity levels. Also bodily movements such as walking, running, or jumping up and down can be effective for pre-exercise stimulation. In weight lifting it is not uncommon for athletes to be physically slapped in by the training partner or coach to increase arousal levels. The underlying theory being that the pain increases adrenaline levels and improves subsequent performance. High energy self-talk (stay pumped) in combination with high energy body movements (pumping fist, slapping thigh) can also help improve performance [16, 17]. Similarly, inspirational team talks by the coach combined with aggressive gestures can increase arousal levels. Finally, many athletes use music prior to performance or during training to increase arousal [18]. Inspirational music might help prepare the body for the upcoming event by raising adrenaline levels and thereby increasing heart rate.

Increasing alertness with the use of legal substances is also used by athletes to raise their performance levels. In Australian Rules Football (AFL) it is common practice for players to consume caffeine pills (up to 600mg) under the assumption that it increases alertness and lowers perceptions of fatigue. Similarly, in weight lifting events athletes commonly use smelling salts or ammonia prior to lifting to increase alertness and provide an additional surge of energy.

Probably the most important tool to achieve cognitive control over situations is self-talk. Positive self-talk has the potential to improve athletic performance and increase self worth. It has the capacity to alter cognitions, regulate arousal levels through power or relaxing words and maintain focus. On the other hand self-talk can also undermine or decrease performance when it is negative, causes distraction from the task at hand or is too frequent that it interrupts automaticity [19]. In particular the use of negative labels (e.g. I am a loser) can become problematic to performance, self-esteem, well-being and mental health [20].

Positive self-talk can influences an athlete's self-concept, self-confidence, self-efficacy beliefs and sporting performance. In their review Zinsser, Bunker and Williams [19] outline that self-talk can, for example, help the athlete to focus on what is required in the here and now, create or change desired mood states through power words, and control and direct effort. There are a number of strategies from cognitive behavioural therapy (CBT) which allow athletes to control self-talk. These include thought-stoppage, reframing, ABC cognitive restructuring, affirmative statements, mastery or coping tapes and countering. As with physical skills it takes systematic practice to develop positive self-talk and the help of an appropriately qualified psychologist would be recommended.

Finally, imagery has consistently been shown to be an effective strategy to optimize performance in power, strength and speed activities. We all use imagery on a daily basis for example when anticipating upcoming events (a date, job interview or public speaking engagement). Similarly, athletes can positively visualize about an upcoming competitive event. Imagery not only enhances competitive performance but can also be used in skill learning. It also improves self-confidence and self-efficacy, enhances motivation, attention control and can change arousal and affect [21].

6.5. PACING FOR POWER, STRENGTH AND SPEED

For power, strength and speed activities, empirical data support the use of a fast start/all-out effort pacing strategy with which to accomplish optimal performance [22, 23] (Figure 6.1). This can easily be observed in an elite 100m running race. For example, Usain Bolt may know that as the world record holder he is capable of running 9.58s, but a fast start is still of sufficient strategic importance to him that he 'jumped the gun' in the 2011 World Championship 100m final and was disqualified. It is unlikely he would false start in a race against recreational athletes or sedentary volunteers. Clearly in that scenario, he would not perceive a fast start as necessary and would adopt a different pacing strategy.

A fast (all-out) pacing strategy is commonsensical for very short duration competitive races as the subtleties of a complex, conscious pacing plan are unlikely to prevail where the pressing issue is to apply maximal effort and rapidly attain maximal muscle tension. In response to activities requiring the application of maximal force, it is not possible to increase motor unit recruitment beyond the limits of voluntary stimulation. Maximal or near maximal voluntary effort can be applied instantaneously in response to a voluntary desire. For example, at the start of a sprint, the athlete's immediate aspiration for maximal effort must be matched by a physiological response, such that the body must catch up to the desire of the mind. This is rapidly accomplished via neural stimulation to the motor cortex which invokes subsequent voluntary recruitment of motor units to innervate the desired muscles [24]. Physiological adjustments accompany motor drive and collectively ensure that the body is working optimally to match physical output to the required effort. In this regard, decision making for single bout, maximal activities of very short duration is relatively simple. The athlete initiates a desire for maximal effort and if that desire is sufficiently compelling, there is no reason to assume that maximum effort does not equal voluntary maximal force [25-27]. However, as we have previously noted, skeletal muscle motor unit recruitment is never 100% even in supposedly maximal isometric contractions [28]. The brain ensures a reserve of motor units is retained so that potentially damaging full muscle recruitment does not occur [29]. This suggests that maximal voluntary force could theoretically be increased if the central (brain) regulator could be overridden.

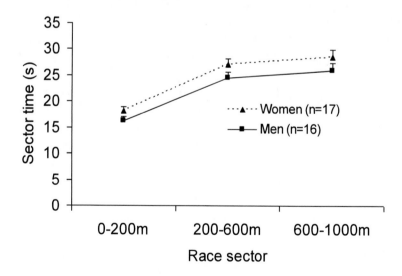

Figure 6.1. Pacing of 1000m sprint performance in speed skating in experienced men and women. The fast start approach to speed skating is clearly evident from sector 0-200m. Performance profiles are parallel for experienced male and female skaters. Original drawing from published data [23].

In response to most short duration events, athletes may perceive reaching the endpoint of the task is attainable without the need for any conscious planning or adjustments to pace. The athlete may simply apply maximal effort until the bout is concluded; however, pacing becomes more complicated for longer duration power or strength activities, such as those observed in response to the 30s Wingate cycle ergometer protocol. In this test, the athlete is expected to sustain maximal voluntary effort for the full 30s duration at a pre-determined resistance based on an individualised body mass (e.g. 0.075 – 0.12 kg/kg body mass) [30, 31]. However, as peak power is almost always attained in the first 2-3s of this protocol, the remaining 27-28s of exercise require considerable motivation and the conscious desire to sustain maximal effort. As afferent feedback from active muscles bombard the brain with negative sensations such as muscle pain and nausea, the desire for continued maximal effort must be consciously weighed against the perceived importance of the task. The more important the task or the more stimulated the athlete, the better the retention of power. Similar issues arise when the task has high accuracy demands. For example in both the high and long jump the athletes would like to take-off with the highest speed possible. However, regulation of the last few strides is paced in such a way (using perceptual information) that the athlete hits the appropriate spot to initiate the jump.

As a means to augment sensory stimulation and thus override central regulation, strategies such as motivational music have occasionally been demonstrated to improve performance. A recent study [18] showed that music significantly motivated a mixed gender population (males = 43, females = 28) to improved performances in a traditional Wingate test (Figure 6.2). This not only augmented average power output across the 30s bout, but also diminished the rate of fatigue, and resulted in the attainment of greater peak power output. This supports the view that there remains some protective mechanism restricting to the execution of power output in supposed maximal performance.

During maximal repetitive sprints, studies have shown that peak power outputs for each bout are less than when compared to single maximal effort bouts (e.g. [32]). This is likely to be a pacing response in the repetitive series, either as a consequence of prior experiences, or as a precautionary response in anticipation of physical cost for the session. In any case, 'maximal' is not truly maximal in these circumstances. Even in response to the first sprint of a repetitive series there is likely to be some degree of neural inhibition so to regulate exercise performance and help avoid the occurrence of premature fatigue prior to completion of the series. As experience grows in completing repeated sprint activities, it is likely that pace judgment will improve, power will be better retained and consequent physiological adaptations to this form of overload training will also be improved [22]. Similarly, when accuracy is required in jump events the athlete learns to achieve the highest speed possible when taking-off.

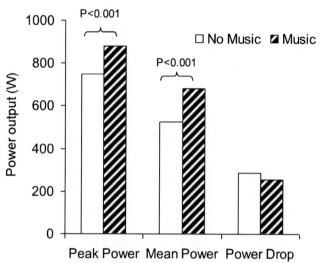

Figure 6.2. Power output in response to 30s Wingate testing, either with or without motivational music. Original drawing from previously published data [18].

Repetition training is not the sole preserve of sprint athletes. This form of training is also the common stratagem for resistance training [33]. It is broadly recommended that novice to intermediate athletes utilise resistance loads corresponding to 60–70% of 1 repetition maximum (RM) for 8–12 repetitions for maximal strength training, while advanced athletes may be able to train with a lower number of repetitions but with higher loads (e.g. 80–100% of 1 RM). It is typical that one to three sets of repetitions per exercise are performed and data tend to support the use of multiple sets of repetitions in comparison with a single set, both for strength gains and strength-endurance [34].

In response to resistance training, the effects of pacing may be observed by the velocity of muscle action. Numerous studies have demonstrated less peak force, power, and numbers of repetitions are performed with enforced 'super slow' repetition velocity compared with a self selected velocity exercise when matched for intensity [35]. One study compared very slow repetition velocity to a normal condition and identified ~40% reductions in training loads were needed to attain the same number of repetitions in this slow/unfamiliar method [36]. Conversely, attempting to lift weighs at too fast a velocity appears to result in the expenditure of excess effort and premature sensations of fatigue.

Inadequate inter-set rest periods are known to impede performance of subsequent sets in resistance training and also diminish metabolic adaptations [37]. In common with all other forms of physical training, the effort distributed across the entire session should be carefully considered, such that the effort is distributed across both repetitions and sets. Power and strength based training sessions should be considered as subject to the same principles of pacing as endurance activities.

6.6. SELF-PACED ANAEROBIC TRAINING

Training adaptations are not instantaneous and depending on factors such as the initial conditioning of the athlete, may take many months of dedicated training and practice. In addition, the principles of training overload suggest that athletes will necessarily experience periods of reduced capabilities during the training period, usually prior to attaining physiological adaptations and consequent performance gains [38]. Overload training specifically requires the individual to train at intensities greater than normal to stimulate specific physiological, muscular adaptations so the body may function more efficiently in the future. This requires planning of the training programme such that frequency, intensity, duration, and mode of exercise are regularly manipulated to cause overload. Training is therefore a period of highs and lows as the body responds to new training stimuli [38, 39]. Athletes should be prepared and advised that performance gains and training experiences will oscillate around a general progression, rather than displaying continual gains [38].

In response to resistance training, research indicates that for most individuals, a load of approximately 60–75% of an individual's 1 repetition maximum (1RM) is required to induce strength gain and muscle hypertrophy [40]. In general, intensities less than 60% of 1RM are considered suboptimal for resistance training when a moderate (e.g. 8-10) number of repetitions are performed. Common exercise prescription methodology in resistance training involves the use of an initial 1RM or 6RM test to establish maximal strength for a given exercise [41]. Training intensity is then usually based on a percentage of this maximum [37]. However, in a health and fitness setting, individuals are often not able to complete 1RM testing because of either a lack of support personnel, time constraints, or the perceived risks associated with

1RM testing [42]. It is possible to broadly estimate 1RM based on performance of multiple repetitions in the knowledge that untrained subjects can usually move a load of 68% of 1RM for 7-10RM and trained subjects can move 79% [43]. However, this only provides a broad index and many individuals intuitively self select training load based on 'feel'.

Lagally and co-workers [44] examined ratings of perceived exertion (RPE) and electromyographic (EMG) responses to chest press exercise. They found that RPE increased similarly to EMG as exercise intensity increased from 60% 1RM to 80% 1RM. However, although RPE closely matches changes to the exercise intensity across most types of resistance training (Figure 6.3), this strategy is less effective for small muscle activities such as bicep curls [45]. This is probably due to the relatively minor muscle activation in a bicep curl and small absolute differences in load (kg) in that exercise [45]. Nevertheless, RPE does appear sensitive to change across large muscle resistance training activities.

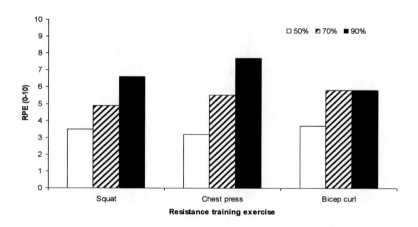

Figure 6.3. Rating of perceived exertion (RPE) values at 50, 70, and 90% of 1 repetition maximum. RPE appears effective to discriminate between 3 levels of intensity for large muscle group exercise, but less so for smaller muscle activities (e.g. bicep curl). Original drawing from previously published data [45].

The greatest advantage of a self-paced (self-selected) approach to resistance training is the ease of use and prospects for increased exercise adherence by adopting this method. By self-selecting exercise intensity, the individual requires less support and instruction and is more likely to increase work volume as individually tolerated rather than as dictated by an external stimulus. However, using self-regulation to perform resistance training at a fixed perception of effort is a relatively new area of research. A number of studies have examined perceptual responses to externally fixed workloads but rarely consider using self-regulation as a means of determining exercise intensity. This is surprising as numerous studies have demonstrated a linear relationship between work intensity and perception of effort [46] and that trained and untrained subjects perceive the intensity of resistance exercise similarly when performing exercise at the same % 1-RM [47].

Data regarding the performance of resistance training at self-selected intensities are relatively scarce, but weight training at light loads (approx 50% 1RM) appears to positively influence state anxiety [48], while heavy loads increase anxiety. However, it is also common for individuals to self-select lighter loads than typically prescribed for resistance training. Glass and Stanton [40] observed that when requested to self-select training loads for resistance training, novices all chose loads beneath 60% 1RM. Consequently this may infer a problem for self-regulated exercise by novices in a resistance training setting as the load required for strength gain and muscle hypertrophy is 60-75% 1RM [49].

If novices do not choose a load that is intense enough to evoke strength and hypertrophy changes, these individuals may not notice strength or substantial gains and this would most likely negatively influence long term exercise adherence. There are, however, several reasons for novices' choice of training load, such as anxiety for personal safety and fear of injury when exercising alone with heavy weights. This is a natural instinctive response to a potentially threatening situation and perfectly sensible. Research has shown that anxiety is reduced following experience [48, 50] as presumably self-confidence improves through task familiarity. However, it is still likely that performance adaptation will not be optimal for an individual if solely relying on self-regulation as the means of determining exercise intensity for resistance training.

A means of optimizing performance outcomes in response to resistance training AND using self-regulation is relatively simple. In a study by Mazzetti et al. [51], two groups performing self-regulated resistance training over the course of 12 weeks were compared. One group was supervised while the other group was unsupervised. The study reported that the supervised training group was able to train with heavier loads, showed a greater rate of increase in training loads, and showed a greater increase in 1RM squat and chest press compared to the unsupervised group. It appears therefore that athletes train at greater relative intensities and progress at a greater rate when their workouts are supervised or supported by a peer. For safety reasons when lifting heavy weights it is common practice for athletes to work in pairs, or to have the assistance of a coach or personal trainer. From the findings of Mazzetti's study, supervised (yet self-regulated) training appears to increase participant self-confidence and perceptions of competence, and importantly to improve the relative percentage of 1RM self-selected for exercise intensity [45].

A coach or trainer could support and/or advise the individual regarding lifting in the presence of fatigue sensations and instil greater motivation, self-confidence and perceptions of competence that the situation is safe and the work achievable [42]. Resistance training lifts are often performed beyond the point of voluntary physical fatigue, such that the final repetitions in a set may occasionally require external support (e.g. a spotter) for completion. This often represents either a resignation that the load is too heavy, or that attempting it will incur damage or injury, or that completion of the final repetition is beyond the tolerable limits of discomfort the individual is prepared to endure. In each case, external support is useful, optimal, and probably necessary, if individuals are to maximally train for strength adaptation. With greater experience of self-regulating performance, the athlete can become more skilled and competent at self determining a suitable load and better perceive their limits of tolerable exercise.

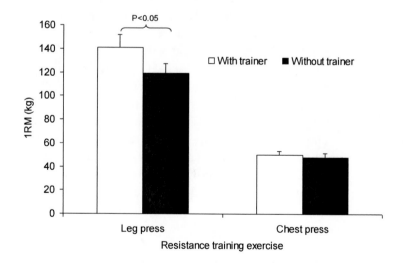

Figure 6.4. One repetition maximum (1RM) strength across leg press and chest press exercise both with and without a personal trainer being present. Data are mean ±SD. Original drawing from published data [42].

The results of a recent study [42] also support the development of a pacing-based approach to strength training under the supervision of a personal trainer (Figure 6.4). That study provided further evidence that the presence of a personal trainer leads to greater initial 1RM strength, improved self-selection of exercise intensities, and greater ratings of perceived exertion values during resistance exercise. As selection of an appropriate intensity is critical to obtaining benefit from resistance training, exercise performed under the supervision of a personal trainer leads to improved performances and, therefore, supervised resistance training via a coach or personal trainer appears to be advantageous.

6.6.1. Self-Paced Anaerobic Training Programme

In this section we have provided an example training schedule for an experienced male 400m runner who would be expected to rely on power, strength and speed for training and performance. This example is provided for the purpose of examining how a self-paced training schedule could be devised, implemented and monitored for anaerobically trained athletes. The principles of the system are exactly the same as for endurance athletes identified in chapter five. The technique requires the coach and athlete to plan out the categories of training considered pertinent to their event and, within each category, list all sessions for possible implementation (Tables 6.1-6.3). For this example, three categories have been devised: 1) interval training (Table 6.1), 2) continuous training (Table 6.2), and 3) resistance training (Table 6.3). Within each table, different sessions have been listed and could be expanded to include further sessions as required. The different sessions have an estimated *duration* and a target *intensity of effort* based on RPE (0-10). These two factors (duration x RPE) produce a session-RPE score with which to develop an accumulative weekly sum for training load. These sessions can therefore be placed in the weekly calendar to form a training schedule (Table 6.4). This schedule can be easily organized into different mesocycles for the purpose of emphasizing different attributes at key stages of the training programme.

In contrast to interval training performed by endurance athletes, sprint/power trained athletes commonly train in groups rather than individually. Performing repetitive efforts in a group can be a motivational strategy to ensure all athletes persevere with the training session despite negative afferent information such as considerable sensations of nausea and pain. In these cases, it is preferential to adopt a common duration of inter-repetition recovery. Clearly, a shorter inter-repetition recovery serves to dampen down interval pace and so the duration of recovery periods may vary according to the place of the session in the training programme (i.e. shorter recovery durations are common in high volume, out of season training). Each individual would therefore know the number of repetitions to be performed and the duration of recoveries when determining their requisite pace for each exercise bout. They would therefore have both a fixed variable (recovery duration) and a flexible variable (individual performance pace).

As with endurance training, the coach should consider the maximal weekly accumulative session-RPE score that would be ever realistically be prescribed in a single week (microcycle) over the year. This estimate thereafter becomes the 100% maximum with which intensity descriptor categories can be developed (Table 6.5). In this case, the maximal load has been estimated to be a score of 1800, which is consistent with the endurance training example. Thereafter, 5 zones have been identified to provide categorical information of intensity levels. From the example, week 1 is regarded as a moderate-high training load (Table 6.5), whereas week 2 is a 'hard' week's training. The training load can clearly be seen to reduce from weeks 1-2 of the schedule to weeks 7-8 as the latter are tapering and race performance weeks. Clearly, the load should be reduced in those weeks as the athlete prepares for a meaningful race.

The session-RPE scores can also be used to compare whether the athlete perceives the load similarly to the purpose for which it was prescribed. In Table 6.6, the athlete can score the weekly load from 1-5 (low-hard) and also provide a coping score (0-10 which is the athlete's view of their ability to cope with the training load). Coping scores outside of the usual range for the athlete may identify potential problems with the load, possible illness, or other issues affecting the athlete. It is a practical means of matching the stimulus (training load) with the response of the athlete. All responses can be coupled with quantifiable performance and physiological outcomes to provide a thorough profile of the athlete.

Table 6.1. Preliminary profiling of interval training sessions

Name	Session Detail	Duration	RPE (L)	Intensity option (Low) Session-RPE (L)	RPE (H)	Intensity option (High) Session-RPE (H)
Int$_1$	300m, 200m, 100m	35min	5	175	8	280
Int$_2$	4 x 200m	35min	5	175	8	280
Int$_3$	8 x 100m	35min	5	175	8	280
Int$_4$	8 x 150m	40min	5	200	8	320
Int$_5$	8 x 200m	45min	5	225	8	360
Int$_6$	4 x 300m	45min	5	225	8	360
Int$_7$	3 x 500m	45min	5	225	8	360
Int$_8$	2(300m, 200m, 100m)	50min	5	250	8	400
Int$_9$	6 x 300m	50min	5	250	8	400
Int$_{10}$	500m, 400m, 300m, 200m, 100m	50min	5	250	8	400
Int$_{11}$	2(500m, 400m, 300m, 200m, 100m)	60min	5	300	8	480
Int$_{12}$	800m, 600m, 400m, 200m	60min	5	300	8	480

*For sprint athletes it is common to train in groups and consequently it is appropriate to manage interval sessions by using a fixed duration recovery (e.g. as set by the coach) for the group. Individuals are able to self-pace the repetitive bouts according to their needs, based on their knowledge of the recovery durations and the overall session demands. The duration of recovery periods (e.g. 2, 3, 4 or 5 min) for sprinters will manipulate the performance outcomes (e.g. so that faster performance times will occur in response to longer recovery periods) and therefore the coach will need to determine optimal duration of recovery for the training period (e.g. the specific mesocycle). The session-RPE will need to be adjusted accordingly (e.g. high intensity session Int$_1$, with a 3min inter-repetition recovery (2 recovery periods in that session) is estimated as 35 min x 8 = 280 session-RPE. Changing the session to use a 5 min recovery will add 4 min to the session duration (and greater physical cost due to the expected rise in the pace of the exercise bouts when greater inter-repetition recovery is provided); therefore the revised session would be: 39 x 8 = 312 session-RPE).

Table 6.2. Preliminary profiling of continuous-run sessions

Category	Session Type	Session Detail	Duration	Intensity option (Low) RPE (L)	Intensity option (Low) Session-RPE (L)	Intensity option (High) RPE (H)	Intensity option (High) Session-RPE (H)
Recovery run	RR_1	Easy run	15min	3	45	-	-
Recovery run	RR_2	Easy run	20min	3	60	-	-
Recovery run	RR_3	Easy run	25min	3	75	-	-
Steady state	SS_1	Constant pace	30min	3	90	5	150
Steady state	SS_2	Constant pace	35min	3	105	5	175
Tempo run	T_1	Variable pace	25min	4	100	7	175

Table 6.3. Preliminary profiling of resistance training sessions

Category	Session Type	Session Detail	Duration	Intensity option (Low) RPE (L)	Intensity option (Low) Session-RPE (L)	Intensity option (High) RPE (H)	Intensity option (High) Session-RPE (H)
Weights (upper body)	W_1	4 sets of exercise (6-8 stations)	40min	6	240	7.5	300
Weights (lower body)	W_2	4 sets of exercise (6-8 stations)	40min	6	240	7.5	300
Weights (whole body)	W_3	3 sets of exercise (10 stations)	45min	6	270	7.5	300
Circuit training	CT_1	Multi-station, speed session	40min	-	-	7	280

Table 6.4. The training schedule and system for monitoring training load

Training phase	Week		Monday	Tuesday	Wednesday	Thursday	Friday	Saturday	Sunday	Session-RPE Weekly load
Mesocycle 1 (Race preparation)	1	Session-RPE	Rest	$Int_{9(H)}$ 400	$W_{1(H)}$ 300	$Int_{3(L)}$ 175	$W_{2(H)}$ 300	Rest	$Int_{10(H)}$ 400	**1575**
	2	Session-RPE	RR_2 60	$Int_{5(H)}$ 360	$W_{1(H)}$ 300	$Int_{7(L)}$ 225	$W_{2(H)}$ 300	Rest	$Int_{10(H)}$ 400	**1645**
Mesocycle 2 (Race tapering)	7	Session-RPE	$SS_{1(L)}$ 90	$Int_{6(H)}$ 360	CT_1 280	Rest	$Int_{2(H)}$ 280	Rest	$SS_{1(L)}$ 90	**1100**
	8 (Race)	Session-RPE	$Int_{1(H)}$ 280	Rest	CT_1 280	$Int_{3(H)}$ 280	Rest	Rest	**Race**	**840**

* Only weeks 1-2 and 7-8 are included in this schematic view of how to schedule and monitor a training programme for a 400m runner. Training should be individualised and the use of session descriptors, options and weekly assessments of weekly RPE loads enables comparison of overall in training. Balance of training load can therefore be maintained using a simple monitoring technique.

Table 6.5. Benchmarked descriptors and evaluation of training load. The coach must determine a maximal achievable weekly score as a benchmarked criterion (e.g. the hardest possible week he/she would ever realistically prescribe). In this case 1800 has been estimated as the maximal load likely to be prescribed in any one week of training. Thereafter, zones (%) similar to those of the heart rate zone TRIMP method can be applied (see Table 4.2, chapter four). Note the values provided in this example are purely for academic purposes and are not meant as a prescription for all 400m runners

Weekly RPE-Load	% of maximum	Load Descriptor	Score
1620 - 1800	90-100	High	5
1440 - 1619	80-89	Moderate – high	4
1260 - 1439	70-79	Moderate	3
1080 - 1259	60-69	Low – moderate	2
< 1079	50-59	Low	1

Table 6.6. Weekly training load (taken from table 4) and description (taken from table 5), coupled with the athlete's self assessment of coping

Training week	Weekly RPE-Load	Load Descriptor	Athlete evaluation (1-5: Low-High)	Athlete self coping (0-10)
Week 1	1575	Moderate-high		
Week 2	1645	High		
Week 7	1100	Low-moderate		
Week 8	840	Low		

The weekly accumulative score for training load can be compared against the zone descriptors for low-high loads. The athlete should also score the weekly load according to their self perception of low-high (1-5) and their ability to cope with that load (0-10: none to maximum).

6.7. ATHLETE COMMENT: POWER, STRENGTH, SPEED

An integral element of any athlete's development is to understand and learn how best to distribute effort across both training and racing. This will help the athlete maximise adaptation to the training stimuli. I have coached athletes with differing strengths and weaknesses who all have the same goal and, in my opinion; the best coaches have the ability to manipulate programmes to facilitate the greatest individual gains. Racing in training is not always productive and session objectives can often be lost in the pursuit of maximal exertion and/or competitive instinct. Therefore, specificity is paramount to setting training and managing the distribution of effort across the session by determining specific, individualised performance targets. Athletes have differing limitations based on physiological and psychological attributes, so the coach must vary the programme to suit their needs, be it by reducing the session by 2 runs, or increasing recovery duration according to their needs. Of course, this doesn't mean training should be easy. The athlete must have self-awareness of how to pace themselves in a session in accordance with their own capabilities and this comes with experience. Athletes must push the barrier to succeed, but trying break down the barrier is self defeating. Listening to how the body reacts to exercise, working with it to better pace a session, and learning to overcome those negative sensations telling you to stop are all important considerations for athletes. As an athlete and coach, I believe there is a fine line between success and failure; a better understanding of self-regulation and pacing can help the athlete gain the greatest adaptation.

Chris Rawlinson, Olympian, Commonwealth Games 400m Hurdles champion (2002), 300m Hurdles world record holder and International coach

CONCLUSION

- For very short duration maximal exercise, the primary source of energy for peak force output is from the ATP-PCr system, supplemented by energy derived from glycolysis.
- Neural activity increases when new movements are being learned and, as a consequence, untrained individuals usually display suboptimal coordination of motor unit recruitment, until patterns of motor unit recruitment are well established.

- Neural adaptations to anaerobic training precede structural change in skeletal muscles and occur within the early days and weeks of training. An increase in neural drive is critical to maximising strength and power and occurs via increases to the firing rate, timing and pattern of coordinated impulse discharge to the major muscles.
- Skeletal muscle adapts to anaerobic training primarily by increasing its size and enhancing its biochemical and ultra-structural components
- Pacing may not directly influence the performance of very short duration maximal events, but it is likely to be highly influential in the training for these events.
- Activities which require high intensity effort from the start (e.g. weight lifting, sprinting) benefit from preparatory strategies. In particular, strategies which psych-up the athlete by increasing arousal levels or strategies which increase expectancies have been shown to enhance performance levels.
- At the start of a sprint, the immediate aspiration for maximal effort must be matched by a physiological response, such that the body must catch up to the mind's desire.
- For power, strength and speed activities, empirical data support the use of a fast start/all-out effort pacing strategy with which to accomplish optimal performance.

REFERENCES

[1]   Costill, D., et al., Adaptations in skeletal muscle following strength training. *Journal of Applied Physiology*, 1979. 46: P. 96-99.

[2]   McArdle, W., F. Katch, and V. Katch, Exercise physiology: nutrition, energy and human performance. 7 Ed. 2010: *Lippincott Williams & Wilkins.*

[3]   Gastin, P., Energy system interaction and relative contribution during maximal exercise. *Sports Medicine,* 2001. 31: P. 725-741.

[4]   Gladden, L., Lactate uptake by skeletal muscle. *Exercise and Sports Science Reviews,* 1989. 17: P. 115-156.

[5]   Hampson, D., et al., The Influence of sensory cues on the perception of exertion during exercise and central regulation of exercise performance. *Sports Medicine,* 2001. 31: P. 935-952.

[6] Sharp, R., Et Al., Effects of eight weeks of bicycle ergometer sprint training on human muscle buffer capacity. *International Journal of Sports Medicine,* 1986. 7: P. 13-17.

[7] Sale, D., Neural adaptation to resistance training. *Medicine & Science in Sports & Exercise,* 1988. 20: P. S135-S145.

[8] Aagaard, P., Training-induced changes in neural function. *Exercise and Sports Science Reviews,* 2003. 31: P. 61-67.

[9] Adams, G., et al., Skeletal muscle myosin heavy chain composition and resistance training. *Journal of Applied Physiology,* 1993. 74: P. 911-915.

[10] Pensini, M., A. Martin, and N. Maffiuletti, Central versus peripheral adaptations following eccentric resistance training. *International Journal Of Sports Medicine,* 2002. 23: P. 567-574.

[11] Sale, D., Influence of exercise and training on motor unit activation. *Exercise and Sports Science Reviews,* 1987. 15: P. 95-152.

[12] Staron, R., et al., Skeletal muscle adaptations during early phase of heavy-resistance training in men and women. *Journal of Applied Physiology,* 1994. 76: P. 1247-1255.

[13] Gettman, L., L. Culter, and T. Strathman, Physiologic changes after 20 weeks of isotonic vs isokinetic circuit training. *Journal of Sports Medicine and Physical Fitness,* 1980. 20: P. 265-274.

[14] Kindermann, W., et al., Catecholamines, growth hormone, cortisol, insulin, and ex hormones in anaerobic and aerobic exercise. *European Journal of Applied Physiology,* 1982. 49: P. 389-399.

[15] Neiss, R., Expectancy in motor behaviour: A crucial element of the psychobiological states that affect performance. *Human Performance,* 1989. 2: P. 273-300.

[16] Weinberg, R., D. Gould, and A. Jackson, Cognition And motor performance: Effect of psyching-up strategies on three motor tasks. *Cognitive Therapy and Research,* 1980. 4: P. 239-245.

[17] Crust, L. and K. Azadi, Mental toughness and athletes' use of psychological strategies. *European Journal of Sport Science,* 2010. 10: P. 43-51.

[18] Brooks, K. And K. Brooks, Difference in Wingate power output in response to music as motivation. *Journal of Exercise Physiology Online,* 2010. 13: P. 14-20.

[19] Zinsser, N., L. Bunker, and J. Williams, Cognitive techniques for building confidence and enhancing performance, In *Applied sport psychology: Personal Growth to peak performance.* J. Williams, Editor. 2010, Mcgraw Hill: New York.

[20] Seligman, M., Learned optimism. 1991, New York: *Knopf.*

[21] Murphy, S., S. Nordin, and J. Cumming, Imagery in sport, exercise, and dance, In *Advances in sport psychology* T. Horn, Editor. 2008, Human Kinetics: Champaign, Il. P. 297-324.

[22] Muehlbauer, T. and C. Schindler, Relationship between starting and finishing position in short track speed skating races. *European Journal of Sports Science,* 2011. 11: P. 225-230.

[23] Muehlbauer, T., C. Schindler, and S. Panzer, Pacing and sprint performance in speed skating during a competitive season. *International Journal of Sports Physiology and Performance,* 2010. 5: P. 165-176.

[24] Amann, M. and J. Dempsey, Locomotor muscle fatigue modifies central motor drive in healthy humans and imposes a limitation to exercise performance. *Journal of Physiology,* 2008. 586.1: P. 161-173.

[25] St Clair Gibson, A. and T. Noakes, Evidence for complex system integration and dynamic neural regulation of skeletal muscle recruitment during exercise in humans. *British Journal of Sports Medicine,* 2004. 38: P. 797-806.

[26] Fuglevand, A. and D. Keen, Re-evaluation of muscle wisdom in the human adductor pollicis using physiological rates of stimulation. *Journal of Physiology,* 2003. 549.3: P. 865-875.

[27] Herbert, R. and S. Gandevia, Muscle activation in unilateral and bilateral efforts assessed by motor nerve and cortical stimulation. *Journal of Applied Physiology,* 1996. 80: P. 1351-1356.

[28] Ikai, M. and A. Steinhaus, Some factors modifying the expression of human strength. *Journal of Applied Physiology,* 1961. 16: P. 157-163.

[29] Noakes, T., A. St Clair Gibson, and E. Lambert, From catastrophe to complexity: A novel model of integrative central neural regulation of effort and fatigue during exercise in humans: Summary and conclusions. *British Journal of Sports Medicine,* 2005. 39: P. 120-124.

[30] Zajac, A., R. Jarzabek, and Z. Waskiewicz, The diagnostic value of the 10- and 30-second Wingate test for competitive athletes. *Journal of Strength and Conditioning Research,* 1999. 13: P. 16-19.

[31] Bar-Or, O., The Wingate anaerobic test: An update on methodology, reliability, and validity. *Sports Medicine,* 1987. 4: P. 381-394.

[32] Chasiotis, D., M. Bergstrom, and E. Hultman, ATP utilization and force during intermittent and continuous muscle contractions. *Journal of Applied Physiology,* 1987. 63: P. 167-174.

[33] Whaley, M., et al., ACSM's guidelines for exercise testing and prescription. 7th Ed. 2006, Philadelphia: *Lippincott Williams & Wilkins.*

[34] Wolfe, B., L. Lemura, and P. Cole, Quantitative analysis of single- vs. multiple-set programs in resistance training. *Journal of Strength and Conditioning Research,* 2004. 18: P. 35-47.

[35] Hatfield, D., et al., The impact of velocity of movement on performance factors in resistance exercise. *Journal of Strength and Conditioning Research,* 2006. 20: P. 760-766.

[36] Hunter, G., D. Seelhorst, and S. Snyder, Comparison of metabolic and heart rate responses to super slow vs. traditional resistance training. *Journal of Strength and Conditioning Research,* 2003. 17: P. 76-81.

[37] Kraemer, W. and N. Ratamess, Fundamentals of resistance training: progression and exercise prescription. *Medicine & Science in Sports & Exercise,* 2004. 36: P. 674-688.

[38] Flueck, M. and W. Eilers, Training modalities: Impact on endurance capacity. *Endocrinology and Metabolism Clinics of North America* 2010. 39: P. 183-200.

[39] Fleck, S. and W. Kraemer, The ultimate training system: Periodization breakthrough. 1996, New York: *Advanced Research Press.*

[40] Glass, S. and D. Stanton, Self-selected resistance training intensity in novice weightlifters. *Journal of Strength and Conditioning Research,* 2004. 18: P. 324-327.

[41] Fleck, S., Periodized strength training: A critical review. *Journal of Strength and Conditioning Research,* 1999. 13: P. 82-89.

[42] Ratamess, N., et al., Self-selected resistance training intensity in healthy women: The influence of a personal trainer. *Journal of Strength and Conditioning Research,* 2008. 22: P. 103-111.

[43] Braith, R., et al., Effect of training on the relationship between maximal and submaximal strength. *Medicine & Science in Sports & Exercise,* 1993. 25: P. 132-138.

[44] Lagally, K., et al., Ratings of perceived exertion and muscle activity during the bench press exercise in recreational and novice lifters. *Journal of Strength and Conditioning Research,* 2004. 18: P. 359-364.

[45] Day, M., et al., Monitoring exercise intensity during resistance training using the session RPE scale, *Journal of Strength and Conditioning Research,* 2004. 18: P. 353-358.

[46] Chen, M., X. Fan, and S. Moe, Criterion-related validity of the Borg ratings of perceived exertion scale in healthy individuals: A meta-analysis. *Journal of Sports Sciences,* 2002. 20: P. 873-899.

[47] Young, G., et al., Ratings of perceived exertion and muscle activity during resistance exercise in trained and untrained women. *Medicine & Science in Sports & Exercise,* 2002. 34: P. S153.

[48] Focht, B., Influence of resistance exercise of different intensities on state anxiety and blood pressure. *Medicine & Science in Sports & Exercise,* 1999. 31: P. 456-463.

[49] ACSM, ACSM's guidelines for exercise testing and prescription 6th Edition Ed. 2000: *Lippincott Williams and Wilkins.*

[50] Focht, B., Pre-exercise anxiety and the anxiolytic responses to acute bouts of self-selected and prescribed intensity resistance exercise. *Journal of Sports Medicine and Physical Fitness,* 2002. 42: P. 217-223.

[51] Mazzetti, S., et al., The influence of direct supervision of resistance training on strength performance. *Medicine & Science in Sports & Exercise,* 2000. 32: P. 1175-1184.

Chapter 7

PACING FOR TEAM SPORTS

7.1. ABSTRACT

Team sports such as invasion games require complex movement patterns, frequent changes in pace and considerable endurance. As such, physiological and psychological responses to these activities have been sources of fascination for many years. The purpose of this chapter is therefore to examine whether or not the principles of pacing apply to team game situations. Until recently, fatigue in invasion games was attributed to several individual physiological or psychological factors such as blood lactate accumulation, glycogen depletion, dehydration, motivation and so on. However, as suggested elsewhere this book, it seems likely that a psychophysiological system regulates the physical capabilities of each individual within the team. This chapter will examine the requirements of team sports, evidence for self-pacing within a team context and apply the principles of self-regulation as a practical means of devising and monitoring the training of team sport athletes.

7.2. INTRODUCTION

Team sports present an intriguing set of physical and psychological challenges for competitors. Team sports can cover a broad range of activities such as 2 vs. 2 net games like beach volleyball, to 15 vs. 15 rugby union games. There are generic demands of these activities such as cooperative team play, team strategy, and, of course, sensations of fatigue specific to each activity. As there is such a large range of games, the focus of this chapter will examine invasion-type games such as hockey, rugby, netball and soccer. The predominant sports science research area within team sports appears to lie within the sport of soccer and consequently substantial parts of this chapter relate heavily to this sport.

The occurrence of fatigue in team sports is of considerable interest and debate [1-3]. Until recently, the theory of terminal (i.e. depletion/system capacity) fatigue has been proposed within various individual physiological systems [1, 2, 4] although data do not consistently support such observations [5]. The principle of a psychophysiological system which controls physical capabilities appears applicable to all types of exercise including team games. This does not diminish the importance of each physiological system providing negative afferent sensations which alert the brain to homeostatic threats. It merely indicates that the ultimate form of performance regulation is performed by the brain at either consciously aware (when negative sensations are so severe as to reach conscious awareness) or sub aware (when sensations are within normal homeostatic range the response/regulation is automated) levels. This means individuals are able to regulate (self-pace) their own performance across a match. This is a process informed by knowledge of the activity (e.g. match demands, duration and its importance), in addition to various forms of feedback sensations such as lethargy, soreness, pain, nausea, and thirst. The combined regulation of these factors is a psychophysiological process controlled by the brain.

7.3. MATCH DEMANDS

Invasion games require movements described as variable, random, acyclical and intermittent [6]. In sports such as netball, players change activity approximately every 4.1s while also covering significant distances across a game [7]. Distances covered vary with field position such that the Centre position players cover greater distances (7984m) than Goal Shooters (4210m) and Goal Keepers (4283m) [7]. In rugby union, positional group comparisons indicate that the greatest differences exist between forwards and backs such that the activity profiles of performers within the same team cover a vast array of activities [8]. It is particularly difficult to generalize physiological observations of exercise intensity to the whole team in rugby. Forwards typically perform significant strength and power activities when rucking or scrummaging, while backs spend considerable time working aerobically until called upon to make tackles or intermittently accelerate at discreet times within the game [8].

There are also differences in distances covered and activity profiles between positions in a soccer team [9]. Midfielders are the most frequently engaged in sustained low to moderate intensity activity during competition, covering distances of 9-13km in a single match [10]. They are also less likely to be stationary than other outfield players [10] and this is a consistent movement pattern across similar sports such as hockey and netball [7, 11]. Forwards in soccer, on the other hand, perform more maximal sprints for longer duration than midfielders and defenders [6]. Defenders in turn perform more backward movements. Such backward (and lateral) movements are associated with 20-40% higher energy expenditure than forward running [12]. This is also true for a number of other soccer related activities like slide tackling, powerful heading, and long passing [5]. Again, player position influences these game behaviours. Strikers and centre backs are significantly more engaged in situations where they have to jump or are required to head the ball whereas defenders tend to make more tackles [12]. Furthermore, an added exertional cost when dribbling a soccer ball has been reported at 5.2 kJ·min-1 [12], although most players are only in possession of the ball for 2-5% of the total game time [13].

Approximately 80-90% of performance in invasion games is generally spent in low to moderate intensity activity and 10-20% in high intensity activities [14]. Match play intensity of effort broadly appears consistent with the individual's heart rate attained in tests of anaerobic threshold. This is similar across invasion games such as both rugby codes, hockey, netball and soccer [6-8, 11]. This is also consistent with activities requiring substantial aerobic energy metabolism for prolonged periods, although clearly there are intermittent requirements in all games for bursts of anaerobic energy.

In soccer, it has been reported that between 1000 and 1500 discrete movement changes occur within each match at a rate of every 5-6s, having a pause of 3s every 2min [12, 15]. Using relatively broad based categories research suggests that in top-class level, Danish soccer players stand 19.5%, walk 41.8%, jog 16.7%, run 16.8%, sprint 1.4%, and do other activities 3.7% of the time [4]. In the FA Premier League soccer players conduct a mean number of 19 sprints within match-play which occurs every 4- 5min (e.g. [16]) and there is an average change in activity every 3.5s. A bout of high-intensity activity occurs every 60s, and a maximal effort every 4 minutes [15].

7.4. PACING FOR TEAM SPORTS

It has previously been suggested that the development of fatigue in team sports may be causally linked with physiological factors such dehydration, hydrogen ion accumulation, potassium imbalance and substrate depletion [2, 5]. However, laboratory-based investigations have not found any single factor or combination of factors that could definitively explain fatigue during match play [5]. This is not surprising when viewed from the perspective of psychophysiological control. For example, well-trained team sport players do not reach core temperatures considered critical [17], they lose relatively modest amounts of body fluids across most match-play conditions (e.g. approx. 1-2% of body mass) [18] and are able to regulate metabolite concentration such as blood lactate (at approx. 3-4 mmol/L) and effort at sustainable levels for the match duration [7, 8, 11, 17].

It is well established that the distances covered by team sport players and the intensity of physical work declines from the first to second half of a match across outfield positions [3, 5]. For example, a second half drop of ~5-10% has been reported in elite and recreational soccer [4]. When considered in isolation, this could suggest that either accumulative fatigue is a feature of match play or perhaps that there is a defined pacing strategy in place with which to self-regulate match performance.

In games such as rugby, soccer and hockey, longer sprints (e.g. 30m) demand markedly longer recovery than the average sprints (10 – 15m) during a game [3, 8, 11]. This suggests that fatigue occurs both acutely during the game (momentary sensations of fatigue) and also as a developing, accumulative feature of prolonged intermittent exercise [3]. Nevertheless, as discussed earlier, despite numerous attempts, no researchers have identified a precise cause of fatigue in team sports [1, 2, 4, 13].

Relatively few studies have examined the influence of pacing as an explanation of reduced work outputs in team sports [3]. This is presumably due to the difficulties in identifying an appropriate model that adequately represents the complex movement patterns and the unpredictable energetic demands of game play. However, as described in chapter two, Edwards and Noakes [3] recently proposed that a multi-level psychophysiological pacing plan may be in place during match play. This model suggests that players modulate effort according to a pacing strategy based on both pre-match (e.g., prior experience in similar circumstances, fitness levels, match importance) and dynamic considerations during a game (skin temperature, accumulation of metabolites in the muscles, plasma osmolality, and substrate availability).

Players' perception of a developing cellular homeostatic disturbance evokes behavioural changes, such as choosing to cover an opponent's movement rather than performing a more energetic interception when momentarily tired. This type of pacing is an individual response and enables the athlete to avoid unsustainable elevations in physical discomfort at a premature stage of a match.

During a game, each 'all-out' sprint is likely to be paced in relation to an overall pacing plan [3]. This inevitably means that all match-play sprints will be slower than non-match 'one-off' sprints, with fewer (or slower) sprints performed while there is a sustained threat to homeostasis. This results in muscle power output being continuously modified in relation to an overall pacing strategy [19]. Consequently, significant feedback to the brain evokes a behavioural decision either to employ a temporary reduction from vigorous work when tired, or to maintain a continuation at a similar level if the peripheral physiological information does not reach such severity that the brain perceives that a gross change in effort compromises the pacing strategy.

The model proposed by Edwards and Noakes [3] indicates that the physical responses of team sport players in a match all conform to an individualised homeostatic set point theory, yet within the context of a generic (across all outfield positions) pacing strategy operating at three connected levels (Figure 7.1). It was proposed that the main (meta) pacing strategy of each player is to reach the conclusion of a match having physically worked at a vigorous, yet sustainable level of performance. This level corresponds to the maintenance of tolerable physical discomfort the player is pre-prepared to endure for the match. Homeostatic processes subsequently serve a protective function, informing the brain of how the strategy is working. The characteristics of the multi level pacing plan for team sports are shown in Table 7.1.

According to this model, the brain initiates a strategy at the start of a match, based on both the knowledge of the duration of the game and prior experience [20, 21]. Prior experience explains the sport-specific fitness observations of both greater total and higher intensity work by experienced players [6], despite similarities in aerobic capabilities with less experienced players [17]. Other factors considered within the overall (meta) pacing decision include variables such as current environmental conditions, health status, and metabolic fuel reserves [22]. All these factors mediate changes in pre-match decisions over the precise regulatory level of physical discomfort each player is willing to endure, for themselves and for the team.

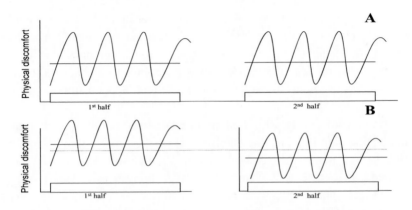

Figure 7.1. Multi level model of pacing in team sports. (A) represents a schematic view of the 'meta' pacing strategy pre-set by each player at the start of the match. The horizontal line represents exercise homeostasis (tolerable discomfort) the player expects to endure during the game. The oscillations represent the dynamic (micro) pacing strategy to release energy and sustainable effort in relation to the long term objectives. (B) represents the meso pacing strategy (first and second halves of the match). The second half level is down regulated from the first half, although the mean of the two (dotted line) broadly equates to the expectations of the player. Taken with permission [3].

Table 7.1. A summary of characteristics within the multi-level pacing model in elite team sport activities

Pacing strategies	Purpose and characteristics
Macro pacing	Overall pacing plan for the match. A subconsciously pre-conceived strategy based around a set point of tolerable physical discomfort expected over the duration of the game.
Meso pacing	Inter-half pacing plan. This variation from the macro plan enables up-and down-regulation of effort during a match based on tactical and specific match considerations.
Micro pacing	Dynamic pacing plan. This strategy enables the player to evaluate the impact of acute periods of intense exercise on the set point strategies. For example, a prolonged sprint late in a game may require an extended recovery to protect homeostasis.

A regulatory level of tolerable physical discomfort (exercise homeostasis) within the meta-pacing strategy would also be affected by extrinsic factors such as the importance of the occasion, future game commitments, formations of team play, and tactical strategies. However, the dynamics of activity during a game mean that not all aspects of the players overall pacing strategy can simply be pre-determined and must be free to vary. Consequently, while the regulatory (tolerable physical discomfort) set point represents a behaviourally 'defended' level of homeostasis, factors such as the quality of the opposition, crowd support, match score, tactical and positional considerations mean that players may or may not reach this level. These factors require the presence of additional intra-match pacing strategies to support the main plan of reaching the end of the match without experiencing total system failure and remain within the pre-set expectations of the individual player.

While this is mostly a theoretical perspective, evidence of pacing within a game can be identified by re-examining existing data from the perspective of central (brain) regulation [23]. For example, Ekblom [23] first identified heart rate dynamics during a game and, on close inspection of those data, it seems clear that match-play heart rates oscillate in a non-random pattern (Figure 7.2). Each heart rate peak is rapidly followed by a sudden and substantial drop beneath a sustained mean rate. This is consistent with match-play video analysis [4] in which longer sprints and greater periods of sustained effort require prolonged (yet temporary) periods of recovery [2]. Consistent evidence across team sports supports the observation that exercise heart rates are regulated at a higher level earlier in a game as a consequence of performing more work [3, 7, 11]. This is both non-random and predictable. Players consciously seek temporary tactical alternatives to maximal work when homeostasis is threatened and this occurs to a greater extent later in a game. The regulation of effort enables the player to manage important metabolic factors such as blood lactate accumulation at a relatively constant level (Figure 7.2) [23] and thus avoid an unsustainable change in any one physiological system.

The presence of a dynamic pacing strategy (micro pacing) in team sports protects the integrity of the longer term aim of the player (macro pacing) to finish the match in a reasonable condition. This is probably functioning at three levels such as 1) the macro plan to finish the game at the level of physical discomfort considered acceptable to the player (i.e. depending on the importance of the game etc.), 2) the meso plan, whereby the player re-evaluates the game at half-time in consideration of tactical changes, match score and review of physical responses to the 1st half, and 3) the micro plan whereby continual movement stresses with a game are performed as necessary, but also in relation to the overall macro plan to finish the entire game at a level of physical discomfort considered appropriate by the individual.

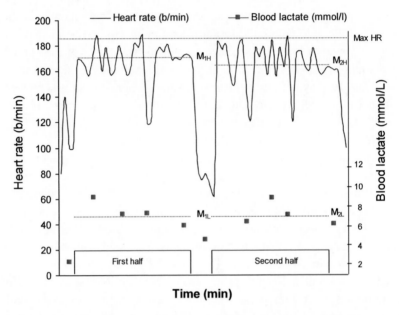

Figure 7.2. An example of soccer match-play pacing strategy in operation. M_{1H} and M_{2H} = mean of first and second half heart rates, respectively. The difference between M_{1H} and M_{2H} lines demonstrate the down regulation of heart rate in the second half of match play. M_{1L} and M_{2L} = mean of first and second half blood lactate concentrations, respectively. Blood pH is a defended variable and consequently blood lactate does not demonstrate substantial change between halves of the match. Taken with permission [3].

The team sport pacing strategy therefore connects both meso and macro strategies with a micro strategy to enable frequent bursts of effort in relation to the overall plan. It is therefore with consideration to the longer term objectives that a player will only expend maximal effort at any one time during the match if it is consistent with the objectives of the meso and macro pacing strategies. Where the match play requirements incur a prolonged threat to homeostasis, the player will require extended recovery to reduce the intracellular threat and so will consciously seek tactical alternatives to short-term high-intensity efforts. As such, players performing either a long sprint, or a rapid series of high intensity activities should be expected to seek extended opportunities to minimise energy expenditure as has been observed in motion analysis of match play (e.g. [4, 6, 10, 24]. This multi-level pacing strategy for team sports requires further exploration utilising a combination of heart rates, movement analysis and regular intra-match evaluations of perceived exertion.

7.5. PREPARATORY PSYCHOLOGICAL SKILLS FOR TEAM SPORTS

As a coach, it is crucial to prepare a team mentally for upcoming competition. A difficulty is that athletes are all different and that a motivational strategy which might work for one athlete might not work for another. Psychological self-regulatory skills training would prepare the players to have the ability to self-control their behaviours in difficult or adverse situations during competition. Prior to the match, the coach's main role is to get the team in the appropriate frame of mind as players have to believe in their ability, be at the right arousal levels and be able to concentrate optimally for the upcoming event [25]. Having an established routine is an important way to prepare the athletes. For example, gathering at a particular time and place prior to the match and having a meal together will increase familiarity and therefore take away unnecessary uncertainty and anxiety. It is not uncommon for coaches to place slogans or mottos on the wall of the dressing room. These can help athletes to get motivated and create the appropriate atmosphere. Again, creating a routine is important. The warm up should be familiar to the players and be structured in the same way for each competition. In the dressing room, music (for the group as a whole or using individual music players) can be used to regulate arousal levels. The coach, prior to the competition, has the ability through pre-performance talk to inspire, motivate and arouse the players. This is probably not the time for long tactical considerations but a well executed team-talk can help athletes to get in the right frame of mind. On the whole, familiarity and having a routine are probably the key ingredients of successful preparation.

In common with physical training, some psychological skills are more important than others during particular phases of the competitive season. In addition, some training phases will make it more difficult to acquire certain psychological skills. For example, learning to relax or use of imagery or mental practice might be difficult in the pre-season when athletes engage in heavy training sessions which result in high sustained levels of fatigue and muscle soreness. When engaging in imagery, kinesthetic feedback received from the muscles is likely to be very different following these training sessions than during other phases of the season and might result in receiving conflicting information limiting the usefulness of this technique [26, 27] That said, it would be extremely useful for athletes if they are able to appropriately use muscular relaxation techniques during the pre-season. Such techniques may help the athlete speed up the recovery process and indirectly help with other behaviours like sleep or diet. As such, when integrating the learning of psychological skills in a macro training cycle, coaches should be aware of the different needs and demands during a season. Careful planning and allowing athletes to master the psychological skill in dedicated sessions or integrated into physical training sessions before using them in competitive situations will allow athletes to raise their performance. If each athlete in a team improved performance by 1% through the mastery of psychological skills this could have a significant effect on the performance of the team as a whole.

The integration or training of psychological skills may also benefit from periodization [26, 27]. Coaches and athletes often only consider mental skill training programmes when there is some sort of performance slump. In the desperation to find a solution, sport psychologists are often engaged by sports clubs as a last resort to improve performance. In these cases, there might be a short-term placebo effect whereby the athletes expect the psychological intervention to improve performance and therefore for a short while it does. However, as soon as the novelty wears off, athletes drop back to previous performance levels [28] Therefore a systematic approach to mental skill training is warranted.

There are facilitative psychological skills which are beneficial throughout the athletes career and life in general (e.g. lifestyle management, media skills and interpersonal or communication skills). There are also psychological skills which are more basic in nature but essential for optimal functioning. These include motivation, self-awareness, self-esteem, self-confidence and inter-personal skills [29]. Finally, there are so called performance skills or skills which are likely to help the athlete to improve performance. These are skills which help with the self-regulation of arousal and affect (e.g. breathing, progressive muscular relaxation, meditation), self-regulation of attention (e.g. concentration training, goal-setting, imagery) and self-efficacy (e.g. modeling)[29].

Psychological factors and skills also play an important role in optimizing training programmes, recovery and maximizing performance. Performance profiling can be deployed in team sports, similarly to other contexts, and can include physiological, biomechanical and psychological aspects [30]. Performance profiling allows for the integration of the team and individual needs and development of training programmes which cater for both these requirements. If conducted correctly performance profiling for teams can have the same psychological benefits as for individual athletes and allow for a systematic approach to training programmes and assessment of progress. Research suggest that athletes experience a more open atmosphere of communication following performance profiling and feel appreciated for their input in determining nature of the training programme [31].

Situational constraints play an important role in the development of psychological skills. However, following a defeat or poor performance, coaches or athletes seldom report that they were not sufficiently physically prepared for the completion [32]. More often than not poor performance or a game lost is attributed to a lack of concentration or lack of motivation. Mastery of psychological skills will allow a reduction in fluctuation in mental states and therefore increase control over performance. Any good training programme at the macro, meso and micro level will include some form of development of psychological factors [33, 34].

7.6. TRAINING FOR TEAM SPORTS

Classical models of periodization do not fit well with the preparation of athletes for team sports [35]. Periodization was originally developed for track athletes to prepare for a small number of major championships a year [36] and is difficult to apply within a team sport context where regular fixtures of equal importance occur continually across a season. In seasonal team sports, high-quality performances are routinely expected 1-2 times a week and therefore a training plan in which performance is developed towards a single peak is not useful. For sports like basketball, rugby and soccer, the season can span in excess of 25-30 weeks. If coaches were to follow a traditional (linear) periodization model, this would mean tapering training towards a specific target outcome (e.g. a cup final) to the likely detriment of routine match play. These factors reinforce the unique challenges faced by coaches when designing training for team sports. However this does not mean that team sports cannot utilize a training system of periodization, but rather than the model should be non-linear, whereby discreet periods of the competitive season (mesocycles) identify different aspects of training for greater emphasis [35]. Therefore, basic conditioning remains intact by using non-linear periodization while particular attention can be given to aspects of conditioning considered of greatest importance at that time by the coach. This is likely to relate to issues such as addressing accumulative fatigue during the season with lighter loads and making amendments to training, or conversely identification of periods in the schedule where additional conditioning work can be conducted without impediment to short or long term performances.

Team sports require several disparate training goals, including metabolic physical conditioning, muscular strength and power development, whilst also trying to prevent injury [37]. Due to the diverse demands and complex mix of physical requirements for team sports, much of what is known about the design of effective training is experiential. However, in recent years, the emergence of sports science and scientifically-informed professional coaching certifications (such as UEFA coaching certifications in soccer) has standardized approaches to training and created more of a culture of shared professional experiences. Nevertheless, considerable divergence of opinion remains within applied coaching practice concerning the optimal design of training for team sports. It is perhaps the case that successful training methods can be confused and/or associated with successful teams regardless of the merits of the training regime. It is quite possible for a team to achieve success in spite of their training methods due to effective match-day strategy and positive characteristics of the playing squad. In addition, wealthy owners of some professional sports clubs are able to regularly purchase the services of highly sought after elite players which may, in some cases, cover deficiencies in the design of team training. Consequently the notion of simply adopting training routines already utilized by successful teams is probably naive and is certainly unscientific. However; the development of professional coaching practice for team sports has seen an increase of sport scientists among the support team of elite sports clubs. The combination of skilled sports coaches and sports scientists may assist in the development of rigor and systematic approaches to the design and monitoring of training.

For the purpose of designing and implementing a training regime for team sports, the training year can generally be viewed as comprising three main parts: 1) Pre-season 2) Competitive season, and 3) Off-season.

Much of the developmental physical conditioning work of team sport athletes is accomplished in the pre-season period [38]. Pre-season training enables coaches to prescribe training practices that would be impractical during the competitive season due to the regularity of matches [35]. Consequently, pre-season training represents the only realistic opportunity to utilise training techniques with the aim of improving squad-wide fitness in situations other than match play. However, despite its importance to the conditioning of players, few published studies have reported typical activities comprising the pre-season training period for team sports. This is surprising as it is well known physical conditioning can be improved following systematic training [39], that players' fitness tends to decline over the course of a season [40] and that fitness fluctuates from season-to-season [40, 41]. Pre-season training is therefore widely regarded as a crucial preparatory phase for professional team sport players [38]. A poorly designed pre-season training programme can also have negative consequences and result in players being overexerted physically and mentally thereby reducing performance levels and increasing susceptibility to injury [42, 43].

The training stimulus utilised during the pre-season phase is a key consideration for maximising potential physiological adaptations and developing technical/tactical team skills. As this is a relatively brief but crucial period, there is a strong temptation to apply heavy loads to this phase of training. However, this could be counterproductive as an abrupt introduction to high intensity activities immediately following the off-season period could lead to injuries [44]. Injuries incurred during pre-season training may subsequently affect players' contributions over the upcoming competitive season. Interestingly, a study of Rugby League players [44] demonstrated that injury rates were lower in the subsequent season when pre-season training loads were reduced from normal levels. This has implications for the design of pre-season training such that the blend of activities is sufficiently stimulating to engender physiological adaptation but not so severe as to pose significant risk of soft tissue injury or illness. As a consequence, expected gains from intense physical work in the pre-season phase must be weighed against maintaining a fit and healthy squad of players over the season. Hence, a recent study demonstrated that excessive training volume, number of pre-season matches and the shortness of recovery periods affected professional rugby union athletes diet, sleep and resulted in them experiencing significant stress and negative affective states [42]. Whereas an excessive reduction of the training stimulus may compromise performance an overly intense load may expose players to elevated risk of injury or illness [44-46].

During the competitive season, the main aims are to ensure players are in sufficient physical condition to perform to their capabilities in each match. Therefore, the training programme within the competitive season must facilitate both adequate post-match recovery, and a sufficient training stimulus to ensure match to match residual fitness is not diminished. This requires careful planning, coupled with a robust system for monitoring the training load and individual responses to it [34, 35]. It is still possible to adopt a periodization approach to training in team sports, but this may be best described as non-linear periodization whereby the stimulus undulates and is acutely varied [47]. Therefore, training can still conform to an overall (macrocycle) plan, separated into distinct phases (mesocycles) for changes of training emphasis across the season, and small discreet periods of specific match-preparation (microcycles).

Reilly [38] suggested monitoring of performance and fitness attributes should be assessed through observational characteristics of routine soccer performance such as work rate analysis of training and match-play and that fitness work should be holistically integrated into coach sport-based training rather than conducted as an isolated component. In this regard, sports science support is best placed as an integrated component of planned *training* rather than additionally imposed *testing* activities. Additional testing activities in a congested playing season can severely disrupt match preparations. Consequently, the design of training sessions can best be accomplish by liaison between sports coaching and sports science staff to ensure satisfactory outcomes are attained. A system of logging the intensity and responses to training can easily be accomplished with prior planning.

The session-RPE method identified in earlier chapters of this book (e.g. see chapter four) is well suited to designing and monitoring responses to training for team sports [34]. In this system, each type of training session can be allocated a session-RPE training load, regardless of its diversity and a target training session intensity identified, based on a pre-determined RPE (e.g. pre-set the expectation of intensity for the session as RPE 7/10: very hard). All prospective training sessions can be logged in a series of categorical tables for the coaches to integrate into the training plan to ensure balance is attained. Thereafter, the training schedule can be assembled into the specific order of mesocycles considered appropriate by the coach across the season (or pre-season) so to maintain the required cyclic (e.g. weekly) training load.

Examples of training-type sessions for team sports are provided in this chapter for reference purposes only. These are intended to identify the practicalities of the self-regulatory system rather than providing a prescriptive training schedule for all team sports. It is therefore an example of how the system might work rather than a unilateral blueprint. Nevertheless, the advantage of this system is fairly obvious in so far as it enables quantification of cyclic training load when setting a balanced training programme, it facilitates a simple system to adjust week to week training loads where needed, it provides a mechanism to check players responses to training, and also facilitates variation in training stimulus via use of different session options to achieve the required training load. Modifications to load can therefore be considered by the coaching team depending on observable responses of individuals in the squad and objective performance outcomes.

The example training schedule for team sport players has been derived from allocating different types of training into categorical tables across an eight week pre-season training period. Only weeks 1-2 and 7-8 are included for the purpose of demonstration.

Table 7.2 contains examples of interval training (Int) sessions coaches may use as a strategy in the pre-season phase when developing repeat sprint skills. Table 7.3 captures several small sided game (SSG) activities which could be constructed in accordance with the requirements of the coaches. The exact formatting and manipulations of time, pitch dimensions and rules are likely to be specific to the coach. In this example, session durations have been estimated for different game situations from the authors' soccer experiences and also, from manipulations of team size such that 3 vs.3 games can be developed into 6 vs. 6 games and so on. Session RPE scores can easily be developed in this way from duration x RPE calculations as with all other types of training (see chapters five-six for other examples). Table 7.4 contains skill based training (SBT). Table 7.5 is intended for occasions where the coach may wish to set continuous run sessions (CON), such as for post-match active recovery purposes to dissipate muscle metabolite accumulation. Table 7.6 is included as a store of strength and conditioning sessions (SCT).

As team sports differ from other sports by requiring regular performances of matches, it is important that an estimate of match demands is also captured in the cyclic training load. For the purpose of this example, competitive and non-competitive matches have been included (Table 7.7). The training schedule (Table 7.8) for team sports captures all activities relevant to the holistic training process, including fitness training, match play, skill based activities and tactical sessions.

To appropriately estimate the accumulative load of all session-RPE scores in each week, it is important for the team coach to consider the maximal weekly session-RPE score that would ever realistically be prescribed in any single week. As with the endurance and power, strength, speed examples, this estimate therefore becomes the 100% maximum with which training load intensity categories can be developed (Table 7.9). In this case, the maximal load has been estimated to be a score of 2400. Thereafter, 5 zones have been identified to provide categorical information of intensity levels. From the example, week 1 is regarded as a moderate training load (Table 7.10), whereas week 2 is a 'hard' week's training.

Table 7.2. Preliminary profiling of interval training (Int) sessions

Session		Duration	Intensity option (Low)			Intensity option (High)	
Name	Detail		RPE (L)	Session-RPE (L)	RPE (H)	Session-RPE (H)	
Int_1	Sprint drills with active recovery	30min	5	150	8	240	
Int_2	10 x 100m	35min	5	175	8	280	
Int_3	8 x 200m	40min	5	200	8	320	
Int_6	8 x 400m	45min	5	225	8	360	
Int_7	4 x 800m	45min	5	225	8	360	
Int_8	2(500m, 400m, 300m, 200m, 100m)	60min	5	300	8	480	
Int_9	800m, 600m, 400m, 200m	60min	5	300	8	480	

For sprint & team game athletes it is common to train in groups and consequently it is appropriate to manage interval sessions by using a fixed duration of inter-repetition recovery (e.g. as set by the coach) for the group. Individuals are therefore able to self-pace the repetitive bouts according to their needs, based on their knowledge of the recovery durations and the overall session demands. The duration of recovery periods (e.g. 2, 3, 4 or 5 min) will manipulate the performance outcomes (e.g. so that faster performance times will occur in response to longer known recovery periods) and therefore the coach will need to determine the optimal duration of recovery for the training period (e.g. within the mesocycle). The session-RPE will need to be adjusted accordingly. For example, the high intensity session Int_3, with a 2 min inter-repetition recovery (6 recovery periods in that session) is estimated as 45 min x 8 = 360 session-RPE. Changing the session to use a 3 min inter-repetition recovery will add 6 min to the session duration (and therefore become more intense due to the expected gains in pace as a consequence of greater known inter-repetition recovery); therefore the revised session would be: 51 x 8 = 408 session-RPE. Interval training may also be useful OCCASIONALLY for the purpose of deception as a means to override brain regulatory control and experience greater than usual metabolic disturbance. This would mean adding an additional repetition with no prior warning on completion of the last bout in the interval series. Note: overuse of this strategy may lead to athletes retaining an extra reserve of energy in anticipation of it, therefore reducing the quality of all subsequent interval training sessions.

Table 7.3. Preliminary profiling of small-sided games (SSG)

Session		Intensity option (Low)			Intensity option (High)		
Name	Detail	Duration	Session-RPE	Session-RPE (Load)	Duration	Session-RPE	Session-RPE (Load)
SSG_1	2 vs. 2 to 4 vs. 4	15min	9	135	25min	9	225
SSG_2	3 vs. 3 to 6 vs. 6	15min	9	135	25min	9	225
SSG_3	5 vs. 5	20min	9	180	30min	9	270
SSG_4	6 vs. 4 to 4 vs. 6	20min	8	160	30min	8	240
SSG_5	8 vs. 6 to 6 vs. 8	20min	7	140	35min	7	280
SSG_6	8 vs. 8	25min	7	175	40min	7	280
SSG_7	9 vs. 9 to 11 vs. 11	30min	6	180	40min	6	240

SSGs in this programme are designed to interchange between team sizes within a given session. For example, a 2 vs. 2 game may develop into a 4 vs. 4 game depending on the requirements of the coach. The coach would vary the team dynamics, permitted/conditioned rules (e.g. 2 x touch play) and the pitch dimensions to achieve the required intensity and purpose.

Table 7.4. Preliminary profiling of skill-based training (SBT)

	Session		Session-RPE	
Name	Detail	Duration	RPE	Session-RPE (Load)
SBT_1	Team formation and game practice	20min	4	80
SBT_2	Set piece direction	25min	3	75
SBT_3	Skill games (conditioned tasks)	30min	3	90

Table 7.5. Preliminary profiling of continuous-run sessions (CON)

Category	Type	Session Detail	Duration	Intensity option (Low) RPE (L)	Intensity option (Low) Session-RPE (L)	Intensity option (High) RPE (H)	Intensity option (High) Session-RPE (H)
Recovery run	RR$_1$	Easy run	20min	3	60	-	-
Recovery run	RR$_2$	Easy run	25min	3	75	-	-
Steady state	SS$_1$	Constant pace	30min	3	90	5	150
Tempo run	T$_1$	Variable pace	25min	4	100	7	175

Table 7.6. Preliminary profiling of strength and conditioning (SCT)

Category	Session Type	Detail	Duration	Intensity option (Low) RPE (L)	Intensity option (Low) Session-RPE (L)	Intensity option (High) RPE (H)	Intensity option (High) Session-RPE (H)
Weights (upper body)	W$_1$	4 sets of exercise (6-8 stations)	40min	6	240	7.5	300
Weights (lower body)	W$_2$	4 sets of exercise (6-8 stations)	40min	6	240	7.5	300
Weights (whole body)	W$_3$	3 sets of exercise (10 stations)	45min	6	270	7.5	300
Conditioning drills	CD$_1$	Power and speed activities	20min	-	-	7	280

Table 7.7. Match-play situations

Name	Session Detail	Duration	RPE	Session-RPE (Load)
MT_1	Competitive match	90min	7	630
MT_2	Non-competitive match	90min	6	540

Table 7.8. The training schedule and system for monitoring training load during the pre-season period of training (8 week programme)

Training phase	Week	Monday	Tuesday	Wednesday	Thursday	Friday	Saturday	Sunday	Session-RPE Weekly load
Mesocycle 1 (Pre-season – conditioning 1)	1	$T_1(L)$ & SBT_3	$SSG_6(H)$ & $W_1(L)$	$Int_7(H)$ & SBT_3	$SSG_7(L)$ & SBT_3	SBT_3 & SBT_2	$Int_9(H)$	Rest	
	Session-RPE	100 & 90	175 & 240	360 & 90	180 & 90	90 & 75	300	630	1790
	2	$SSG_5(L)$ & SBT_3	$Int_6(H)$ & SBT_2	$W_3(H)$ & $SSG_4(L)$	$SSG_3(L)$ & $T_1(H)$	SBT_1 & SBT_2	MT_2	Rest	
	Session-RPE	140 & 90	360 & 75	300 & 160	180 & 175	80 & 75	540	540	2175
Mesocycle 4 (Season – maintenance 1)	7	SBT_1 & $SSG_2(L)$	$W_3(L)$ & SBT_3	$SSG_4(L)$ & SBT_2	Rest	SBT_1 & SSG_2	MT_1	Rest	
	Session-RPE	80 & 135	270 & 90	160 & 75		80 & 135	630	630	1655
	8	RR_2 & SBT_3	$W_3(H)$ & SBT_3	$SSG_4(L)$ & $SBT2$	$SSG5(L)$ & CD_1	Rest	SBT_1 & SSG_2	MT_1	1900
	Session-RPE	60 & 90	300 & 90	160 & 75	140 & 140		80 & 135	630	

Note: Only weeks 1-2 and 7-8 have been included in this example. Training loads prescribed are clearly dependent on individual requirements and should not be considered generic across all sports codes and performance levels.

Table 7.9. Benchmarked descriptors and evaluation of training load

Weekly RPE-Load	% of maximum	Training Load Descriptor	Score
2160 - 2400	90-100	High	5
1920 - 2159	80-89	Moderate – high	4
1680 - 1919	70-79	Moderate	3
1440 - 1679	60-69	Low – moderate	2
<1439	50-59	Low	1

Table 7.10. Weekly training load and description, coupled with the athlete's self assessment of coping

Training week	Weekly RPE-Load	Training Load Descriptor	Athlete evaluation (1-5: Low–High)	Player self coping (0-10)
Week 1	1790	Moderate		
Week 2	2175	High		
Week 7	1655	Low-moderate		
Week 8	1900	Moderate		

This table is used to compare the weekly load with zoned descriptions. This information is coupled with individual players' retrospective (end of the week) perception of weekly load (Table 7.9) and their perception of coping with the prescribed load (0-10: not coping to maximal coping).

The session-RPE scores can also be used *ex post facto* to compare whether or not the athlete perceives the load similarly to the purpose for which it was prescribed. In Table 7.10, the athlete can score the weekly load from 1-5 (low-hard) and also provide a coping score (0-10 which is the athlete's view of their ability to cope with the training load). Coping scores outside of the usual reporting range for an athlete may identify potential problems with the load, possible illness, or other issues affecting the athlete. It is a practical means of facilitating regular feedback and matching the stimulus (training load) with the response of the athlete. All responses can be coupled with quantifiable performance and physiological outcomes to provide a thorough profile of the athlete.

7.7. PRACTITIONER COMMENT: TEAM SPORTS

The management of training load for a professional soccer team can be very challenging as variables such as fixture schedule, team selection and player fitness all have to be considered. It is vitally important therefore to ensure the training loads for players are individualised if they are to remain in optimum physical condition during the course of a season. General assessments of squad training load are insensitive to individual player needs and can actually be detrimental to a player's physical development.

A very practical and inexpensive method of monitoring an individual players training load is the use of RPE. Asking players to self report how hard they thought they exercised allows an exertion score (RPE x duration of session) to be assigned to the training session that is individual to that player. The collation of such data then allows the sport scientist to assess how hard each player is working in all the different areas of their physical training.

Alternative methods such as heart rate and GPS analysis are restricted to work done on the pitch, whereas RPE assessment of training load can be used for any mode of training, whether it be football, strength or sprint work, thus providing a holistic indicator of a players training load, which for a multi-faceted sport such as soccer is vital.

Dr Carl Wells. Sports Scientist, Sheffield Wednesday Football Club, UK

CONCLUSION

- Team sports are generally characterized as intermittent in nature requiring both aerobic and anaerobic energy systems.
- Match demands differ for players in different team positions. This suggests that training programmes need to be adapted to these individual demands.
- During competition more work is generally performed early on in the game with reductions in work-rate of 5-10% towards the end of the game.
- Team athletes appear to regulate their behaviour during the game based on the energetic demands. Longer periods of work are generally followed by longer periods of recovery.
- Because of the different physical demands throughout the season periodization of psychological skill training is required.
- Periodization for most team sport is likely to be non-linear. Discreet periods of the competitive season (mesocycles) requiring a focus on different aspects of training.
- Careful planning is required in order that players are in sufficient physical condition to perform to their capabilities in each match during the season. Therefore, the training programme within the competitive season must facilitate both adequate post-match recovery, and a sufficient training stimulus to ensure fitness is not diminished.
- Coaches can use the session-RPE method to design and monitor training for team sports.

REFERENCES

[1] Reilly, T., B. Drust, and N. Clarke, Muscle fatigue during football match-play. *Sports Medicine,* 2008. 38: p. 357-367.

[2] Mohr, M., P. Krustrup, and J. Bangsbo, Fatigue in soccer: a brief review. *Journal of Sports Sciences,* 2005. 23: p. 593-599.

[3] Edwards, A. and T. Noakes, Dehydration: cause of fatigue or sign of pacing in elite soccer? *Sports Medicine,* 2009. 39: p. 1-13.

[4] Mohr, M., P. Krustrup, and J. Bangsbo, Match performances of high-standard soccer players with special reference to the development of fatigue. *Journal of Sports Sciences,* 2003. 21: p. 519-528.

[5]   Bangsbo, J., The physiology of soccer – with special reference to intense intermittent exercise. *Acta Physiologica Scandinavica,* 1994. 15: p. 1-156.

[6]   Bangsbo, J., L. Norregaard, and F. Thorso, Activity profile of competition soccer. *Canadian Journal of Sport Science,* 1991. 16: p. 110-116.

[7]   Davidson, A. and G. Trewartha, Understanding the Physiological Demands of Netball: a time-motion investigation. *International Journal of Performance Analysis in Sport,* 2008. 8: p. 1-17.

[8]   Deutsch, M., G. Kearney, and N. Rehrer, Time-motion analysis of professional rugby union players during match-play, *Journal of Sports Sciences,* 2007. 25: p. 461-472.

[9]   Bloomfield, J., R. Polman, and P. O'Donoghue, Physical demands of outfield positions in FA Premier League Soccer. *Journal of Sports Science and Medicine,* 2007. 6: p. 63-70.

[10]   Reilly, T. and V. Thomas, A motion analysis of workrate in different positional roles in professional football match-play. *Journal of Human Movement Studies,* 1976. 2: p. 87-97.

[11]   Boyle, P., C. Mahoney, and W. Wallace, The competitive demands of elite male field hockey. *Journal of Sports Medicine and Physical Fitness,* 1994. 34: p. 235-241.

[12]   Reilly, T., Motion analysis and physiological demands., in *Science and Soccer,* A.W.T. Reilly, Editor. 2003, E & FN Spon: London. p. 59-72.

[13]   Reilly, T., Energetics of high intensity exercise (soccer) with particular reference to fatigue. *Journal of Sports Sciences,* 1997. 15: p. 257-263.

[14]   Rienzi, E., et al., Investigation of anthropometric and work-rate profiles of elite South American international soccer players. Journal of Sports Medicine and Physical Fitness, 2000. 40: p. 162-169.

[15]   Strudwick, A., T. Reilly, and D. Doran, Anthropometric and fitness profiles of elite players in two football codes. *Journal of Sports Medicine and Physical Fitness,* 2002. 42: p. 239-242.

[16]   Weston, M., B. Drust, and W. Gregson, Intensities of exercise during match-play in FA Premier League referees and players. *Journal of Sports Sciences,* 2011. 29: p. 527-532.

[17]   Edwards, A., Thermoregulatory observations in soccer match-play: professional and recreational level applications using an intestinal pill system to measure core temperature. *British Journal of Sports Medicine,* 2006. 40: p. 133-138.

[18] Edwards, A., et al., Influence of moderate dehydration on soccer performance: physiological responses to 45 min of outdoor match-play and the immediate subsequent performance of sport-specific and mental concentration tests. *British Journal of Sports Medicine,* 2007. 41: p. 385-391.

[19] Tucker, R., et al., Non-random fluctuations in power output during self-paced exercise. *British Journal of Sports Medicine,* 2006. 40: p. 912-917.

[20] Lander, P., R. Butterly, and A. Edwards, Self-paced exercise is less physically challenging than enforced constant pace exercise of the same intensity: influence of complex central metabolic control, *British Journal of Sports Medicine,* 2009. 43: p. 789-795.

[21] Lambert, E., A. St Clair Gibson, and T. Noakes, Complex systems model of fatigue: integrative homoeostatic control of peripheral physiological systems during exercise in humans. *British Journal of Sports Medicine,* 2005. 39: p. 52-62.

[22] Rauch, H., A. St Clair Gibson, and E. Lambert, A signalling role for muscle glycogen in the regulation of pace during prolonged exercise. *British Journal of Sports Medicine,* 2005. 39: p. 34-38.

[23] Ekblom, B., Applied physiology of soccer. *Sports Medicine,* 1986. 3: p. 50-60.

[24] Bangsbo, J. and M. Mohr, Variations in running speed and recovery time after a sprint during top-class soccer matches. Medicine & Science in Sports & Exercise, 2005. 37: p. S87.

[25] Dosil, J., Psychological interventions with football (soccer) teams. , in The sport psychologist's handbook: A guide for sport-specific performance enhancement J. Dosil, Editor. 2006, Wiley: Chichester. p. 139-158.

[26] Holliday, B., et al., Building the better mental training mousetrap: Is periodization a more systematic approach to promoting performance excellence. *Journal of Applied Social Psychology,* 2008. 20: p. 199-219.

[27] Balague, G., Periodisation of psychological skills training. *Journal of Science and Medicine in Sport,* 2000. 3: p. 230-237.

[28] Beedie, C. and A. Foad, The placebo effect in sports performance: A brief review. *Sports Medicine,* 2009. 39: p. 313-329.

[29] Vealey, R., Future directions in psychological skill training. *The Sport Psychologist,* 1988. 2: p. 318-336.

[30] Jones, G., The role of performance profiling in cognitive behavioural interventions in sport. *The Sport Psychologist,* 1993. 7: p. 160-172.

[31] Dale, G. and C. Wristberg, The use of a performance profiling technique in a team setting: getting the athletes and coach on the "same page". *The Sport Psychologist*, 1996. 10: p. 261-277.

[32] Miller, R., Mental preparation for competition., in *Sport psychology: A self-help guide*. S. Bull, Editor. 1997, Crowood Press: Marlborough.

[33] Flouhaug, C.F.J., et al., A new approach to monitoring training. *Journal of Strength and Conditioning Research*, 2001. 15: p. 109-115.

[34] Impellizzeri, F., et al., Use of RPE-based training load in soccer. *Medicine & Science in Sports & Exercise*, 2004. 36: p. 1042-1047.

[35] Gamble, P., Periodization of training for team sports athletes. *Strength and Conditioning Journal*, 2006. 28: p. 56-66.

[36] Plisk, S. and M. Stone, Periodization strategies. *National Strength and Conditioning Association*, 2003. 25: p. 19-37.

[37] Drust, B., G. Atkinson, and T. Reilly, Future perspectives in the evaluation of the physiological demands of soccer, *Sports Medicine*, 2007. 37: p. 783-805.

[38] Reilly, T., An ergonomics model of the soccer training process. *Journal of Sports Sciences*, 2005. 23: p. 561-572.

[39] Bangsbo, J. and M. Mizuno, Morphological and metabolic alterations in soccer players with detraining and retraining and their relation to performance., in *Science and Football*, A.L. T. Reilly, K. Davids and W.J. Murphy, Editor. 1988, E.& F.N. Spon: London. p. 114-124.

[40] Clark, N., et al., Season-to-season variations of physiological fitness within a squad of professional male soccer players. *Journal of Sports Science and Medicine*, 2008. 7: p. 157-165.

[41] Edwards, A., N. Clark, and A. Macfadyen, Lactate and ventilatory thresholds reflect the training status of professional soccer players where maximum aerobic power is unchanged. *Journal of Sports Science and Medicine*, 2003. 2: p. 23-29.

[42] Nicholls, A., et al., Overtraining during pre-season: The perceived causes of stress and negative affective states among professional rugby union players. *Journal of Clinical Sport Psychology*, 2011. 5: p. 211-222.

[43] Polman, R. and K. Houlahan, A cumulative stress and training continuum model: A multidisciplinary approach to unexplained underperformance syndrome. *Research in Sports Medicine: An International Journal*, 2004. 12: p. 301-316.

[44] Gabbett, T., Reductions in pre-season training loads reduce training injury rates in rugby league players, *British Journal of Sports Medicine,* 2004. 38: p. 743-749.

[45] Coutts, A., et al., Monitoring for overreaching in rugby league players. *European Journal of Applied Physiology,* 2007. 99: p. 313-324.

[46] Sari-Sarraf, V., et al., The effects of single and repeated bouts of soccer-specific exercise on salivary IgA *Archives of Oral Biology,* 2007. 52: p. 526-532.

[47] Kraemer, W. and N. Ratamess, Fundamentals of resistance training: progression and exercise prescription. *Medicine & Science in Sports & Exercise,* 2004. 36: p. 674-688.

Chapter 8

PACING FOR SPECIAL POPULATIONS

8.1. ABSTRACT

Pacing has been described throughout this book as a means of self-regulating exercise; however this may not be an optimal approach for all populations. It is likely that specific situations could be viewed as exceptions to this practice and such cases are discussed in this chapter. Specific examples are provided of exercise practice in selected populations such as children, those with acute and chronic illness and overweight/obese individuals. In these cases, homeostatic processes may either be developmental, temporarily altered or require extrinsic support to regulate exercise performance. It may therefore be appropriate to consider a support-based exercise environment, facilitating supervised self-regulation until such time as fully self-regulated exercise is feasible.

8.2. INTRODUCTION

In earlier chapters, the role of pacing in response to exercise has primarily been examined in accordance with psychophysiological control as a preferable mechanism with which to individually manage performance. However, self-regulation of exercise may not be optimal for all individuals and, as such, considerations for several specific population groups are investigated in this chapter.

As self-regulation relies on an accurate self-perception, factors such as maturation, disorders of motor coordination, or an acutely altered physical/psychological state (e.g. in the presence of an illness) can affect homeostatic control. In addition, populations with lack of self-confidence, motivation or experience of exercise practices may need greater extrinsic support and facilitation such as from an exercise professional, coach, rehabilitation specialist and/or physiological monitoring devices. Nevertheless, positive behaviours such as adherence to physical activities are reliant on engagement with exercise and this requires positive experiences such as those in which the individual enjoys the experience and/or can see purpose and some tangible gain from the task. Therefore in some cases, fully self-regulated exercise is not optimal and individuals will benefit from external facilitation and supervision within an environment where the individual still perceives value and engagement. This is not an easy mix and several example situations are provided in this chapter.

8.3. CHILDREN AND PACING

The definition of what constitutes exercise often differs between children and adults. While adults may consider exercise to be a formal activity requiring the performance of a specific routine in a fixed environment, for children it is much less complicated [1]. Typically, this could be unstructured play or engaging in almost any form of physical activity [2, 3]. Structured activities such as swimming, soccer or dance clubs often compliment free play activity, but should not replace it.

Unstructured, free form play is one of the cornerstones of children's physical development and an important feature of learning self-regulatory exercise skills [4]. In infants, reflex movements are practiced with actions such as grabbing, before eventually moving on to more deliberate movements like pushing, pulling, lifting and touching [5]. All these developmental movement skills strengthen neurological and musculoskeletal systems and are experienced with great frequency during free form play (e.g. [5, 6]).

As the child matures, free play is gradually replaced with more adult-like formal play or game opportunities such as competitive sports [4]. These activities are also crucial stages in childhood physical development. However, this development also progressively requires children to follow rules, coaches' instructions, limit individual flair or inventiveness for the sake of the team, and generally diminish individual self expression. These developments are important features of physical and social maturation; however, they could also be counterintuitive for the development of self-regulatory fundamental motor skills. Nevertheless, self-regulation requires experience, prior knowledge and an accurate assessment of individual capabilities in a specific situation. Children cannot be expected to derive these qualities entirely from free form physical activity. Direction, encouragement, guidance and technical instructions are all important features of facilitating self-awareness. The difficulty is, of course, finding a balance between (fun) free form activity and overtly structured physical training sessions [4, 7, 8].

Currently, nearly half of modern adolescent youth (aged 12-21 years) are not vigorously active on a regular basis and by age 15, evidence suggests that daily physical activity commonly declines to less than 50 min per day [3]. There are many reasons for this; school physical education classes often become optional, sports teams become more selective, and pastimes such as video gaming become more interesting to the child.

Although physical activity plays important roles in determining cardiorespiratory, skeletal and psychological health of children, young children and adolescents tend not to see health as a motivational factor [9]. Motivation is usually derived from enjoyment, feelings of competence, socialization and engagement. That requires engagement with activities the child enjoys, is able to do, and perceives the environment to be supportive and fun [4]. If the child does not enjoy the experience it is highly unlikely that a sustainable exercise practice will be established.

The teaching of sport often embraces the skill/drill focus associated with the 'technical' [10] or 'traditional' model of coaching/teaching [11]. The underlying principle of this model emphasizes the transfer of knowledge from a coach to the athlete. The emergence of teaching games for understanding (TgfU) [12], Game Sense [8] and Play for Life [13] models of teaching sport are child/athlete centered and focus on a more holistic approach. For example, the TgfU approach shifts the teaching emphasis from technique to total performance in game situations. Consistent with constructivist learning theory, these approaches try to engage children in meaningful and enjoyable physical activity or sport, social interaction, problem-solving and decision-making [14]. Such methods allow children to self-pace their activities and gain the necessary awareness and self-regulatory skills to successfully execute sporting activities in the future.

The long-term health effects of exercise on children include a lower risk of developing conditions such as diabetes, obesity, and cardiovascular disease, all of which can lead to lifelong medical difficulties [15, 16]. Children who are physically active are also more likely to continue exercising regularly as adults [17]. Considering the many advantages of regular exercise during childhood, parents should encourage their children to be physically active as much as possible in areas enjoyable to the child. Strategies for motivating a reluctant child to feel engaged with exercise include suggesting fun physical activities suitable for the child's age, allow for variation due to the stage of development (maturation), enabling the child to take some ownership of the experience (i.e. self-regulation) and for parents to serve as role models by exercising frequently with the child, as a family.

8.3.1. Specific Exercise Considerations for Children

There are several specific differences in the physiological responses to exercise between children and adults that can affect both the design of appropriate exercise training sessions and the interpretation of session outcomes. For example, during endurance activities such as cycling, swimming, walking or running, oxygen consumption is approximately 10-30% higher for children than for comparatively sized adults at a given sub-maximal pace [18, 19]. This represents lower exercise economy and metabolic cost for children, driven by several factors such as lower ventilatory efficiency, a greater body surface area to body mass ratio, shorter stride length, and greater stride frequency which all make a standard cycling, swimming, walking or running pace physiologically more stressful and outcomes therefore different to adults [19].

In young children, fitness gains from sustained physical activity or endurance training largely result from improvements to mechanical efficiency (e.g. neuromuscular coordination) rather than a large change in aerobic power (see [20]). Maximal aerobic power gradually improves in accordance with maturation but such developmental changes limit the usefulness of performance tests to predict $\dot{V}O_2$ max throughout childhood and adolescence [21]. Meaningful training for children should therefore combine both aerobic exercise and substantial activities to augment coordinative and efficient movements.

Children consistently perform worse than adults on tests of anaerobic power [22, 23]. This may be attributable to children's low intramuscular levels of the glycolytic enzyme phosphofructokinase compared to adults, which performs an important regulatory role in anaerobic glycolysis [22]. Consequently, children cannot generate sufficiently high anaerobic metabolism that would lead to substantial accumulations of blood lactate during maximal exercise [23]. Instead, energy is predominantly provided via aerobic metabolism with less production of blood lactate compared to adults

[24]. This undoubtedly influences maximal sprint and power performances among children. Very little is known about the trainability of anaerobic capacity in children and further work in this area is warranted. However, parents and coaches need to be aware of this to understand children's physical capabilities.

In terms of perceptual responses to exercise, children tend to score higher than adults when both exercise at equivalent percentages of aerobic power [25]. This may be a result of greater sensitivity to pulmonary discomfort owing to the higher respiratory rate and ventilatory equivalent of children [26]. These considerations can also be meaningful in the design, implementation and monitoring of training conducted by children.

Because of the physiological and physical differences between children and adults most sports have developed adapted versions or have introduced modified equipment as a means of graduated technical and physical demands. Such approaches are sensible means of facilitating coordinative development, facilitating task success and enjoyment in the activity. Practical examples include children running or swimming shorter distance races, using lower basketball rings or volleyball nets, and playing on smaller pitches with small soccer goals and soccer balls. Such modifications allow children to increase their efficacy beliefs. There is, however, a need to establish how the self-regulatory skills developed by children in modified games translate to participation in the adult versions.

8.4. Chronic or Acute Illness

The progression of chronic illness is physiologically similar to physical deconditioning, in that over time people show impaired exercise capacity, strength/power, cardiac and vascular function, reduced muscle mass, and in some cases increased body fat [27]. Chronic and acute illnesses differ in that pathophysiological changes to tissues are generally indicative of acute, rather than chronic illness. For example, the first line of immune system defence in response to a pathogen is to increase temperature by the actions of inflammatory cytokines [28]. This leads to raised tissue temperature which is indicative of an acute infection. Consequently, individuals with an acute illness will experience more profuse sweating and elevated core temperature at lower work rates than usual. These sensations will ordinarily result in a premature perception of fatigue; however, medications to alleviate these symptoms can mask this important regulatory information. As a consequence, it is conceivable that exercise could continue to the usual (illness free) training intensity in the presence of symptom relieving medication, but at an elevated core temperature which could cause harm to vital organs. In response to chronic conditions, sustained, yet only moderately elevated temperatures are often observed which are of little diagnostic value. Nevertheless, both acute and chronic illnesses influence homeostasis, the system which self-regulates exercise performance and determines our exercise capabilities [29].

Many people with chronic illnesses experience both premature and residual fatigue over sustained periods that can lead to reductions in the desire to perform physical activity [30]. Sustained sensations of fatigue are common symptoms in chronic illness and because of this; people may become more sedentary as the illness further develops. Consequently, some of the negative consequences of the illness may be exacerbated by physical inactivity. Acute illnesses, such as in response to viral or bacterial infections, can also affect daily functionality. Performing exercise in the presence of acute illness will put strain on the immune system and could prolong the illness. However, if properly treated and managed, these can be quickly overcome and fitness remains largely unaffected.

The importance of establishing an appropriate training stimulus (see chapter four) may be described by examining associations between exercise and illness. Reports from early in the twentieth century demonstrated that overt exercise practices increase susceptibility to illness (see [31]). In studies among boys in boarding houses, respiratory illnesses more readily progressed to pneumonia among those who had participated in heavy sports training. More recent work has supported the contention that strenuous exercise affects the immune system [32, 33]. Repeated heavy training sessions interspersed with inadequate recovery periods particularly increase susceptibility to upper respiratory tract infections (URTI) [31]. The association between exercise and susceptibility to infection has been described by a general J-shaped curve, whereby both no exercise and too much exercise appear to pose greater risk of illness susceptibility than maintaining moderate physical activity [31]. Therefore, acutely high, or chronically sustained, exercise presents greater risk for illness susceptibility and particularly for the development of URTI. For example, marathon runners have been reported to be of particular susceptibility to URTI infection with ~13% of runners reporting infection in the week following a race compared with residual infection rates of 2% [32].

Many patients undergoing medical treatments experience a loss of energy and impaired physical performance. Up to 30% of cancer survivors report reduced performance status even years after treatment [34]. This problem has been linked to several factors including nutritional status, protein turnover, anaemia, sleep disturbances, increased production of pro-inflammatory cytokines, psychosocial situation, mood disorders and amount of physical activity (e.g. [35]). However, in most studies, endurance and resistance exercise programmes prior to and following treatment have resulted in improvements to quality of life and mood state, and also to physical performance. Rehabilitation programmes based on professionally facilitated self-paced activities have the potential to increase adherence and develop life-long health behaviour change.

8.4.1. In Focus: Multiple Sclerosis

Multiple Sclerosis (MS) is a chronic, unpredictable, progressive, disabling neurological disease of the central nervous system that most commonly affects young adults [36]. This condition presents a complex challenge to homeostatic control mechanisms in response to exercise. Some of the symptoms and functional limitations associated with MS are fatigue, muscular/motor weakness, spasticity, impairment of balance, difficulty walking, heat sensitivity, depression, cognitive impairments and autonomic dysfunction [36, 37]. These impairments typically decrease functional capacity, reduce daily activity and increase fatigue [38]. Individuals with MS are therefore challenged by their condition when attempting to lead an active lifestyle. Not surprisingly, MS is associated with reduced physical activity levels [39]. Increased inactivity has two major consequences. Firstly, individuals with MS are at increased risk of secondary diseases like coronary heart disease, obesity, diabetes and osteoporosis which affect the general population [40]. Secondly, increased inactivity has been shown to be indirectly associated through functional limitations with the disablement process [41].

Current treatments of MS focus on slowing progression, managing symptoms, and preventing co-morbidities [42]. The incorporation of formal exercise or regular physical activity may particularly be helpful for individuals with MS to manage symptoms and slow the rate of functional decline [36]. The effect of exercise prescription, however, is still relatively under-researched in MS in comparison to other populations with or without diseases (e.g. cardiac rehabilitation). Despite physical inactivity often being identified as an important risk factor in disease prevention and management, it is not uncommon for individuals diagnosed with MS to reduce their engagement in daily physical activity or exercise because concerns of exacerbating MS-related symptoms. Decreased activity levels, in turn, might augment the already diminished physical functioning of individuals with MS. Reduced activity levels could lead to reduced social interactions and poorer well-being and quality-of-life [43]. Therefore, engagement of individuals with MS in daily physical activity or formal exercise, either as a complimentary therapy or a therapy in its own right, would be beneficial. Especially, that exercise/physical activity participation could increase or help maintain their movement repertoire, their ability to live independently through managing activities of daily living, as well as it could improve their psychological well-being [36, 43].

Reviews on exercise and MS have noted that exercise does not exacerbate MS related symptoms or cause symptom instability but can positively influence cardiopulmonary fitness levels, muscular strength and endurance, mobility, bone health, flexibility, fatigue, improve disease related psychological states and low self-rated quality-of-life, and reduce the risk of secondary disorders (e.g. [44]). Regular physical activity or formal exercise in this respect, is non-invasive, and appears to have few side effects, which are very common in pharmacological interventions to alleviate MS symptoms.

MS may be a condition in which self-pacing would benefit from additional external support, facilitation and education. For example, individuals may use heart rate monitoring as an extrinsic aid to avoid exercising at high intensities. In addition, as people with MS experience elevated body temperatures during exercise [45], it is possible that exercising in a swimming pool could be useful as water is 20-25 times more effective than air for the purpose of heat dissipation.

Not surprisingly, Kasser [46] found that individuals with MS preferred to exercise in a programme specifically for people with MS. The social support experienced in such a setting allowed for comparative targets as well as feelings of acceptance and self examination. The environment had a positive impact on self-perceptions, comfort, and outlook. Individuals with MS, who have been active prior diagnosis, are more able to regulate and pace their activities when living with MS [38]. They are more body aware and able to recognize what and when can do, which helps them with pacing their energy through the different periods of MS, including fatigue. In general, when they are in the MS fatigue stage they need to preserve all their energy for everyday living and exercise or physical activity for health is not seen as possible.

8.5. Pacing for Overweight and Obese Individuals

According to the 2003 Health Survey of England [47] only 37% of men and 24% of women reported meeting the recommended physical activity target (moderate activity for at least 30 minutes on at least 5 days per week). Studies have additionally shown an inverse association between body weight and physical activity (e.g. [48, 49]). Obesity is now an important public health problem and is associated with many serious health conditions. The risk of developing obesity depends on many lifestyle considerations but is heavily influenced by food intake and physical activity levels [50]. Low physical activity, combined with heavy consumption of energy-dense, nutrient-poor foods has increased the prevalence of obesity in modern society to such an extent that the majority of the western population is now either overweight or obese [51]. Overweight and obese individuals also pose a major risk for serious chronic diseases, including diabetes, cardiovascular disease, hypertension and stroke, and certain forms of cancer.

Since the early 1970s, studies consistently confirmed that body fatness reduction could be achieved through relatively moderate exercise without calorie restrictions, when administered over a longer period of time [50, 52]. Also, diet-plus-exercise interventions are generally associated with improved weight loss for up to 36 months in comparison to either diet or exercise alone [53]. For example, diet and exercise together results in greater weight loss than diet-alone immediately after intervention periods (20% greater initial weight loss) and at one year follow up (20% greater sustained weight loss). These reductions are of clinical significance, leading to cardiovascular risk factor reductions in patients. Unfortunately, half of the initial weight loss is regained after one year, suggesting that combined exercise and diet treatments do not result in better long term maintenance of the initially lost weight suggesting that obese individuals have difficulties in maintaining long term the lifestyle changes associated with intervention programmes [54].

Qualitative research has shown that obese individuals find exercising difficult. There are a number of reasons for this, including functional limitations due to excess adipose tissue, physical health problems, and joint and lower back pain. In addition, costs of gyms, subscriptions, or personal trainers, lack of suitable facilities or exercise opportunities and the notion that exercise requires significant emotional and physical effort have also been mentioned as barriers. Furthermore, increased risk of orthopaedic injury is often poorly understood by those who run obesity interventions, unless is it based in a specialist clinic, where often previously sedentary individuals are closely monitored to achieve higher intensity exercise outputs [52].

The motivational significance of the type of physical activity stimulus itself represents one of the most understudied and underexploited factors possibly underlying physical inactivity. Common sense suggests that, if people derive pleasure, a sense of energy or enjoyment, they will probably seek to repeat this activity. Alternatively, if people derive displeasure, discomfort, pain or a sense of exhaustion from exercise the chances of them repeating the activity or adhering to it over the long run will be diminished.

Self-determination theory [55] indicates that a lack of perceived autonomy and control in externally imposed exercise would result in less positive affective exercise experiences. It has already been demonstrated that in most cases, self-selected intensity is similar to or exceeds the minimum level of the range recommended by the American College of Sports Medicine [56]. For example, Murtagh et al. [57] found the average walking intensity of habitual adult walkers to be 67.3% HRmax and 59.0% $\dot{V}O_2$ max which is well within the ACSM guidelines. In addition, Spelman et al. [58] had earlier found the average walking intensity of adults to be approx 70% of HRmax and 52% $\dot{V}O_2$ max which strongly suggests individuals are able to pace themselves at an appropriate intensity for potential weight loss and cardiovascular benefit.

A recent study [59] has also demonstrated that, when allowed to self-select exercise intensity, individuals tend to choose a level that approximates anaerobic threshold. This appears to allow them to maintain a positive affective state as if this level were exceeded; most participants would enter supra-threshold exercise where negative affective associations are common. Supra-threshold exercise intensities are well known to be accompanied by significant declines in pleasure [60].

Without exercise, rates of weight re-gain when solely dieting often approach or exceeds 100% [61]. This clearly indicates a combined approach to weight management is required. Drastic dieting can have short term and spectacular results but make little sense to the stable and sustained management of weight whereas a behavioural change should ensure life-long successful weight management. How to best manage this process is an open ended question, but by identifying an effective range of low risk physical activity options for fitness and health which are both interesting and sustainable may help develop behavioural change. When most adults are allowed to self-select their exercise intensity and homeostasis has not been compromised such as in the presence of acute or chronic illness, they are known to choose a level within the range considered safe and effective for the development and maintenance of cardiorespiratory fitness. For individuals who are obese, formerly sedentary or older, this finding appears consistent.

Exercise is a beneficial and rewarding aspect of human life that can improve our self worth, mood state, aid our longevity and improve recovery from debilitating illnesses. Nevertheless, the style, mode, volume, intensity and frequency of exercise must be carefully considered in instances where the protective mechanism of homeostasis has been compromised. In situations where homeostasis has been affected either acutely or chronically, exercise should be performed with caution and most likely under the guidance of a supporting exercise professional who has the experience to act in a protective capacity while the individual's self-regulation is sub-optimal. Exercise rehabilitation programmes play important roles in re-establishing functionality after either an operation or a significant trauma. Such exercise practices are best facilitated in a supervised environment while the patient recovers to the extent of self managing basic exercise and/or following recommendations. In situations where the individual is able to establish stable and non-medicated exercise practices he/she will be able to become once again self-regulatory.

8.6. Exercise Practitioner's Comment: Obesity

For individuals with moderate to morbid obesity status, regular habitual physical activity and structured exercise are very hard. Working with such individuals, practitioners have to forgo their normal routine and start thinking outside the box: 'What is the most useful movement for my client?' or 'Should I run small classes?' First aid and emergency plans are also a must. You'll also need to teach your clients to monitor their breathing and heart rate and get them to recognize physical sensations if they are reaching 'their limit.' Explain to them the physical signs of moderate intensity exercise and assure them that it's okay to perspire and to be slightly out of breath. Self-pacing is crucial in this population. When I was a new Exercise Practitioner I didn't know what to expect and I thought I was prepared, but I was very surprised to learn how little my clients could actually do. Most managed about 5 minutes of continuous, low intensity movement in a 45 minutes class. The good news was that with support and facilitation, people build up to a full 45 minutes of moderate exercise per class within a year. To achieve that, they participated in a minimum of 2-4 hours of self-paced, but structured exercise per week over this period. I found a circuit-type class with built-in progression to be the best mode of exercise. I lowered the beat of music to evoke a motivated yet calm environment and avoided prescribing movements that made clients turn fast or use steps. From my experience, facilitated and diverse exercise options work well. There are plenty of alternative modes of exercise, such as seated exercise. Also a buddy system increases motivation, while educating people about 'correct' exercise movements improves confidence. Remember, many people may have never exercised before, and they have no idea how any form of exercise should feel or which physical sensations are important. This all requires facilitation, support and understanding. Helping people to develop the skills and confidence to become independent and hopefully lifelong exercisers can be extremely rewarding.

Dr Erika Borkoles, Victoria University, Melbourne, Australia

CONCLUSION

- As self-regulation relies on an accurate self-perception, factors such as inexperience (e.g. in children) or acutely altered physical/psychological state (e.g. in the presence of acute or chronic illness) can affect homeostatic control and hence distort our innate sense of our own capabilities.
- Support from extrinsic regulation mechanisms such as external input from an exercise professional, coach, rehabilitation specialist or physiological monitoring devices is purposeful until such time as fully self-regulated physical activity is feasible.
- Unstructured, freeform play is one of the cornerstones of children's physical development and an important feature of learning self-regulatory exercise skills.
- Strategies for motivating a reluctant child to feel engaged with exercise include suggesting fun physical activities and facilitating an environment in which the child is able to take some ownership of the experience (i.e. self-regulation).
- Both acute and chronic illnesses influence homeostatic processes, the system which facilitates self-regulatory exercise performance.
- Multiple Sclerosis (MS) is a chronic, unpredictable, progressive, disabling neurological disease of the central nervous system that most commonly affects young adults [36]. This condition presents a complex challenge to

homeostatic control mechanisms in response to exercise. Supportive exercise environments are likely to benefit people with MS.

- Obesity is an important public health problem and is associated with many serious health conditions. The risk of developing obesity depends on many lifestyle considerations but is heavily influenced by food intake and physical activity levels. Facilitating a supportive environment of exercise participation is likely to be beneficial for obese individuals.

REFERENCES

[1]   Kohl, H., J. Fulton, and C. Caspersen, Assessment of physical activity among children and adolescents: a review and synthesis. *Preventive Medicine*, 2000. 31: p. S54-S76.

[2]   Lorenzo, T.D., et al., Determinants of exercise among children. II: a longitudinal analysis. *Preventive Medicine*, 1998. 27: p. 470-477.

[3]   Nader, P., et al., Moderate-to-vigorous physical activity from ages 9 to 15 years. *JAMA*, 2008. 300: p. 295-305.

[4]   Burdette, H. and R. Whitaker, Resurrecting free play in young children: looking beyond fitness and fatness to attention, affiliation, and affect. *Archives of Pediatrics & Adolescent Medicine*, 2005 159: p. 46-50.

[5]   Gallahue, D., J. Ozmun, and J. Goodway, Understanding motor development: infants, children, adolescents, adults. 7th ed. 2012: McGraw Hill.

[6]   McGraw, M., Development of neuromuscular mechanisms as reflected in the crawling and creeping behaviour of the human infant. *The Pedagogical Seminary and Journal of Genetic Psychology*, 1941. 58: p. 83-111.

[7]   Byers, J. and C. Walker, Refining the motor training hypothesis for the evolution of play. *The American Naturalist*, 1995. 146: p. 25-40.

[8]   Duyen, N., Why it makes sense to play games! *Sports Coach*, 1997. Spring: p. 6-9.

[9]   Sallis, J. and K. Patrick, Physical activity guidelines for adolescents: consensus statement. *Pediatric Exercise Science*, 1994. 6: p. 302-314.

[10]   Griffin, L., R. Brooker, and K. Patton, Working towards legitimacy: two decades of teaching games for understanding. *Physical Education & Sport Pedagogy*, 2005. 10: p. 213-223.

[11] Pill, S., Teacher engagement with teaching games for understanding-game sense in physical education. *Journal of Physical Education and Sport*, 2011. 11: p. 5-13.

[12] Bunker, J. and R. Thorpe, A model for the teaching of games in the secondary school. *Bulletin of Physical Education*, 1982. 18: p. 5-8.

[13] ASC, The final report of the evaluation of the Australian Sports Commission's Active After-School Communities Program. Australian Sport Commission, 2008.

[14] Dyson, B., L. Griffin, and P. Hastie, Sport education, tactical games and cooperative learning: theoretical and pedagogical considerations. *Quest*, 2004. 56: p. 226-240.

[15] Boreham, C. and C. Riddoch, The physical activity, fitness and health of children. *Journal of Sports Sciences*, 2001. 19: p. 915-929.

[16] Sothern, M., Obesity prevention in children: physical activity and nutrition. *Nutrition*, 2004. 20: p. 704-708.

[17] Taylor, W., et al., Childhood and adolescent physical activity patterns and adult physical activity. *Medicine & Science in Sports & Exercise*, 1999. 31: p. 118-123.

[18] Walker, J., et al., The energy cost of horizontal walking and running in adolescents. *Medicine & Science in Sports & Exercise*, 1999. 31: p. 311-322.

[19] Armon, Y., et al., Oxygen uptake dynamics during high-intensity exercise in children and adults. *Journal of Applied Physiology*, 1991. 70: p. 841-848.

[20] Magill, R., Motor learning and control: concepts and applications. 9th ed. 2011, New York: McGraw Hill.

[21] Cureton, K., et al., Metabolic determinants of the age-related improvement in one-mile run/walk performance in youth. *Medicine & Science in Sports & Exercise*, 1997. 29: p. 259-267.

[22] Eriksson, B., P. Gollnick, and B. Saltin, Muscle metabolism and enzyme activities after training in boys. *Acta Physiologica Scandinavica*, 1973. 87: p. 485-497.

[23] Inbar, O. and O. Bar-Or, Anaerobic characteristics in male children and adolescents. *Medicine & Science in Sports & Exercise*, 1986. 18: p. 264-269.

[24] Mero, A., Blood lactate production and recovery from anaerobic exercise in trained and untrained boys. *European Journal of Applied Physiology*, 1988. 57: p. 660-666.

[25] Mahon, A., J. Gay, and K. Stolen, Differentiated ratings of perceived exertion at ventilatory threshold in children and adults. *European Journal of Applied Physiology*, 1998. 18: p. 115-120.

[26] Timmons, B. and O. Bar-Or, RPE during prolonged cycling with and without carbohydrate ingestion in boys and men. *Medicine & Science in Sports & Exercise*, 2003. 35: p. 1901-1907.

[27] Painter, P., Exercise in chronic disease: physiological research needed. *Exercise and Sports Science Reviews*, 2008. 36: p. 83-90.

[28] Tracey, K., The inflammatory reflex. *Nature*, 2002. 420: p. 853-859.

[29] Lambert, E., A. St Clair Gibson, and T. Noakes, Complex systems model of fatigue: integrative homoeostatic control of peripheral physiological systems during exercise in humans. *British Journal of Sports Medicine*, 2005. 39: p. 52-62.

[30] Morgan, A., et al., Effect of attitudes and beliefs on exercise tolerance in chronic bronchitis. *British Medical Journal*, 1983. 286: p. 171-173.

[31] Nieman, D., Exercise, upper respiratory tract infection, and the immune system. *Medicine & Science in Sports & Exercise*, 1994. 26: p. 128-139.

[32] Nieman, D. and B. Pedersen, Nutrition and exercise immunology. 2000: Boca Raton, FL: CRC Press.

[33] Malm, C., Susceptibility to infections in elite athletes: the S-curve. *Scandinavian Journal of Medicine & Science in Sports*, 2006. 16: p. 4-6.

[34] Dimeo, F., et al., Effect of aerobic exercise and relaxation training on fatigue and physical performance of cancer patients after surgery: a randomised controlled trial. *Support Care Cancer*, 2004. 12: p. 774-779.

[35] Gutstein, H., The biologic basis of fatigue. *Cancer*, 2001. 92: p. 1678-1683.

[36] Snook, E. and R. Motl, Effect of exercise training on walking mobility in multiple sclerosis: A meta-analysis. *Journal of Neurologic Rehabilitation*, 2009. 23: p. 108-116.

[37] Andreasen, A., et al., Fatigued patients with multiple sclerosis have impaired central muscle activation. *Multiple Sclerosis*, 2009. 15: p. 818-827.

[38] Borkoles, E., et al., The lived experiences of people diagnosed with multiple sclerosis in relation to exercise. *Psychology and Health*, 2008. 23: p. 427-441.

[39] Motl, R., Physical activity and its measurement and determinants in multiple sclerosis. *Minerva Medica*, 2008. 99: p. 157-165.

[40] Stuifbergen, A., Physical activity and perceived health status in persons with multiple sclerosis. *Journal of Neuroscience Nursing*, 1997. 29: p. 238-243.

[41] Motl, R. and E. McAuley, Longitudinal analysis of physical activity and symptoms as predictors of change in functional limitations and disability in Multiple Sclerosis. *Rehabilitation Psychology*, 2009. 54: p. 204-210.

[42] Roullet, R., Treatments of multiple sclerosis. *Revue du Praticien* 1991. 41: p. 1919.

[43] Motl, R. and J. Gosney, Effect of exercise training on quality of life in multiple sclerosis: *A meta-analysis. Multiple Sclerosis*, 2008. 14: p. 129-135.

[44] Rietberg, M., et al., Exercise therapy for multiple sclerosis. *Cochrane Database of Systematic Reviews*, 2004(3): p. CD003980.

[45] Watson, C., Effect of lowering of body temperature on the symptoms and signs of multiple sclerosis. *New England Journal of Medicine*, 1959. 261: p. 1253-1259.

[46] Kasser, S., Exercising with multiple sclerosis: insight into meaning and motivation. *Adapted Physical Activity Quarterly*, 2009. 26: p. 274-289.

[47] Stamatakis, E., Physical activity. In: SprostonK, Primatesta P, editors. *Health survey for England* 2003,. Vol. 2. 2004, London: The Stationery Office. 107-141.

[48] Armstrong, T., et al., Physical activity patterns of Australian adults: results of the 1999 National Physical Activity Survey. 2000, Canberra (ACT): Australian Institute of Health and Welfare.

[49] Blair, S., M. LaMonte, and M. Nichaman, The evolution of physical activity recommendations: how much is enough? *American Journal of Clinical Nutrition*, 2004. 79: p. 913S-920S.

[50] Tremblay, A., E. Doucet, and P. Imbeault, Physical activity and weight maintenance. *International Journal of Obesity*, 1999. 23: p. S50-S54.

[51] Deitel, M., Overweight and Obesity Worldwide now Estimated to Involve 1.7 Billion People Obesity Surgery, 2003. 13: p. 329-330.

[52] Carroll, S., E. Borkoles, and R. Polman, Short-term effects of a non-dieting lifestyle intervention programme on weight, cardio-metabolic risk and psychological well-being in obese pre-menopausal females with the metabolic syndrome. Applied Physiology, Nutrition and Metabolism, 2007. 32: p. 125-142.

[53] Avenell, A., et al., What interventions should we add to weight reducing diets in adults with obesity? A systematic review of randomized controlled trials of adding drug therapy, exercise, behaviour therapy or

combinations of these interventions. *Journal of Human Nutrition and Dietetics,* 2004. 17: p. 293-316.

[54] Wu, T., et al., Long-term effectiveness of diet-plus-exercise interventions vs. diet-only interventions for weight loss: A meta-analysis. *Obesity Reviews,* 2009. 10: p. 313-323.

[55] Deci, E. and R. Ryan, The "what" and "why" of goal pursuits: human needs and the self-determination of behaviour. *Psychological Inquiry,* 2000. 11: p. 227-268.

[56] Whaley, M., et al., ACSM's guidelines for exercise testing and prescription. 7th ed. 2006, Philadelphia: Lippincott Williams & Wilkins.

[57] Murtagh, E., C. Boreham, and M. Murphy, Speed and exercise intensity of recreational walkers. *Preventive Medicine,* 2002. 35: p. 397-400.

[58] Spelman, C., R. Pate, and C. Macera, Self-selected exercise intensity of habitual walkers. *Medicine & Science in Sports & Exercise,* 1993. 25: p. 1174-1179.

[59] Lind, E., S. Vazou, and P. Ekkekakis, The affective impact of exercise intensity that slightly exceeds the preferred level: "pain" for no added "gain". 2008, 2008. 13: p. 464-468.

[60] Rose, E. and G. Parfitt, A quantitative analysis and qualitative explanation of the individual differences in affective responses to prescribed and self-selected exercise intensities. *Journal of Sport and Exercise Psychology,* 2007. 29: p. 281-309.

[61] Ekkekakis, P., E. Lind, and S. Vazou, Affective responses to increasing levels of exercise intensity in normal-weight, overweight, and obese middle-aged women. *Obesity,* 2009. 18: p. 79-85.

INDEX

C

N

O